The Management of Maritime Regulations

T0362112

Ship management is a worldwide activity. Modern ships are sophisticated designed structures equipped with several automatic devices. It is estimated that 90 per cent of commodities transported worldwide are carried by ships. Therefore there is great interest from many private and public organizations that those ships are operating, manned, designed and maintained within international acceptable standards. The obligation of stakeholders to comply with maritime regulations is included in most statutory and commercial agreements and therefore inadequate implementation of maritime regulations exposes stakeholders to commercial risks.

This book explores how the application of mathematical decision-making tools could be used to manage maritime regulations. Performance management tools are proposed which would allow stakeholders to monitor the regulatory performance of their organization in order to reduce or eliminate those commercial risks. The process of introducing an implementation process for maritime regulations worldwide is described within this text. An emphasis is put on the role of main stakeholders in the regulatory process and reasons that increase the willingness of stakeholders to participate in the implementation of regulations.

This book will be of interest to scholars and students interested in the management of the shipping industry as well as ship owners and managers who are charged with implementing maritime regulations.

Hristos Karahalios is Maritime Consultant in the fields of ship management and quality control, Piraeus, Greece.

Routledge studies in transport analysis

The Management of Maritime Regulations

Hristos Karahalios

Routledge
Taylor & Francis Group

LONDON AND NEW YORK

First published 2015 by Routledge

2 Park Square, Milton Park, Abingdon, Oxfordshire OX14 4RN
52 Vanderbilt Avenue, New York, NY 10017

Routledge is an imprint of the Taylor & Francis Group, an informa business

First issued in paperback 2020

British Library Cataloguing in Publication Data
A catalogue record for this book is available from the British Library

Library of Congress Cataloging in Publication Data
Karahalios, Hristos.
The management of maritime regulations / Hristos Karahalios.
   pages cm
   1. Shipping–Management. 2. Maritime law. I. Title.
   HE571.K37 2015
   387.5068'1–dc23   2015000965

ISBN: 978-1-138-80713-6 (hbk)
ISBN: 978-0-367-59896-9 (pbk)

Typeset in Times New Roman
by Wearset Ltd, Boldon, Tyne and Wear

Contents

Figures

Tables

Acknowledgements

This book is based on research that was carried out over the past nine years and is something that I would never have achieved if some people did not support and guide me through this process. I now have the opportunity to express my sincere gratitude to all of them.

The first person I would like to thank is Professor Jin Wang, a person who accepted me as a research student based more on my willingness to carry out research rather than my typical academic skills. In all my research efforts he always provided me with quick and useful feedback.

Special thanks are due to Captain Vincent Williams for encouraging me. With his excellent knowledge of the shipping industry, he provided me with valuable feedback and comments in order to take my research to a higher level. Additionally, I would like to thank Dr Zaili Yang (Reader in Maritime Transport) for his interest in my research; he was always available when I needed his advice. Additional thanks should also be given to Associate Professor Metin Celik. Furthermore, I would like to personally thank Ms Anna Tsioukla for her proofreading and editorial contributions.

Finally, I would like to express my gratitude to my family, friends and all those people who have supported me daily to achieve this goal.

1 Introduction

1.1 Historical review

The maritime industry is believed to be the oldest international industry in the world (King 2001). The introduction of new technologies such as satellite navigation systems (Beukers 2000) improved safety at sea in terms of navigation. Ships sail all over the world, transferring 90 per cent of the world's commodities relatively cheaply and safely between countries. Such trade contributes to an increase in wealth for countries and their citizens. However, seafarers and their ships are still exposed to many dangers such as storms and piracy.

For centuries, the dangers of shipping were so widely accepted by people that there was not a significant attempt by many administrators to develop a regulatory regime that would improve safety at sea and trade. There were limited examples of nations that imposed regulations, but such rules were restricted to ships flying that nation's flags. Early in the twentieth century, the situation changed when the world's nations realized that it would be to their benefit if they could agree to a common regulatory framework that would enhance the standards of safety at sea. The common regulatory regime became reality when, in 1948, the United Nations adopted the convention that established the International Maritime Organization (IMO) (originally IMCO) (Smith 1999). To some degree the regulations imposed by the IMO established a common and acceptable foundation, and as a result safety at sea was improved significantly within just a few decades. As a consequence of safer ships, there was a corresponding increase in the efficiency of sea trade.

The IMO has produced numerous codes, conventions and resolutions, which are referred as 'Maritime Regulations'. The most known is the International Convention for the Safety of Life at Sea 1974 (SOLAS), which is generally considered as one of the most important of all international conventions concerning maritime safety at sea. Similarly, the International Convention for the Prevention of Pollution from Ships 1973/1978 (MARPOL) was adopted to cover prevention of pollution of the marine environment by ships; the International Convention on Standards of Training, Certification and Watchkeeping for Seafarers 1978 (STCW) sets minimum requirements for training, certification and watchkeeping for seafarers in international standards.

The SOLAS Convention, in its successive forms, is generally regarded as the most important of all international treaties concerning the safety of merchant ships. It is composed of 12 chapters, all listed in Table 1.1. The sequence of the chapters shows the prioritization of concerns of the maritime community with respect to safety for each type of ship. Construction of technically reliable ships is the first concern described in Chapter II-1. Firefighting is described in Chapter II-2 as the next major threat. When a ship loses its stability or fire is spread, the crew should have the means to abandon the ship or rescue other seamen. Consequently, Chapter III refers to the lifesaving equipment required on board a ship. Emergency radio communication and navigation equipment are described in Chapters IV and V, respectively.

A ship, in order to be seaworthy, should also be able to carry goods without any risk to its safety. With respect to this issue, Chapter VI of SOLAS refers to principles of safe carriage of cargoes. However, the global need for carrying more specialized cargoes contributed to the addition of Chapter VII for carriage of dangerous goods. Despite those requirements, the tragic losses of several bulk carriers led to the adoption of Chapter XII, for additional safety measures. When technological innovations brought nuclear science to ships, Chapter VIII was written to include safety issues. In a similar way, Chapter X includes safety measures for high-speed craft.

The latest trend in SOLAS development is to regulate management systems. This trend appears in Chapter IX, which highlights significant issues to management of the safe operation of ships. In a similar way, Chapter XI-1 lists special measures to enhance maritime safety and Chapter XI-2 contains special measures to enhance maritime security. Those three chapters are an expected regulatory development since a technically reliable ship with insufficient management could still be unsafe.

The MARPOL Convention is the main international convention covering prevention of pollution of the marine environment by ships from operational or accidental causes. It is a combination of two treaties adopted in 1973 and 1978,

Table 1.1 SOLAS 74 Chapters

Chapter I – General Provisions
Chapter II-1 – Construction – subdivision and stability, machinery and electrical installations
Chapter II-2 – Fire protection, fire detection and fire extinction
Chapter III – Life-saving appliances and arrangements
Chapter IV – Radio-communications
Chapter V – Safety of navigation
Chapter VI – Carriage of cargoes
Chapter VII – Carriage of dangerous goods
Chapter VIII – Nuclear ships
Chapter IX – Management for the safe operation of ships
Chapter X – Safety measures for high-speed craft
Chapter XI-1 – Special measures to enhance maritime safety
Chapter XI-2 – Special measures to enhance maritime security
Chapter XII – Additional safety measures for bulk carriers

---

respectively, and updated by amendments through the years. The Convention includes regulations aimed at preventing and minimizing pollution from ships – both accidental pollution and that from routine operations – and currently includes six technical annexes that appear here in Table 1.2. The development of MARPOL reveals the understanding of the maritime community regarding the harm that is causing to the environment. The establishment of oil as a primary fuel in industries and the larger ships carrying huge quantities of oil was the reason to draft Annex I with respect to prevention of pollution by oil as either a cargo or fuel. The transportation of hazardous liquids for industrial purposes generated an additional concern about ships' ability to control pollution by noxious liquid substances, which resulted in Annex II. The introduction of containers and the growth of door-to-door trade created the risk of losing a container from a ship at sea, causing pollution. Consequently, Annex III was prepared to address the issue of harmful substances in packaged form.

Apart from cargoes and bunkers, ships pollute due to routine operations. The incredible size and number of ships sailing around the world means there is a the need to regulate these issues as well. One of these forms of pollution is the dispersion of sewage, which is regulated with Annex IV. Another form of pollution is created with the disposal of garbage, especial when it contains plastic and recyclable material. Therefore, Annex V concerns preventing this form of pollution from ships, with particular interest in specialized areas. Finally, there are ports that suffer air pollution because they serve numerous ships. This health concern has led to the introduction of Annex VI, regulating air pollution from ships.

The STCW Convention chapters, which are shown in Table 1.3, aim to standardize training standards at a state level. Starting from the deck department, a seaman should follow certain training courses in combination with sea service in order to be promoted to the rank of master mariner, as described in Chapter II. Similar requirements are detailed in Chapter III for the engine department. The establishment of communications between a ship and shore, and with other ships, for a distress situation requires skilful radio users. Chapter IV specifies the appropriate training for radio personnel.

Apart from requirements for certain ranks, the STCW puts emphasis on training. Chapter V covers the need for special training requirements for personnel on certain types of ships, with particular focus on oil tankers and passenger ro-ro

Table 1.2 MARPOL 73/78 Contents

1973 Convention
1978 Conference
Annex I: Prevention of pollution by oil
Annex II: Control of pollution by noxious liquid substances
Annex III: Prevention of pollution by harmful substances in packaged form
Annex IV: Prevention of pollution by sewage from ships
Annex V: Prevention of pollution by garbage from ships
Annex VI: Prevention of Air Pollution from Ships

Table 1.3 STCW 95 Chapters

Chapter I: General provisions
Chapter II: Master and deck department
Chapter III: Engine department
Chapter IV: Radiocommunication and radio personnel
Chapter V: Special training requirements for personnel on certain types of ships
Chapter VI: Emergency, occupational safety, medical care and survival functions
Chapter VII: Alternative certification
Chapter VIII: Watchkeeping

---

ships. In case of an emergency, some crew members will be appointed with specific duties such as firefighting, medical care and operation of rescue boats. Chapter V addresses these issues and specifies certification and minimum acceptable training standards. Chapter VII, titled 'Alternative Certification', gives the ability for officers to gain a single certificate of competency combining deck, engineering and radio competencies. Of course, such certification requires a specific education and training path. Specific emphasis in STCW is given in Chapter VIII with respect to watchkeeping. A main concern in this chapter is to avoid human fatigue of personnel who have watchkeeping duties. The recent Manila amendments to the STCW Convention are evidence that maritime regulations are constantly developing to cover new training needs for seamen. In the amended STCW references are made to resource management, leadership, teamwork and managerial skills.

MLC 2006 has been designed to become a global instrument. Its contents are shown in Table 1.4. It is deemed as the 'fourth pillar' after the SOLAS, MARPOL and STCW Conventions of the international regulatory regime for quality shipping. From this convention, which is an amendment of existing ILO requirements, two groups could be separated. The first is existing requirements and the second comprises new requirements.

In the first group there are regulations such as minimum age (Reg 1.1), medical certification (Reg. 1.2), qualifications of seafarers (Reg. 1.3), seafarer employment agreements (Reg. 2.1) and hours of work or rest (Reg. 2.3). These regulations should already be in place to ensure a healthy environment for seamen. In addition, these regulations emphasise seamen's rights under contract, such as payment.

The second group is innovative for the shipping industry. The signatory state now has the obligation to develop the skills of seamen (Reg. 2.8). Emphasis therefore is given to the quality of the human element on board ships. Occupational safety and health incidents should now be processed through statistics (Regs 4.3.5, 4.3.6, 4.3.8). Such a requirement generates the demand for employees ashore that can understand and carry out studies using statistics. Crew complaints (Reg. 5.1.5) are also creating grounds for transparency. Therefore, since the voice of the crew could reach headquarters of a ship's management company, the liability of top managers is increased. Eventually, the right of detentions (Reg. 5.2) will place a significant burden on ship management companies for compliance.

Although the main regulatory framework is given from the above convention, the IMO is producing several codes which, if they accepted by a state, make them mandatory ships flying that state's flag. In Table 1.5 there is a list of approved codes of practice in the UK. The areas covered are very broad, covering cargo handling, construction, equipment and management. Those codes are in addition to conventions and are usually followed by circulars. It is not within the scope of this book to describe those codes, but to give emphasis to the plethora of maritime regulation that currently exists in the shipping industry.

Table 1.4 MLC 2006 titles and regulations

Title 1 Minimum requirements for seafarers to work on a ship
• Regulation 1.1 – Minimum age
• Regulation 1.2 – Medical certificate
• Regulation 1.3 – Training and qualifications
• Regulation 1.4 – Recruitment and placement

Title 2 Conditions of employment
• Regulation 2.1 – Seafarers' employment agreements
• Regulation 2.2 – Wages
• Regulation 2.3 – Hours of work and hours of rest
• Regulation 2.4 – Entitlement to leave
• Regulation 2.5 – Repatriation
• Regulation 2.6 – Seafarer compensation for the ship's loss or foundering
• Regulation 2.7 – Manning levels
• Regulation 2.8 – Career and skill development and opportunities for seafarers' employment

Title 3 Accommodation, recreational facilities, food and catering
• Regulation 3.1 – Accommodation and recreational facilities
• Regulation 3.2 – Food and catering

Title 4 Health protection, medical care, welfare and social security protection
• Regulation 4.1 – Medical care on board ship and ashore
• Regulation 4.2 – Shipowners' liability
• Regulation 4.3 – Health and safety protection and accident prevention
• Regulation 4.4 – Access to shore-based welfare facilities
• Regulation 4.5 – Social security

Title 5 Compliance and enforcement
• Regulation 5.1 – Flag state responsibilities
• Regulation 5.1.1 – General principles
• Regulation 5.1.2 – Authorization of recognized organizations
• Regulation 5.1.3 – Maritime labour certificate and declaration of maritime labour compliance
• Regulation 5.1.4 – Inspection and enforcement
• Regulation 5.1.5 – On-board complaint procedures
• Regulation 5.1.6 – Marine casualties
• Regulation 5.2 – Port state responsibilities
• Regulation 5.2.1 – Inspections in port
• Regulation 5.2.2 – Onshore seafarer complaint-handling procedures
• Regulation 5.3 – Labour-supplying responsibilities

Table 1.5 Approved codes of practice in the UK

- BC Code – Code of Safe Practice for Solid Bulk Cargoes
- BC Code 2004 – Code of Safe Practice for Solid Bulk Cargoes, 2004
- BLU Code – Code of Practice for the Safe Loading and Unloading of Bulk Carriers
- CSS Code – Code of Safe Practice for Cargo Stowage and Securing
- DS Code – Code of Safety for Diving Systems, 1995
- DSC Code – Code of Safety for Dynamically Supported Craft
- FSS Code – Fire Safety Systems
- FTP Code – International Code for Application of Fire Test Procedures
- Grain Code – International Code for the Safe Carriage of Grain in Bulk
- HSC Code – International Code of Safety for High-Speed Craft
- HSC 2000 Code – International Code of Safety for High-Speed Craft, 2000
- IBC Code – International Code for the Construction and Equipment of Ships Carrying Dangerous Chemicals in Bulk
- IGC Code – International Code for the Construction and Equipment of Ships Carrying Liquefied Gases in Bulk
- IS Code – Intact Stability for All Types of Ships Covered by IMO Instruments
- ISM Code – International Management Code for the Safe Operation of Ships and for Pollution Prevention
- ISPS Code – International Code for the Security of Ships and of Port Facilities
- LSA Code – International Life-Saving Appliance Code
- Noise Levels – Code on Noise Levels on Board Ships
- NOx Technical Code – Technical Code on Control of Emission of Nitrous Oxides from Marine Diesel Engines
- OSV Code – Code of Safe Practice for the Carriage of Cargoes and Persons by Offshore Supply Vessels
- Port State Control – Procedures for Port State Control
- SPS Code – Code of Safety for Special Purpose Ships
- STCW Code – Seafarers' Training, Certification and Watchkeeping
- Timber Code – Code of Safe Practice for Ships Carrying Timber Deck Cargoes, 1991

1.2 Implementation issues

The aim of these maritime regulations is to ensure a high level of safety standards at sea, minimize pollution caused by ships and establish a secure environment for ships and ports. The IMO's purpose is to bring these maritime regulations to the attention of world states by organizing international conferences (Kopacz *et al.* 2001). The ultimate responsibility for adoption and enforcement of maritime regulations depends on the world states themselves (Odeke 2005).

One might expect that the majority of states would act in a responsible way and implement the IMO's maritime regulations. However, many states, often due to their lack of knowledge, fail to achieve this goal (Klikauer and Morris 2003). This stems from the rather complicated shipping industry, which consists of a large number of organizations, companies and a variety of specialized ships. These sophisticated ships, which today sail in the world's oceans, require highly educated and skilful personnel to operate, control and monitor them. It can be readily appreciated that some developing countries in need of utilizing the services of specialist ships are likely to experience difficulties in employing staff familiar with the practices associated with such ships. Furthermore, this staff should be able both to comprehend and enforce the legal requirements.

It is apparent that many states lack the willingness to rigorously enforce maritime regulations (Llacer 2003). A reason for this unwillingness could be that the economies of some states are likely to be dependent on the shipping industry. Consequently, they find it necessary to provide a shield for the foreign companies based in the developing countries, which would otherwise fall foul of the criteria set by the regulations.

Such situations as referred to above have caused difficulties to the IMO in fulfilling its objective. On one hand, the standards of a proposed regulation should be minimal in order to achieve ease of ratification by a greater number of states. On the other hand, new scientific findings, especially with regard to forms of pollution from ships or design innovations, lead the IMO to introduce numerous regulations. The IMO, in recognizing the potential risk of excessive regulatory obligations which lack adequate enforcement, has decided to implement a new strategy targeting the worldwide implementation of the existing maritime regulations to an acceptable level (IMO 2000).

It is of utmost importance to address the risk of excessive regulations and their effect on the shipping industry. A cursory look at the conventions promulgated by the IMO reveals that most of them were introduced after 1970. After 1970 there was a plethora of regulations all needing the compliance of those within the shipping industry. Notwithstanding their justification, such regulations have imposed significant changes upon the ship operators who are a keystone within the industry. Such legislation has often been accompanied by the imposition of heavy monetary penalties and even criminal convictions.

1.3 The significance of measuring implementation performance

Many academics have found the maritime regulations to be an interesting field for research. Such research has focused on the impact of maritime regulations affecting safety at sea, pollution from shipboard operations, the performance and analysis of various ship-related operations. Additionally, some academics have explored the potentials and limitations of existing regulatory tools such as the Formal Safety Assessment (FSA) and the International Management Code for the Safe Operation of Ships and for Pollution Prevention (ISM Code 1998). To date no academic has offered a method capable of dealing with the worldwide implementation of maritime regulations issue. Moreover, there is only limited research directed at strategies or methodologies designed to improve the implementation of the maritime regulations. Nevertheless, there is a debate that a worldwide implementation could be easily achieved if the stakeholders in the shipping industry had an increased role in the regulatory process (Chantelauve 2003).

There is a need for the introduction of new solutions applicable in the current status and practices of the IMO for implementation of maritime regulations. An investigation of the current status by analysing the process of implementing the IMO regulations and its implications into the shipping industry is the key to better regulations. Furthermore, the current implementation practices that have been adopted by the IMO need to be examined for possible challenges and any potential improvement. An exhaustive literature review exposes the challenges of the implementation of the maritime regulations.

A further challenge in this approach is the high number of stakeholders in the industry and also the variety of activities covered by maritime regulations. The approach that is followed is that the stakeholders can be grouped according to their interests. From each group a representative stakeholder can be chosen as a sample of the industry. Thereafter, the sample can be used to investigate the distribution of various costs and benefits in the shipping industry. The terms 'costs' and 'benefits' are used in a wide sense in order to extend the meaning of the possible gains and losses to a stakeholder from the implementation of a regulation and so include non-financial issues such as reputation, innovation and employee skills.

The subject has not previously been approached in this manner. This makes it difficult to collect data from past experience since most researchers have focused either on the effect of a regulation in a localized geographical region, or to specific types of ships or to a specific group of stakeholders. However, the majority of such research can provide valuable information on the implementation of maritime regulations. Furthermore, it is necessary to investigate approaches to the management to the regulations of other industries such as nuclear, chemical process and aviation. These approaches are examined for their applicability to the maritime industry.

The primary purpose of this book is to explain methods of evaluating the implementation burden of a maritime regulation based on a cost–benefit analysis. A cost–benefit analysis of a maritime regulation should assess the gains and losses that will be imposed on certain stakeholders of the shipping industry. Providing such methodologies for the regulators of the shipping industry provides them with a tool capable of assessing the burdens of a maritime regulation. Then the regulators can make a decision on how they will reduce the losses of the stakeholders to an acceptable level. The available methodologies are presented regarding the implementation of the maritime regulations. The methodologies are described from the viewpoint that there is a need for the IMO to adopt a strategy with regard to the implementation of the maritime regulations. The strategy should be based on the evaluation of both an existing and a newly introduced maritime regulation implementation performance through cost–benefit analysis pertinent to the stakeholders of the shipping industry. The applicability of the methods is demonstrated through various case studies.

Adopting contemporary mathematical applications may benefit the maritime management science in many significant ways. The most important issue is that it deals with a crucial issue of current concern to the shipping industry, which is the worldwide implementation of maritime regulations. The issue was examined from a cost–benefit point of view for each stakeholder. It was found that the burden of some regulations is sometimes excessive for certain stakeholders. Additionally, it was found that the current regulatory system is very challenging for small stakeholders.

A more recent work was carried by the author, with an emphasis on implementation of maritime regulations (Karahalios *et al.* 2011a, 2011b; Karahalios 2014). Several conclusions were drawn from this work, the most important of which are as follows. First, it confirmed that the states are the most important stakeholders in the shipping industry with regard to the implementation of maritime regulations, these being followed by classification societies and ship operators. However, the success of a regulation's implementation depends on many other stakeholders. Second, the research introduced the concept of a performance management system including costs and benefits analysis as a strategy to improve the current regulatory environment. Third, it confirmed and emphasized the importance of the economic consequences that a regulation may generate. Such costs should take into account other aspects such as available knowledge and stakeholders' ability to adapt new procedures.

1.4 The need for new management tools

In the modern complex shipping industry, mistakes and omissions are often heavily punished. Therefore, a ranking of the priorities that a stakeholder should consider when he implements maritime regulations is of great importance. In this work it is demonstrated how significant is for a stakeholder to use a detailed performance management system when he evaluates his organization regarding regulatory implementation. In addition, in such a system the most significant management perspectives could be used as an initial prompt appraisal.

A successful implementation of maritime regulations requires tools to be established in order to evaluate the performance of a stakeholder and in particular that of a ship operator. Hence, an effective management system can assist the ship operators and other stakeholders to improve their implementation performance. The proposed management systems in this book do not demand an excessive workload or excessive paperwork. Practices and methodologies currently enforced in many industries and principles to which many developed governments adhere, in order to improve their regulations, are examined for their applicability to the shipping industry. Some common principles such as risk analysis, knowledge management and cost evaluation must be used in their entirety, while the structure of hierarchies can be developed to satisfy the needs of various stakeholders. The combination of these principles could be used as guidance to each stakeholder to monitor his implementation performance regarding maritime regulations.

After the risk assessment introduction it is necessary for the stakeholders to adopt new tools in order to quantify risks. The significance of introducing tools is that existing methodologies have been simplified for both the regulators and the industrial stakeholders. Therefore, it can be easily used by stakeholders in the measurement of their implementation performance without the need to carry out the complicated calculations required. The adoption of such a tool should provide detailed results and indicate early signs when a regulatory deviation appears. The comparison between the detailed implementation of a tool and selective implementation of the tool reveals two significant points. First, it is very costly for a stakeholder to assess in detail his regulatory performance and monitoring. Second, a stakeholder may find it has misleading conclusions for its regulatory implementation performance if it fails to use a management system or a tool in detail.

The risk of inadequate implementation of a regulation due to its excessive costs is not exclusive to the shipping industry. To date, some organizations have developed guidelines on how to reduce the imposed burdens of a regulation. Additionally, many governments have developed new processes, structures and tools to help them develop new regulations, and to review existing ones (Ballantine and Devonald 2006). Some governments and administrations have decided to adopt the Balanced Scorecard (BSC) to evaluate the implementation of a regulation (Ramos *et al.* 2007).

It is important that inadequate operation of the proposed tools by a stakeholder could produce a high degree of uncertainty for their organization's implementation performance. This can be caused because the BSC's elements with small relative weight are numerous; however, these are issues that can expose a stakeholder to risks. This is why it is suggested in this book that although the higher-ranked elements can offer a quick indication of a stakeholder's performance, the remaining elements should be examined thoroughly.

1.5 The system of hierarchical scorecards

The innovative concern in this book is that the current maritime regulatory environment is not managed on a performance basis (Karahalios *et al.* 2014). As a result, many maritime regulations have become ineffective in large geographic regions. One proposed solution to this issue could be to motivate stakeholders, and in particular ship operators, to follow an appropriate performance management system. Such a system should produce results relatively quickly, accurately and without excessive workload. A common regulatory performance management system for the stakeholders in the shipping industry can help in two ways: first, as an assessment of potential limitations of a regulation; and second, as a measurement system of how a regulation is actually implemented and where the stakeholders either fail or face significant challenges.

With this work, performance management for the shipping industry with regard to regulatory implementation is introduced. The potential of a maritime regulation to be implemented worldwide in a short period is defined as its implementation performance. This implementation performance of a regulation can be evaluated by assessing its implementation costs and benefits. For instance, an evaluation of the implementation performance of the ISPS Code should be indicated as very high. The evaluation should include implementation costs such as training, equipment maintenance and additional workload for seafarers. On the other hand, the benefits from the code are minimizing the security threat of ships and ports. These security threats could lead to loss of human lives and reduction of seaborne trade. Obviously the benefits considerably outweigh the costs.

The suggested management system imposes commonly accepted performance indicators for the stakeholders. Thus, it can be used as a tool to assist regulators and stakeholders in implementation of a maritime regulation by evaluating their performance.

One proposed methodology is the System of Hierarchical Scorecards (SHS), which is a unification of methods in an advanced mathematic model. The combination of sound methods such as the Analytic Hierarchy Process (AHP) and the Fuzzy Set Theory produced a decision-making methodology. Regulators can use this methodology as a tool to justify their decision in introducing a regulation based on accurate and reliable results. This approach is in line with many governments that follow the OECD's guidance for improving their regulations and so avoid unnecessary and overlapping regulations.

The developed methodology combined the principles of the BSC as a modern performance management system with a decision-making technique, AHP. The innovation is that a performance management system should be able to highlight the most significant elements of a management system rather than simply to list them. The methodology and its tools were validated through surveys in order to confirm their applicability in the practical world. Advanced research methods such as Delphi and Fuzzy Set Theory were used in order to compensate for the somewhat limited data available for this research.

The BSC is a comprehensive simple performance measurement tool that a regulator can use in order to assess the impact of a regulation on a stakeholder's commercial activities such as costs, profits and human resources availability. Furthermore, a system of many BSCs for a group of stakeholders can be used to evaluate the imposed burdens of a regulation to that group. The group of stakeholders can be an entire industry. Therefore, in this research it is suggested that the BSC is a potential tool to evaluate the implementation burdens of a maritime regulation in the shipping industry. The BSC can be used for a cost–benefit analysis of the shipping industry and its stakeholders. However, in the implementation of a maritime regulation the contribution of each stakeholder may have a different weight. Consequently, the weighting of each stakeholder should be determined. There are many available methods with regard to the weighting of elements of a given problem; however, the AHP has an advantage over other methods due to its simplicity and its ability to rank parts of a multi-criteria problem into a hierarchical structure (Chan 2006). The AHP is significantly improved when it is used with a Fuzzy Scale for measuring weight criteria in hierarchical structures (Cheng 1996).

The methodology is devised to be applicable in a generic form, so capable of including the shipping industry in its entirety. Special consideration is given to the ability of a small stakeholder to implement a maritime regulation because it is suggested in this research that the shipping industry should be open to small stakeholders. To achieve a detailed evaluation of the shipping industry the methodology is divided into two stages: one for an implementation evaluation of the shipping industry and the other for a detailed evaluation of a stakeholder. For each stage of the methodology, a tool is introduced in order to evaluate the implementation performance of a stakeholder either individually or as part of the shipping industry.

To achieve the main aim of the SHS it is necessary to introduce a performance-based evaluation system for maritime regulation by assessing the costs and benefits of a maritime regulation. A main hypothesis in this research is that the stakeholders of the shipping industry will more easily implement a maritime regulation that offers significant benefits while at the same time requiring the minimum costs for its implementation. Therefore, the proposed performance-based methodology includes the commercial activities of the stakeholders. The innovative idea of this methodology is that the implementation of a regulation may be more effective if it is possible to evaluate the implementation performance of a maritime regulation. The main aim was fulfilled by developing a number of BSCs for the main stakeholder of the shipping industry. These BSCs establish a performance-based structure for the implementation performance of a maritime regulation. The performance of BSC perspectives and measures is then evaluated by using AHP and Fuzzy Set Theory.

The introduced methodology addresses various important issues such as rationality of data collection, their utilization and the production of the tools. By adopting this approach the methodology will satisfy the needs of a comprehensive performance measurement system applicable for any stakeholder. To fulfil the above-mentioned issues a number of subsidiary objectives need to be met:

1   Create a system of scorecards that will include the commercial activities of every stakeholder.
2   Evaluate the degree of contribution of each stakeholder to the regulation implementation by using experts' judgements.
3   Evaluate the experts' judgements

1.6 Practical issues, point of consideration when applying management tools

The procedure for the implementation of maritime regulations is a complex one. The maritime regulations already drafted and enacted are numerous. In addition, the maritime regulations are drafted in a variety of formats such as codes, conventions, resolutions and circulars. Hence, an attempt to investigate the implementation procedure poses difficulties. These difficulties are exacerbated mainly due to the many stakeholders in the shipping industry together with the industry's international character, the large number of regulations and the lack of previous related research. Thus, in this research, the definition of a maritime regulation is narrowed to a single requirement of an IMO convention. The scope of this selection is to study the effect and the difficulties experienced by the shipping industry's stakeholders in managing a small change to an already existing regulatory regime.

Considering the above issues, it is nevertheless possible to design a method that will estimate the performance of a maritime regulation. This method will be capable of contributing positively to the implementation of a maritime regulation by examining the difficulties the stakeholders experience when complying with a regulation. In addition, any excessive burden on a stakeholder would be a reliable indication that this stakeholder will either probably try to limit this burden or to avoid it.

A main issue of the proposed methodology is that it is too complicated for the average industrial expert and ship operator, although it follows the proven principles that exist in other business sectors. A reason could be that the majority of people working in the industry have specialized experience in certain fields of shipping, such as surveying, quality assurance and maintenance. Although these people have high levels of education together with many years of experience, they may have difficulties in understanding practices such as economics and knowledge management.

1.7 Structure of the book

To achieve the aims and objectives of this research the book is structured in a rational order to demonstrate the applicability of the proposed methodology capable of dealing with the regulatory issue. The book consists of the following main parts:

1 Introduction to maritime regulatory environment and discussion on the need to quantify and measure.
2 An investigation into the challenges posed by maritime regulations, and also a comparison with the challenges faced by other industries.
3 Description of existing management tools.
4 Description of methodologies applicable to the shipping industry.
5 Discussion on the potentials of a performance management tool capable of measuring the implementation of a regulation within the shipping industry.
6 Discussion on the potentials of a performance management tool capable of measuring the implementation of a regulation by a ship operator.
7 Implementation and validation of the above tools.
8 Conclusions.

This book consists of seven chapters, the contents of which are briefly described below.

Chapter 1 Introduction

The first chapter is a generic introduction to the topic presented in this book. After a brief presentation of the main conventions and code that are implemented in the shipping industry, a discussion follows on the need to introduce decision-making tools for measuring regulatory performance. The non-compliance with maritime regulation may have severe commercial and economic consequence. Therefore, the application of decision-making tools such as BSC, AHP and SHS are presented as potential managerial solutions from a point of view linking commercial costs and regulations.

Chapter 2 The maritime regulatory environment

Due to lack of previous literature and research on a similar topic, the scope of this chapter is twofold: to explain the regulatory process in the shipping industry and then to present the commercial position of the industrial stakeholders due to regulations. In the first part of this chapter the process of implementing an international maritime regulation is described. The role of the IMO is described, highlighting strengths and limitations of the organization's efforts for the establishment of an international regulatory framework. This process is then assessed to identify potential challenges of various stakeholders. In this second part of the chapter the challenges of the main stakeholders of the shipping industry are discussed in relation to their efforts to follow IMO guidance. Those implementation challenges include cost, commercial and managerial issues.

The effectiveness of the current regulatory environment is discussed. The scope of this regime is mainly to minimize accidents at sea and eliminate environmental damage from ship operations. Consequently, the efficiency of maritime regulations is examined in conjunction with the accidents that occur in the shipping industry. Although there has been significant improvement to the above safety and environmental goals, accidents still occur. It is worthy to examine the factors that allow the occurrence of accidents at sea.

Chapter 3 Management tools for implementing maritime regulations

In this chapter, various methods and tools introduced by the IMO to improve the regulatory procedure are described and analysed for their efficiency. Those tools include scientific methods such as formal safety assessments, and management systems such as the International Safety Management Code for the Safety of Ships and Pollution Prevention. Yet there is still a punishment attitude which was enhanced with the involvement of Port State Control. Those tools have contributed to the implementation of maritime regulations; however, they may not be able to offer much more. Consequently, in the second part of this chapter the shipping industry and other high-risk industries which operate in strict regulatory environments are compared. Comparisons are carried out between the shipping industry and other high-risk industries such as nuclear plants, aviation and chemical process in terms of their regulatory regimes. This comparison extends to how governments deal with excessive regulations.

Chapter 4 Evaluating the implementation performance of a maritime regulation

An important conclusion from recent studies is that the implementation of a regulation may increase the cost of the stakeholders' commercial activities and make the operation of the shipping industry more complicated. The stakeholders that suffer most of the burdens from a newly introduced maritime regulation will try to postpone its implementation date. Therefore, the regulators should target a fair balance of commercial costs and benefits in order to facilitate the implementation process. In this chapter a variety of methodologies are presented which can be used to improve the implementation procedures of the IMO and other stakeholders by targeting a worldwide implementation of the maritime regulations. The tools are analysed and discussed for their potentials and limitations.

A system of BSCs that includes the commercial activities of every stakeholder was created. This system was developed by identifying perspectives and measures that describe the operational activities of each main stakeholder of the shipping industry. Through research, the chosen perspectives and measures are justified as valid to evaluate a maritime regulation and they include significant aspects of a cost–benefit analysis.

In the complicated business environment in which various companies are operating, a successful system such as the BSC can only provide a main management framework. It is necessary to adopt additional decision-making tools. Following this concept, other decision-making tools are presented, such as AHP and SHS.

Chapter 5 The role of stakeholders in the implementation of maritime regulations

In Chapter 2 the role of stakeholders in the shipping industry was highlighted as paramount for an effective implementation of maritime regulations. Therefore, in this chapter two main issues are examined: the commercial impact of a regulation to a stakeholder and the authority in the regime that each one has. This book emphasises the impact that a maritime regulation may have on some stakeholders and their activities. In order to investigate the severity of the impact, the costs and benefits for the stakeholders generated by the implementation of a regulation are examined using the BSC. As it would be impractical to examine all stakeholders, a group of ten main stakeholders is examined. The scorecards created in this chapter show that the BSC is applicable to a variety of stakeholders with different structures and needs. However, those scorecards are not of equal weight. The weightings of the perspectives as they are calculated indicate that some commercial activities of a stakeholder due to their high weights are of vital importance for him. Consequently, a maritime regulation may cause a severe impact to a stakeholder if its implementation has a negative effect to these commercial activities.

With respect to the commercial authority of the stakeholders, a ranking of stakeholders shows the primary role of the states in the implementation of a regulation. On the other hand, the significance of the private stakeholders indicates that a maritime regulation can be implemented more easily if they contribute positively. It is shown that some stakeholders, such as states, have a high regulatory authority by definition. On the other hand, a number of private stakeholders have the commercial power to implement some maritime regulations.

The applicability of one or several industrial tools combined can be used for a global monitoring of the implementation performance of a maritime regulation by evaluating the stakeholders' performance. To demonstrate this argument, the case of the marine antifouling convention is presented as it was investigated by Karahalios *et al.* (2011b).

Chapter 6 Implementation of maritime regulations by a ship operator

In this chapter the concept of using a performance management system to evaluate the worldwide implementation of maritime regulations is extended for the study of a single stakeholder. It is shown how scorecards can be used for assessing the regulatory burdens to a stakeholder, in particular the ship operator, by including an analysis of his divisions. This two-stage approach is used to evaluate the impact of a regulation from multiple aspects. At Stage 1 an initial implementation performance evaluation of a maritime regulation can be carried out for the entire shipping industry. If excessive burdens to some stakeholders are detected at Stage 1 then it is necessary to proceed to Stage 2, where a more detailed analysis can be carried out for the affected stakeholders and their divisions. Therefore, the two-stage approach enables a regulator to assess the imposed burdens of a regulation in detail.

In this chapter a particular emphasis is given to a ship operator, who is probably the major stakeholder. The organization of a typical medium ship operator is distinguished by divisions. The divisions are examined via the use of scorecards for their costs and benefits when implementing a maritime regulation. The divisions of a ship operator are then ranked in terms of their importance in the regulatory process. To demonstrate the applicability of this methodology the research findings of Karahalios *et al.* (2011a) are presented in this chapter. Ship operators are requested to evaluate their implementation performance with regard to a certain regulation. The challenges of a ship operator to implement a maritime regulation are then analysed and discussed.

Chapter 7 Evaluation of employees for their expertise in maritime regulations

The concept of the human element is examined in this chapter. The scope is to discuss the contribution of employees to the above decision-making models. The evaluation of knowledge of an individual is assessed and applicable tools are introduced. Studies with respect to formal qualifications and experience of an individual are examined in this chapter. With the means of AHP it is then shown that an absolute reliance to the curriculum vitae of a person may not result in better decision making.

References

Ballantine B., Devonald B. (2006). Modern regulatory impact analysis: the experience of the European Union. *Regulatory Toxicology and Pharmacology*, Vol. 44, pp. 57–68.

Beukers J.M. (2000). Global radionavigation: the next 50 years and beyond. *Journal of Navigation*, Vol. 53, pp. 207–214.

Chan Y.C.L. (2006). An analytic hierarchy framework for evaluating balanced scorecards of healthcare organizations. *Canadian Journal of Administrative Sciences*, Vol. 23(2), pp. 85–104.

Chantelauve G. (2003). An overview of maritime safety assessment trends in a stakeholder perspective. 14th European Safety and Reliability Conference, 15–18 June, Maastricht, Vol. 2, pp. 387–395.

Cheng C.H. (1996). Evaluating naval tactical missile systems by fuzzy AHP based on the grade value of membership function. *European Journal of Operational Research*, Vol. 96, pp. 343–350.

IMO. (2000). *Objectives of the Organization in the 2000s, Resolution A.900 (21)*, IMO Publishing, London.

Karahalios H. (2014) The contribution of risk management in ship management: the case of ship collision. *Safety Science*, Vol. 63, pp. 104–114.

Karahalios H., Yang Z.L., Wang J. (2011a) A study of the implementation of maritime safety regulations by a ship operator. In *Advances in Safety, Reliability and Risk Management*, ed. Berenguer, Grall and Guedes Soares, Proceeding of 2011, Annual European Safety and Reliability Conference (ESREL), Troyes, France, 18–22 September, pp. 2863–2869.

Karahalios H., Yang Z.L., Williams V., Wang J. (2011b). A proposed system of hierarchical scorecards to assess the implementation of maritime regulations. *Safety Science*, Vol. 49, pp. 450–462.

King J. (2001). Technology and the course of shipping. *Ocean and Coastal Management*, Vol. 44, pp. 567–577.

Klikauer T., Morris R. (2003). Human resources in the German maritime industries: 'back-sourcing' and ship management. *International Journal of Human Resource Management*, Vol. 14(4), pp. 544–558.

Kopacz Z., Morgas W., Urbanski J. (2001). The maritime safety system, its main components and elements. *The Journal of Navigation*, Vol. 54(2), pp. 199–211.

Llacer F.J.M. (2003). Open registers: past, present and future. *Marine Policy*, Vol. 27, pp. 513–523.

Odeke A. (2005). An examination of bareboat charter registries and flag of convenience registries in international law. *Ocean Development and International Law*, Vol. 36, pp. 339–362.

Ramos T.B., Alves I., Subtil R., Melo J.J. (2007). Environmental performance policy indicators for the public sector: the case of the defence sector. *Journal of Environmental Management*, Vol. 82, pp. 410–432.

Smith H.D. (1999). The regional management of the seas around the United Kingdom. *Marine Policy*, Vol. 23(4), pp. 525–535.

2 The maritime regulatory environment

2.1 Introduction

The transportation of goods is the foundation of commerce and the shipping industry is a major part of it. The maritime industry is believed to be the oldest international industry in the world. Almost 90 per cent of the world's commodities are estimated to be transported by ships worldwide. Such a maritime transport system includes sophisticated ports that can serve a wide range of ships carrying various commodities. The dependence of a state on the sea trade may vary significantly according to its financial growth and the development of its port facilities. Many people are involved in what is known as the shipping industry, which includes a variety of jobs that cover different parts of the sea trade, such as legal, marine, port administration, cargo handling, etc.

However, even states with less dependence on sea trade are affected by the sea services as consumers of products carried by ships. National economies can achieve optimal competitiveness in external trade markets by implementing and maintaining a cost-effective maritime transport system (Clark *et al.* 2004). One way to reduce costs of transportation services is to improve safety standards of ships, therefore minimizing the probability of cargo damage and delays at port or during the sea voyage.

The significance of sea trade has been recognized and, consequently, unilateral efforts were enhanced early in the last century. However, there were limited examples of nations that imposed regulations, and the applicability of these regulations was restricted to ships flying the flags of those nations. Early in the twentieth century, the situation changed when the world's nations realized that it would be to their benefit if they could agree a common regulatory framework that would enhance the standards of safety at sea.

The significance of the states and the growth of ship-borne trade urged states to cooperate on an international level, to ensure that ships will be safer and, consequently, cargoes will be transferred faster and at minimum risk. After the Second World War states were ready to cooperate on the international level under the umbrella of the United Nations. In 1948 the United Nations adopted the convention that established the Inter-Governmental

Maritime Consultative Organization (IMCO) (Hassler 2010), which was later renamed the International Maritime Organization (IMO). The scope of the IMO is to promote safe, secure and efficient shipping on clean oceans (Dahlstrom *et al.* 2011).

The idea of producing regulations for ships' safety and the protection of the marine environment grew rapidly. The IMO produced several conventions, guidelines and codes that were adopted by the majority of the world's states. However, it was later shown that the generation of regulations is not a panacea that will raise quality standards in the maritime industry. A legislative framework of about 50 IMO conventions is currently enforced worldwide (Perepelkin *et al.* 2010). This framework includes numerous codes, conventions and resolutions, which are commonly referred as 'Maritime Regulations'.

To some degree the regulations imposed by the IMO established a common and acceptable foundation, and, as result, safety at sea was improved significantly within just a few decades. As a consequence of safer ships, there was a corresponding increase in the efficiency of sea trade. Notwithstanding their justification, such regulations have imposed significant changes upon the shipowners and managers who are a keystone within the industry. Such legislation has often been accompanied by the imposition of heavy monetary penalties and even criminal convictions. Although the introduction of all those maritime regulations was a necessity, there are also some objections regarding their contribution to safety. Those objections can be summarized as follows:

1   Technological improvements have contributed more to ships' safety.
2   There are variation of standards among states.
3   Some threats, such as piracy, are beyond regulatory control.

For instance, due to technological advance ships have become safer. Modern ships have been designed and equipped with the most recent technologies in order to achieve high standards. Navigation is achieved with the assistance of satellite navigation systems (Beukers 2000), increasing, therefore, the efficiency of passage planning. In terms of ship design, structural reliability of ships has also been improved (Yu *et al.* 2009).

On the other hand, some threats beyond the technological innovations are still significant. Technological advances did not eliminate the exposure of seafarers and ships to many dangers, such as storms and piracy (King 2005). Adding new regulations is no panacea, as in some cases they negatively affect the functioning of the existing regulations, and sometimes seem to be motivated primarily by the desire to show political alertness (Knudsen and Hassler 2011). The IMO has no enforcement powers and does not directly monitor the performance of its member states (Knapp and Franses 2009). This weak connection to the national maritime administrations has led to a variety of interpretations and practices in implementing maritime regulations.

2.2 The regulatory process

The process of implementing a regulation is described in the IMO Convention and has been developed and specialized in a 50-year period of evolution. In this scheme the IMO is monitoring the regulatory process by bringing to a state level concerns regarding regulatory gaps in the shipping industry. Schematically this process could be described by seven main steps:

1   The appropriate IMO committee drafts a regulation (Stenman 2005).
2   The IMO submits the regulation to its member states at a conference (IMO 2000).
3   A number of states adopt the proposed regulation (IMO 2000).
4   Flag states incorporate the regulation into their national laws and make it compulsory for their ships (Odeke 2005).
5   Coastal states also make the regulation compulsory for the ships visiting their ports (Devine 2000).
6   Ship operators implement the regulation's requirements into their systems (Mitroussi 2004).
7   The crew members conform to the regulation (Talley *et al.* 2005a).

However, in the IMO process, the states are the key players for adopting a regulation at national and international levels. The states that are willing to adopt an IMO regulation incorporate it into their national law and, therefore, it is compulsory for the private organizations. The regulating agencies possess the ability to exercise sanctions, while the private industrial stakeholders accept the use of such sanctions, if they do not behave in accordance with the rules of the game (Lindøe *et al.* 2011). This could be a very good process provided that the private organizations are permanently located. The reality is that in the shipping industry the main transportation instruments are the ships, which naturally relocate frequently to different states. The shipping industry is giving the impression that it is not mature enough to rely on a self-regulation approach, mainly due to the vague sense of safety standards among its stakeholders (Goss 2008; Bennett 2000).

Private stakeholders are not directly involved in the IMO process by voting as member states. However, they can contribute positively to the maritime regulation implementation by excluding the substandard ships and their operators from the market. Lately there is a growing demand for more involvement of private stakeholders in the procedure of maritime regulations' implementation. Their contribution in the maritime regulation process is investigated separately from the implementation process in the IMO jurisdiction. The IMO has the responsibility to convince different stakeholders to understand the necessity of implementing a new maritime regulation.

2.2.1 The appropriate IMO committee drafts a regulation

When there is a need to improve an area in the shipping industry, the IMO develops and proposes a maritime regulation. Such a need is usually revealed after an accident that attracts public attention following coverage in the media. The organization of the IMO is structured in a hierarchical form. The Assembly sits in the highest position and has a session every two years. The Council is elected by the Assembly; the Assembly is the IMO's supreme governing body and is responsible for supervising the work of the organization. From its foundation convention the Council is constituted by representatives of 40 states, ten of which have the greatest interest in providing international services, and ten of which have the greatest interest in international seaborne trade (IMO 1977).

The remaining 20 representative states do not belong to the above categories but represent major geographical areas of the world. The Committees, which consist of all member states, have a meeting at least once per year and draft regulations in the form of conventions, codes, rules and recommendations. Every state participates equally in these Committees as a member with one vote (IMO 2000).

The necessity for specialization within the IMO led to the creation of several subcommittees, each one appointed with a specific scope. Those committees are the Maritime Safety Committee (MSC), the Legal Committee, the Technical Cooperation Committee, the Facilitation Committee and the Secretariat (Stenman 2005) and the Marine Environment Protection Committee (MEPC) (Mingorance *et al.* 2009). The member states participate in those committees and have the right to vote.

2.2.2 The IMO submits the regulation to its member states in a conference

The task of each Committee is to monitor the regulatory needs in the maritime industry. Changes in technology or notable accidents may reveal gaps in the existing regulatory framework. The appropriate Committee prepares and delivers a draft of a regulation to the Council or the Assembly. Then a conference is held at which all UN members are invited to discuss the implementation of the proposed maritime regulation, even if they are not IMO members (IMO 2000). A successful conference will result in the ratification of the maritime regulation by several states. The signatory states may adopt the full text or part of a convention, code or recommendation to their national law (Talley *et al.* 2005a). Each convention describes the procedure to be followed before it enters into force. However, the formal adoption of a convention can take several years, since the costs generated by the implementation of a regulation may discourage some states from ratification. Consequently, the international implementation of a maritime regulation may be slow or even insufficient.

The above process has some ineffectual processes. First is the restriction on the IMO authority implementing regulations itself, as states are still not willing to surrender their authority to a global agency. Therefore, it is up to the states to accept or not any maritime regulation, since the IMO lacks enforcement powers and does not directly monitor the performance of its member states (Knapp and Franses 2009). On the one hand, there are states that adopt all the IMO regulations and often make them stricter in their national laws. On the other hand, at the national level, implementation procedures are not often in accordance with the IMO requirements (Knudsen and Hassler 2011).

Adding new regulations is no panacea, as in some cases they negatively affect the functioning of existing regulations, and sometimes seem to be motivated by political reasons (Knudsen and Hassler 2011). An important clarification to the reasons for such variation of practices is that some states fail to adequately enforce the regulations due to lack of knowledge, and some others because they are unwilling to do so (Alderton and Winchester 2002; Llacer 2003).

The freedom of states to selectively adopt maritime regulations has created various regulatory regimes among the states. The existing regulatory regime is threatened by the decision of some states to go beyond the IMO standards when they are considered to be of low significance. One notable case is the enforcement of the Oil Pollution Act 1990 (OPA 1990) by the United States within its jurisdiction (Robertson 2011). The United States has exercised its right to take further steps than the international community in order to protect its natural resources from risks generated by the maritime industry. The extension of the OPA to bulk carriers has generated a set of regulations that should be followed globally by the majority of ships.

The variety of regulatory regimes has created a concern for some states with regard to the efficiency of the IMO. Some states have realized that, due to their size and power, they can force part of the shipping industry to comply with their unique regulations. This is achieved by exercising their authority to make their unique regulations applicable to all foreign ships entering their jurisdictions. Every coastal state has the right and obligation to protect its natural sea resources from any environmental threat.

A typical example of OPA is the requirement for ships calling US ports to have a non-tank vessel response plan (NTVRP). This means that if a vessel is positioned within US waters, the master should follow the NTVRP procedures. Prior to vessels conducting transfer operations greater than 12 nautical miles from the shore, the vessel master shall ensure that the available resources in the oil spill removal organization(s) identified in the appropriate geographic-specific appendix are able to meet the modified time frame permitted by the alternate compliance proposal approved by the US Coast Guard.

Another US development is the vessel general permit 2013 (VGP). Any vessel which carries ballast water that was taken in areas fewer than 200 nautical miles from any shore, and which will subsequently operate beyond the exclusive economic zone (EEZ) (more than 200 nm from any shore), must carry out an exchange of ballast water for any tanks that will discharge ballast water into waters subject to this permit, unless the vessel meets certain exemptions.

It is very clear from the US example that the practice of unilateral action, such as the United States' OPA, could affect the value of the IMO, which is the leading regulatory authority. Consequently, there is the possibility that the shipping industry will become confused by an overly regulatory regime.

2.2.3 A number of states adopt the proposed regulation

Due to the geopolitical position, every state has developed an economy with a dependence on sea trade. Therefore, each state has an interest in protecting its economy by adopting regulations that will not be in conflict with its industrial activities. Such industrial activity may include imports and/or exports of cargoes by sea, ship ownership and seafarers' rights. As a result, economic interests will determine the willingness of a state to adopt a maritime regulation.

The issue is often more complicated when a regulation needs revision in order to apply stricter requirements. States may not be happy to adopt such new requirements. Consequently, an innovative solution to deal with this issue was the adoption of the principle of 'tacit acceptance' introduced by the IMO, where future amendments apply automatically unless countries oppose them (Glen and Marlow 2009). This provides that amendments will be entered into force by a specific date, unless objections are raised.

2.2.4 Flag states incorporate the regulation to their national law and make it obligatory for their ships

A state that has adopted a maritime regulation should initially implement it on ships that are registered as business entities of that state. This relationship between the ship and the state is described by the term 'flag state', which is the only authority responsible for enforcing safety standards on ships entitled to fly its flag on the high seas (Alderton and Winchester 2002).

The responsibility of a flag state towards its ships is described in Article 91 of the United Nations Convention on the Law of the Sea (UNCLOS 1982). In Section 1 of Part VII of UNCLOS 1982 it is stated that a flag state is obligated to ensure that its ships are operated under safety standards (Odeke 2005). A common practice to ensure this obligation of a flag state could be summarized as follows:

1 inspection of ships;
2 issuance of certificates;
3 endorsement of foreign seamen;
4 establishment of punishment scheme for violations.

However, the above practices have to be exercised from a distance. A flag state that has to monitor thousands of ships will face practical challenges when trying to ensure that its safety standards are being followed by all its ships. A common procedure for a flag state to exercise its authority is by inspecting at regular intervals the ships flying its flag. Undesirable results of such an inspection can lead to penalties for the ship managers and sometimes the ship's detention at port.

The traditional maritime countries constitute a group of registries where restrictions of ownership of a vessel apply (Knapp and Franses 2010). The second group are the open registries, which are states that allow foreign citizens to register their ships under their flags. It is very important to highlight the fact that many of those open registries have achieved exceptional safety standards for their fleets. With respect to the open registries, there is a considerable literature dealing with the subject and, today, there is a consensus, particularly, in not making a simple distinction between 'good' and 'bad' flag countries (Silos *et al.* 2012). A third group is a middle type of registry, between the traditional flags and the open registries. These are the so-called international registries (e.g. the Norwegian International Registry), which were created to retain some vessels under their national flags after an exodus of ships to open registries (Knapp and Franses 2010).

The International Transport Federation (ITF) introduced the term 'Flag of Convenience' (FOC) to describe states unwilling to efficiently implement maritime regulations. This term is adopted in this book as well, in order to describe states with less strict legislative compliance (Li and Wonham 1999), which also offer advantageous regimes by requiring in some cases only an annual registration fee (Odeke 2005).

A significant number of FOCs take advantage of the vagueness of UNCLOS 1982 articles. The tax havens and lack of maritime regulation enforcement offered by various FOCs are very competitive tools in attracting a significant number of ships to their registries. It can be assumed that there is a high degree of competition among FOCs. An FOC's competitiveness against other FOCs depends on the continued and anticipated maintenance of a light regulatory environment (Alderton and Winchester 2002). Consequently, every internal attempt of an FOC to adequately enforce a new regulation is a threat to its own environment. An FOC allows a continuous lax regulatory environment for ship operators (Alderton and Winchester 2002).

The growth of FOCs in terms of ship tonnage is significant. In the previous decade, FOCs controlled 44 per cent of the global tonnage (Li and Wonham 1999), but this was slightly reduced to 41 per cent in 2006 (IMO 2006a). Nowadays, the ten major open registries control 56.6 per cent of the world fleet in terms of tonnage (UNCTAD 2012). Panama, Liberia, Antiqua & Barbuda, Malta and Cyprus have been characterized as FOCs by the ITF, and are at the top of this list. It is noteworthy that during the same period Malta and Cyprus, two countries traditionally recognized as FOCs, joined the European Union (EU) and were removed from the EU Port State Control (PSC) blacklists (Equasis 2005). The deletion of these two countries from the blacklists could be due to the fact that both had to harmonize their laws with the EU's higher requirements, or it could be that they received more favourable treatment from the EU PSC.

However, in the three-year period from 2003 to 2006, Cyprus lost 40 per cent of its tonnage and Malta lost 44 per cent. This could be seen as a clear indication of the consequences to flag states of more rigorous regulation.

2.2.5 The coastal states make the regulation compulsory for the ships visiting their ports

It has been briefly described how a flag state may exercise its authority over the ships that are registered in that state. However, the authority of a state is also extended to foreign ships. A foreign ship may accidentally cause a major environmental catastrophe to a state. The impact of such a catastrophe could be extended to other industries that use the marine environment, such as fishing and tourism. The ineffectiveness of flag states to control the entire world fleet with respect to its safety standards has exposed coastal states to risks of sea trade threats, such as oil and air emissions pollution. The tool to handle this issue is a network for exchanging information about ships' performance in PSC inspections (Perepelkin *et al.* 2010). When a state exercises authority over foreign ships it is referred to as a 'coastal state'.

A state can protect its coasts by inspecting foreign ships when they are in its jurisdiction. According to UNCLOS 1982, there are three recognized areas of jurisdiction of a coastal state, which are the ports, the territorial sea and the exclusive economic zone (EEZ). The actions that a state can use in each of these three areas are very specific. At the port any foreign ship can be inspected by approved inspectors in order for them to verify that it is not a threat to the environment or people. This procedure is known as 'Port State Control'. Originally there were no conventions to guarantee the enforcement of PSC programmes, which refer to a state's jurisdiction over ships in its ports. The final text of the provisions on 'Enforcement by Port States' was completed and included in Article 218 of UNCLOS 1982 (Gan *et al.* 2011).

According to UNCLOS 1982 requirements, a ship is free to navigate in the territorial sea of a coastal state, which could exceed 12 miles from the coast under minimal requirements that are laid in UNCLOS 1982, and is referred to as 'Innocent Passage'. Such requirements exclude smuggling, criminal actions and carriage of weapons. When the state suspects that the passage of a ship is not innocent anymore, then it has the authority to inspect the ship.

In the aftermath of the *Prestige* accident, there is a trend in some countries to impose stricter controls on transient oil tankers through their sea territories. Spain, France, Portugal, Belgium and the UK submitted a petition to the IMO to declare virtually their entire EEZs to be 'particularly sensitive sea areas' which would be completely off-limits for single-hulled oil tankers and other cargo vessels transporting dangerous cargoes (Dyke 2005). In 2006 the IMO recognized in the revised Resolution A.982(24) that, if such initiative is approved, then there is a risk of significantly limiting the old principle of free navigation at sea. However, in the same resolution, paragraph 6.1.2 states as an associated protective measure (IMO 2006b):

> adoption of ships' routeing and reporting systems near or in the area, under the International Convention for the Safety of Life at Sea (SOLAS) and in accordance with the General Provisions on Ships' Routeing and the Guidelines and Criteria for Ship Reporting Systems. For example, a PSSA may be designated as an area to be avoided or it may be protected by other ships' routeing or reporting systems.

Later the following year the Canadian government announced the prohibition of the passage of LNG tankers through the sovereign Canadian waters of Head

Harbour Passage (Dyke 2008). Such prohibition was enforced in the regions where the risks were unacceptably high for the government of Canada. Such an action is based on numerous examples of actions taken by other nations, including the United States. Therefore, countries are allowed to restrict or regulate passage in their coastal waters for environmental and security reasons in order to protect their coastal population and resources (Dyke 2008).

2.2.6 Ship operators implement the regulations' requirements into their management systems

The definition of a ship operator in this book is the person or company who has the responsibility for the operation of its own ships or manages ships of other owners. Typical examples of a ship operator would be a ship owner, ship manager or bareboat charterer. The ship operator makes a profit by hiring the space of each ship that he operates to transfer cargo for a voyage or a specific period (Li and Cullinane 2003). The tools of the marketing mix for a shipping enterprise, active either in the tramp or in the liner shipping market are: the product (tramp or liner service), the price (freight or hire), the process (negotiation procedure and execution of the charter), the people (office personnel and ship's crew), the place (ports and geographical area of the ship's employment), the promotion (advertising programmes), the physical evidence (ship's characteristics and seaworthiness of the vessel) and the paperless trade (Plomaritou *et al.* 2011).

The aim of a ship operator is not different from that of any other company in the business world, which is to ensure that his business is profitable. Profit will necessitate the long-term business survival of the company, especially during depressed market cycles. However, a further challenge for a ship operator is the rapidly changing regulatory environment. The effect of such changes could be more severe when there is not a uniform adoption of these changes. In the case of the shipping industry, a ship operator should maintain his ships to the exclusive standards of every state in the geographical area in which he trades. This practice increases the operating costs but not necessarily the quality standards of shipping.

The variation of the regulatory enforcement generates many challenges for a ship operator regarding his commercial activities. Various regulated issues such as speed, seaworthiness, effective equipment and manning are of primary importance for the ship operator. Furthermore, ships visit ports of different states on a regular basis and, consequently, they are subject to different regulatory regimes. In addition, some states have extended their jurisdiction through their EEZ (Vince and Haward 2009). Hence, a ship sailing in the area of an EEZ, even if it does not intend to call at a port of that state, may have to comply with some restrictions with respect to the environment protection (Keyuan 2002). Violation of such restrictions would be examined by PSC officers (Paris MOU 2006).

Besides the flag state inspection, there are several more inspections that should be carried out on board a ship by the member states. A common practice for flag states is to delegate their authority for such inspection to classification societies, which then issue certificates on their behalf. The certificates required on board a ship are listed in major IMO conventions such as SOLAS, MARPOL and MLC.

The compliance of ships with all national and international requirements is very frequently examined through a complicated inspection programme (Mokashi *et al.* 2002). Knudsen and Hassler (2011) have argued that the involvement of classification societies ensures the flag states' implementation obligations. PSC officers inspect ships to verify their compliance with regulations internationally applied by the IMO and those nationally applied at the port of call. Furthermore, independent surveyors often inspect ships on behalf of third parties, such as P&I clubs, insurance and charterers.

Although any commercial ship is subject to those inspections, it is still possible for it to be involved in an accident. Then, despite its performance in the inspection results and the certification, the crew and the ship operator will be subject to severe penalties. For seamen, a frequent penalty for violations of regulations is the imposition of fines and imprisonment. The criminalization of seamen is an awkward issue which has not proven its contribution to the quality of shipping. Contrarily, seamen will try to mislead the authorities regarding the real cause of any accident. However, US law has pursued such actions (Knapp and Franses 2007). In a similar way, and despite the opposition of many member states, the EU has also been active recently in promoting the criminalization of seafarers for pollution incidents (Roe 2009). Criminalization also applies to the employees of a ship operator. It has been argued that in many cases the media drive authorities to impose severe penalties (Sampson 2004).

In such a demanding environment a ship operator must find the appropriate human resources to fulfil positions on board his ships and ashore, in order to comply with all the maritime regulations. The availability and quality of human resources are the cornerstones for a rational management system of a company. However, due to changes in crew labour resources, it is common for ships to be manned by crew members from the Far East when their company is based in Europe. To illustrate the gap in crew salaries: studies have showed that in 1995 a Japanese seaman earned 41 times more than the lowest paid, a Bangladeshi seaman; in 2009 it was revealed that the average monthly salary had fallen by one-quarter since 1992, at $1,318 (Silos *et al.* 2012). A ship registered under a FOC may have limited restrictions regarding manning, such as crew nationality and manpower. As a result, many companies operate their ships with cheap labour from developing countries, overlooking their lack of skills (Klikauer and Morris 2003). This is an irrational practice; the shipping industry is a high-risk environment, and the crew members of a ship should be considered as vital guards in the process of implementing maritime regulations. Adequate human resources should also be used ashore, so as to implement regulations and provide guidance and assistance to crew members on the ships. The demand for human resources ashore is sometimes generated by regulations, in order to cover specific positions such as the 'Designated Person Ashore' and the 'Company Security Officer' required by the ISM Code (IMO 1993) and the International Code for the Security of Ships and of Port Facilities (ISPS code) (IMO 2002).

Early studies provide considerable evidence that the choice of a ship-owning company giving the management of its fleet to an independent third-party ship-management company may be related to the growth of maritime regulations (Mitrousi 2004). In the third-party management concept some of the responsibilities are delegated to companies depending on the nature of the activities, such as safety management or commercial arrangements. In general, the structure of a modern ship operator consists of ownership, which is the beneficial owner, and the registered owner (normally a brass plate company in a country not related to the location of the shipowner or ship operator) (Knapp and Frances 2010). An independent management company with qualified personnel and experience in the shipping industry can be an attractive option for a shipowner. The use of a third-party management option offers flexibility regarding financial and legislation regimes to a shipowner since it may be difficult to prove responsibility of a shipowner for the seaworthy condition of his ship.

2.2.7 The crew members conform to the regulation

The final stage of the implementation process is that crew members must conform to all applicable IMO regulations. The ability of crew members to conform to maritime regulations is under debate. However, there is a considerable variation of skills among seamen (Vanem *et al.* 2008; Hetherington *et al.* 2006; Klikauer and Morris 2003). Consequently, training, costs, quality and supply of seamen are key elements for which a ship operator should develop commercially and legally accepted solutions. This could be one of the reasons that the salaries of seamen reflect the salary/training ratio that Silos *et al.* (2012) identified. The role of crew members in the implementation of maritime regulations has been well considered by the IMO since most accidents are caused by human error (Talley *et al.* 2005a; Wang 2006). The revised International Convention on Standards of Training, Certification and Watchkeeping for Seafarers 1995 (STCW 1995) and the International Safety Management Code for the Safe Operation of Ships and for Pollution Prevention 1998 (ISM Code) are two steps towards the increased quality of seamen. Although it has been argued that the STCW 1995 scope remains focused primarily on training, since it is adverse to the overall development of human resources, recent policy interventions are significant (Bonnin *et al.* 2004).

2.2.8 The involvement of private stakeholders in the regulations' implementation

A success in the implementation process is a new maritime regulation being uniformly enforced in the shipping industry. The shipping industry consists of several private stakeholders, each one specialized in a particular area of sea trade. Examples of such private stakeholders are insurers, P&I clubs, classification societies, charterers, cargo owners, consultants and shipyards (Chantelauve 2003). The implementation of a new regulation, which has an effect on either operation or design standards of a ship, will affect some of the private stake-holders. Their interest in the regulatory process is so high that they lobby and participate, without the right of voting, in the IMO conferences as non-governmental organizations. Their opinion is frequently requested in certain fields. When private stakeholders recognize the benefit they receive from the implementation of a maritime regulation, they incorporate it in their policies, contributing to the implementation process (Mason 2003). A typical example is the incorporation of the ISM Code as a warranty to charter parties and insurance policies, putting an additional but reasonable burden on the ship operators to comply with this regulation (Katarelos and Alexopoulos 2007).

The private stakeholders can increase safety standards at sea. The above process, however, generates some costs to the private stakeholders. Those costs should include expenses to conform to the existing regulations and to prepare for the forthcoming ones. The regulatory implementation deadlines could overlap with the long recession periods occasionally generated by unpredictable market cycles. It should be stressed that the interests of private stakeholders in regulatory compliance is much narrower than that of states. Consequently, a private stakeholder will usually face a risk of conflicts of interests in controlling clients versus retaining their market share. There has been an attempt by some states to involve private stakeholders in maritime regulations. The European Commission is attempting to enrol as many industry stakeholders as possible in its 'Quality Shipping Campaign', so as to influence regulatory standards. However, when a stakeholder believes the costs to minimize a hazard are not adequately justified by statistics, and they also produce financial costs, he could be tempted to elim-inate those costs. This temptation will be higher when such shortcomings may not be easily detected. Therefore, it can be argued that their willingness to con-tribute depends on the benefits they can gain from the costs they will bear.

2.3 Challenges to the implementation of current maritime regulations

There are a number of private organization referred to in the literature, for example classification societies, charterers, cargo owners, consultants and ship-yards, which are also affected by maritime regulations as they may increase the cost of the stakeholders' commercial activities and make the operation of the shipping industry more complicated. Apart from the ship operator, the literature has mainly been concentrated on the examination of the role of classification societies and insurers with respect to regulatory compliance. More detailed ana-lysis of the main stakeholders offered in Chapter 5.

The classification societies are companies that undertake inspections of ships in order to certify their standards. The classification societies serve shipowners, insur-ance companies and flag states as technical experts to whom much of the flag state's authority is delegated. To perform their function, the classification societies need to 'translate' the IMO decisions into concrete technical or operative standards to be applied on board every vessel they certify for new-building or retrofitting, regardless of the flag state concerned (Knudsen and Hassler 2011). Classification inspections are twofold: first, they verify that their registered ships maintain standards according to their classification society's rules; second, they issue a certificate on behalf of a flag state. Therefore, classification surveyors ensure that there are no violations of the existing IMO regulations when issuing certificates. Since there are several classification societies in the shipping industry, there was an early attempt to make their standards uniform. The International Association of Classification Societies (IACS) aims to eliminate substandard classification societies. However, by examining Equasis' database, it appears that there are still many non-IACS classification societies with poor detention rates (Equasis 2011). It is compulsory for a ship to be classed as it is stated in regulation 3.1 of SOLAS 1974, Chapter II-1 (IACS 2007). However, a ship registered in a non-IACS classification society may be treated by PSC as a potentially substandard ship and so will result in more rigorous inspections.

Another important group of stakeholders are the insurance organizations. The insurers are private companies that undertake to indemnify any party that has an interest in a ship's voyage regarding the exchange of a premium, such as shipowners, cargo owners, mortgages and crew. With respect to the insurance of a ship, it is expected that it is registered in a classification society at all times (Bennett 2000). In addition, insurance policies refer to compliance with maritime regulations. For instance, insurance companies typically require new tankers to be properly equipped and fulfil all relevant regulations before issuing insurances. Since the insurers usually rely on a ship's certification, before they insure a ship it is expected that they must trust the existing maritime regulatory environment and the way this is self-monitored and effectively implemented in the industry (Bennett 2000).

Another group of stakeholders, which is also referred to in the literature for their role in affecting the maritime regulatory environment, are the protection and indemnity clubs (P&I clubs). The P&I clubs are mutual societies of shipowners that have mutual indemnification against third-party liabilities (Bennett 2000). Their scope is to provide indemnity to shipowners for risks not covered by insurers, such as cargo damage, pollution and crew sickness. As Mason (2003) clarified, in the case of an accident, if it is proven that the shipowner was aware of his ship's unseaworthy condition, then it is highly possible that this will expose his club to unlimited claims from any party affected by the ship's accident. Such evidence may be revealed from defective management systems, such as records and communication evidence.

2.4 Regulatory failure analysis

The complexity of the international regulatory regime has been examined in the previous sections. However, questionable whether overall improved safety standards are the outcome of the increasing number of regulations. Therefore, in the following sections there is an investigation into the effect of a regulation on ship safety, pollution and casualties near coasts. The purpose of setting international regulation standards is to make sure ships operate worldwide without any significant risk to human life on board and ashore, are environmentally friendly and not involved in any illegal usage. Any deviation from the above goals should be examined in detail for its causes and results in the shipping industry, giving emphasis to its commercial character.

2.4.1 Accident review regarding ship safety

One way to review the results of regulations regarding ship safety is through a review of accidents that result in loss of ships and lives and cause injuries. Although safety records have significantly improved, the shipping community is still investigating potential threats. A list of factors that contribute to accidents includes flag states' inability to enforce safety standards on board their ships, human error and exclusion of coast trade ships from the IMO requirements. There is also an opinion that the regime is reactive and does not prevent the future occurrence of marine incidents by anticipating possible failure scenarios (Psarros *et al.* 2010).

Limitations of the existing maritime regulatory environment have been identified by Li and Wonham (2001). This study discussed the fact that several incidents occur in relation to ships that are not covered by the IMO conventions, known as non-SOLAS ships. This is applicable in two cases: either when a ship is under a certain size or when it is trading in national voyages. When a ship is not under the international standards, then if it is involved in an accident it is very likely not to be included in the IMO studies. In a complicated governmental structure such as the EU, where many traditional nation-state models are involved in decision making in shipping policy making, this may be the reason why so many failures and problems continue to occur (Roe 2009). The EU maritime safety policy has evolved in the aftermath of major accidents (Pallis 2006).

The inability of flag states to maintain safety standards on ships has been reported in case studies. Although some states have demonstrated exceptional efforts to improve safety at sea, the overall picture is not positive. Roberts and Marlow (2002) identified a correlation between a bulk carrier's safety and its flag. Flag was identified as a risk factor in loss of 125 bulk carriers, often as a consequence of structural failure during the 36-year period from 1963 to 1996. At that time it was alleged that open registries failed to monitor their fleet, which was not proven to be the case with other flag states (Llacer 2003; Alderton and Winchester 2002). The ships registered within OECD states seem to show very good records. A possible explanation could be that the resources from these states are greater than from less financially strong states.

A noteworthy area of research is bulk carriers' losses during the last 20 years as a consequence of the inadequate regulatory environment in which they operated. Some studies have dealt with bulk carriers and their ability to withstand abnormal waves. Older ships are suspected to be more vulnerable when exposed to sea conditions. The IMO introduced several regulations with regard to those issues, the most notable being the Enhanced Survey Programme (ESP). The

IMO Resolution A.744 (18) means that as a result of the introduction of the ESP, oil tankers, combination carriers, chemical tankers and dry bulk cargo ships (bulk carriers) require a Survey Planning Questionnaire and a Survey Programme (planning document) to be prepared in advance of the Special Survey and the Intermediate Survey on ships of over ten years of age. Those surveys reveal corrosion, deformation, fractures, damage or other structural deterioration, as well as the condition of the protective coating.

However, the above studies did not explain the loss of many new ships, as well as why ships older than 20 years had fewer casualties than ships of 15–19 years. The case of the bulk carrier losses should be considered as an example of inadequate design of regulations by the IMO, which allowed structurally defective ships to sail.

Bulk carriers are still seen as potential threats in terms of safety and, therefore, are inspected more rigorously. A study based on PSC inspection showed that bulk carriers and chemical carriers are subject to a higher number of detentions than other types of vessel (Cariou *et al.* 2009). Comparing the sophisticated design of chemical carriers to the simpler design of a bulk carrier, such a finding is peculiar. Nevertheless, the annual average number of bulk carriers lost has fallen to 5.9 for the decade 2001 to 2010, compared to the previous decade, when it was 11.9 (INTERCARGO 2010).

When studies refer to casualties, it should be stressed that those records may include older ships, which are more likely to be declared as total losses compared to newer ships, due to the excessive cost of their repairs (Roberts and Marlow 2002). In addition, the IMO does not have global detailed statistical data (Campa Portela 2005; IMO 2006a). However, the IMO has made significant efforts to develop the GISIS, which is a database via which states report casualties and incidents as per IMO instructions (IMO 2008). Psarros *et al.* (2010) argued that there is evidence of serious under-reporting in accident databases, which can be considered as the main contributor to the questionable nature direct and uncritical use of historical data. In their research, by analysing the ten-year tanker accident data from Lloyd's Register FairPlay (LRFP) and the Norwegian Maritime Directorate (NMD) for vessels registered in Norway, it was found that reported performance was weak. According to a comparison between LRFP data and self-assessment by flag states, the accident records reported by the flag states are also incomplete.

In addition to bulk carriers, other types of ships also suffer from similar regulatory ineffectiveness, such as passenger ships (Lois *et al.* 2004; Kim 2005) and oil tankers (Llacer 2003). For instance, the passenger evacuation analysis in passenger ships has been found insufficient with respect to the IMO requirements (Vanem and Skjong 2006). The same study also suggested that in the current regime it is not sufficient to meet certain performance criteria of the IMO without an adequate study of their impact on the total safety of the ship. In some cases the IMO efforts have mainly concentrated on introducing manuals providing information about different response techniques that can be used (e.g. in the case of chemical spills) (Häkkinen Posti 2013).

Human behaviour is a very important element that designs, develops, builds, operates, manages, regulates and interacts with other elements of the system (Mullai and Paulsson 2011). The main cause of accidents is human error, with 80 per cent of accidents being so attributed (Talley *et al.* 2005a). However, it is not clear whether the human factor can be traced back to errors in design, construction or routine maintenance (Goulielmos and Tzanetos 1997). Analysis of on-board accidents due to human error has found they are often connected to insufficient English-language skills of seamen (Yercan *et al.* 2005). Harrald *et al.* (1998) described an incident as a triggering event, such as a human error or a mechanical failure, that creates an unsafe condition that may result in an accident. Toffoli *et al.* (2005) noted that although many incidents may be related to human errors, accidents still occur due to unexpected and dangerous sea states, which can result in an inability to keep the ship under proper control. Human errors, technical and mechanical failures and environmental factors are commonly underlined as factors leading to shipping accidents. Yip (2008) concluded that there is statistically significant evidence that the port of registration, the vessel type and the accident type are critical to the number of injuries and fatalities. Psarros *et al.* (2010) have provided data regarding the fact that the casualty records provided by NMD include the vessel's dimensions, geographical location and position of the accident, time, environmental conditions (visibility, wind, wave height), operational phase, navigation issues (type of chart, presence of pilot), cargo carried, extent of damage (serious, no damage, unknown), number of dead/injured, as well as details with regard to the causes (human error, procedural, organizational, equipment failure). However, there is no certain consensus on the statistical distribution of the causes of shipping accidents due to the different viewpoints of accident analysis and investigation approaches (Celik *et al.* 2010). Prevention of shipping accidents is still a crucial matter for maritime interests.

2.4.2 Accident review regarding pollution

Pollution prevention from ships is a major issue for the IMO. The International Convention for the Prevention of Pollution from Ships, 1973, as modified by the Protocol of 1978 (MARPOL 73/78) is an attempt to focus on the main issues that harm the environment. Amendments to MARPOL are sometimes due to the necessity for harmonization with other industries. Annex VI, which refers to preventing pollution resulting from air emissions of ships due to combustion of low-quality fuels, was based on the Kyoto Protocol of 1997. The costs that are imposed upon the shipping industry were not really taken into account (Bode *et al.* 2001).

A ship may pollute during its normal operation or in the case of an incident, such as oil discharge from a tanker's cargo tanks, the bunkers of a cargo ship or the discharge of any other hazardous cargo. Pollution from routine operation of a ship may include the transfer of alien species through ballast (Mingorance *et al.* 2009), release of harmful substances from a ship's coating (Karlsson *et al.* 2010), air emissions (Miola *et al.* 2010) and a ship's garbage (Ringbom 1999; Chen *et al.* 2013). All of these pollution threats are subject to maritime regulations, which also cover many additional operational requirements such as sewage treatment, reception facilities and combating of spills in both coastal and deep sea areas (Kopacz *et al.* 2001).

It has been argued that marine pollution could be eliminated due to technological improvements. Modern ship design and equipment can eliminate operational pollution and, therefore, maritime regulations are sometimes a follow-up to these innovations. A few very large spills are responsible for a high percentage of the total amount of oil spilled. Collisions and groundings account for more than 60 per cent of the incidents with more than 700 tons of oil spill (Vanem *et al.* 2008). According to the data of the International Tanker Owners Pollution Federation Limited (ITOPF), oil spills of less than seven tons account for 95 per cent of all oil spills (ITOPF 2012). By examining the ITOPF data, it is revealed that *Erika* (1999) and *Exxon Valdez* (1989) accidents caused more regulatory reaction by enforcing double-hull construction for tanker ships. However, the *Atlantic Empress* collision (1979) and *ABT Summer* (1991) caused 245,000 tons of oil to be spilled, which is almost three times the amount of *Erika* and *Exxon Valdez*. It has been argued that unilateral action may have better results than the agreements of the IMO. Llacer (2003) stated that some unilateral actions, such as OPA 1990 of the United States and 'Erika I' and 'Erika II' packages of the European Union, contributed to a reduction in marine pollution over a 12-year period, although maritime accidents still occur.

The various oil pollution and environmental regulations have generated a great deal of criticism regarding the criminal liability of seafarers, which can arise as a result of pollution incidents. The lack of adequate port facilities for the discharge of oily water, together with the expensive charges, may also lead companies to follow illegal practices (Wonham 1998).

When MARPOL was introduced, its intention was to eliminate pollution at sea. States found that it would be beneficial to impose penalties to the polluters in addition to cleaning costs. The cleaning costs are usually covered by the shipowners' insurance policies, and occasionally states require additional compulsory insurance (Ringbom 1999). Therefore, the main headache for a shipowner is the penalties, the reputation damage due to pollution and the imprisonment risk for his seafarers. Viladrich-Grau (2003) stated that it is difficult to distinguish whether pollution is a result of an accident or negligence. Early studies have estimated that an average spill of 400 tons could result in an average clean-up cost estimated to be approximately $3 million (Vanem *et al.* 2008). These costs could significantly increase if such an accident included loss of lives or damage of natural resources. Consequently, it is very tempting for a ship's master and/or operator not to report an incident if it is not detected by the authorities. This practice is against the scope of MARPOL, but there are several geographical areas where environmental pollution could go undetected, such as the oceans. MARPOL includes the requirement for each state to provide port facilities for the disposal of polluting substances. However, these services are not always free or available to ships. Expensive charges, therefore, for the use of port facilities may be a reason for a ship operator to follow illegal practices (Wonham 1998).

The success of a maritime regulation is in worldwide enforcement in order to applicable for all commercial ships involved in international voyages. However, regarding environmental pollution there are strong indications that it is successful only regionally. The success of pollution prevention regulations in ports and other regulated zones is doubtful (Giziakis and Bardi-Giziaki 2002; Burgherr 2007). In addition, the creation of port facilities at ports of states with weak economies may be a discouraging factor for MARPOL's full implementation (Tan and Khee 2002).

Furthermore, many developing countries may be in a weak position because their economies depend on foreign oil companies. In addition, these countries may not have the funding or the environmental expertise for the monitoring and research, or even the essential technological development in order to use these modern high-technology compounds. Therefore, they may end up with more contamination because they do not have the necessary regulatory structures to prevent it (Champ 2000). In contrast, it is easier for wealthier states to deal with large companies, as has been noted in the case of oil pollution in Europe and North America (Hamzah 2003).

Oil pollution accidents frequently affect more than one state. The European Commission, which aimed to facilitate improved coordination of national and regional research activities and policies, established the Accidental Marine Pollution ERA-Net 'AMPERA' (Garnacho *et al.* 2010). The AMPERA network was established to provide a platform where governmental policy makers and scientists could meet to discuss many aspects of accidental marine pollution, and to provide guidance to implement EU-wide measures as required.

The implementation of a maritime regulation is not an easy task. It needs careful planning from each stakeholder and there is a possibility for that stakeholder to be found in violation of a regulation due to poor implementation. This planning includes the addition of new certification and inspections, as in the case of air emissions (Lin and Lin 2006). Careless certification requirements imposed by authorities may lead to ambiguous results (Talley *et al.* 2005b). Certain ships' characteristics should be examined and prioritized for more rigorous inspections. A ship's age, flag of registry and size should be included in those characteristics. Furthermore, the operational status of a ship should be taken into account, as for example if it is anchored, moored or docked, towed/towing, underway or adrift. It is also very important that the implementation of a new regulation be carefully considered in relation to time frame, in order for a smooth change to be ensured. It has been reported that sudden changes to ship practices due to regulatory changes cause severe damage to the marine environment. For instance, Champ (2003) found that the ban of coatings that contain tributylin (TBT), which is required by the Antifouling Convention, could inadvertently release more TBT to ports and harbours in the five-year compliance period than has been leached from ships in the same waters over the past 40 years.

2.4.3 Accidents in the jurisdiction of a coastal state

The authority that a coastal state could exercise over foreign ships has different forms. The first is to prohibit areas where ships can sail in its territorial waters, if they are designated as highly important for that state. Such area are those related to fishing, tourism or any other environmental issue. However, such measures have not been proven to prevent accidents. For instance, with respect to the geographical distribution, it appears that the majority of collisions occur near coasts; this is in line with the findings from other researchers (Hsu *et al.* 2008; Kokotos and Linardatos 2011; Hsu 2012). Many spills still occur in ecologically sensitive locations because the major maritime transport routes often cross certain geographic areas, such as the Mexico Gulf, the Mediterranean and the Bay Gulf (Burgherr 2007). In some areas with high traffic, natural resources are exposed to human errors. For instance, marine collisions account for over two-thirds of all accidents within Hong Kong waters. About 5 per cent and 20 per cent of these accidents cause fatalities and injuries, respectively (Yip 2008).

Some oil spill cases, like those of the *Torrey Canyon* (1967), *Amoco Cadiz* (1978), *Exxon Valdez* (1989), *Erika* (1999) and *Prestige* (2002), have all led to great public concern and progressively to stricter regulations (Knudsen and Hassler 2011). A remedy for a coastal state is to organize a contingency plan for the case of an accident. Such a plan may include directions to the owner of the ship, its master or to any salvor in possession of the ship. These directions may govern all aspects of the position, movement and salvage of the ship and/or cargo and include even the destruction of the ship (Bywater 1995).

However, in the notable case of the *Prestige* accident, this plan was proven to be inadequate. Initially there was no designated port of refuge, since it was not obligatory in UNCLOS 1982 (Murray 2002). The decision of the Spanish authorities to order the damaged ship to sail into the rough sea had devastating results, causing the loss of the ship and a major oil spill (Roberts *et al.* 2005). The omissions of the Spanish authorities in proper planning put at risk a geographical area that also included other states, such as France and Portugal. Eventually, the ship master and the operator of *Prestige* were blamed through the media for the disaster.

Another similar case includes the *Castor* (2001), which was a cargo ship sailing around the Mediterranean for nearly 40 days with a severe crack on its deck (Murray 2002). The fear of several states of a possible pollution incident prevailed over a rational obligation to offer assistance to the ship and its crew. Another case is that of *Erika*, which was refused assistance by the French authorities, leading to an oil spill on the coast (Murray 2002). The appropriate helicopters to rescue the crew were only available from the UK. Therefore, the lack of sufficient resources, such as helicopters in the case of *Erika*, is an issue that is related to the cost of implementing maritime regulations and/or the superficiality of many states.

The above cases show that the implemented maritime regulations can fail in the event of an emergency. Powerful states with sufficient knowledge in maritime issues failed to respond to ships' requests. The states, fearing the consequences of oil pollution, did not provide adequate assistance. Such attitudes by some states may lead the shipping industry to a blame culture where seamen and sea operators will always be targeted.

References

Alderton T., Winchester N. (2002). Flag states and safety: 1997–1999. *Maritime Policy Management*, Vol. 29(2), pp. 151–162.

Bennett P. (2000). Mutuality at a distance? Risk and regulation in marine insurance clubs. *Environment and Planning*, Vol. 32, pp. 147–163.

Beukers J.M. (2000). Global radionavigation: the next 50 years and beyond. *Journal of Navigation*, Vol. 53, pp. 207–214.

Bode S., Isensee J., Krause K., Michaelowa A. (2001). Climate policy: analysis of ecological, technical and economic implications international maritime transport. *International Journal of Maritime Economics*, Vol. 4, pp. 164–184.

Bonnin D., Lane T., Ruggunan S., Wood G. (2004). Training and development in the maritime industry: the case of South Africa. *Human Resource Development International*, Vol. 7(1), pp. 7–22.

Burgherr P. (2007). In-depth analysis of accidental oil spills from tankers in the context of global spill trends from all sources. *Journal of Hazardous Materials*, Vol. 140, pp. 245–256.

Bywater J. (1995). Government response to marine pollution from ships. *Marine Policy*, Vol. 19(6), pp. 487–496.

Campa Portela R. (2005). Maritime casualties analysis as a tool to improve research about human factors on maritime environment. *Journal of Maritime Research*, Vol. 2(2), pp. 3–18.

Cariou P., Mejia M.Q., Wolff F.C. (2009). Evidence on target factors used for port state control inspections. *Marine Policy*, Vol. 33, pp. 847–859.

Celik M., Lavasani S.M., Jin Wang J. (2010). A risk-based modelling approach to enhance shipping accident investigation. *Safety Science*, Vol. 48, pp. 18–27.

Champ M.A. (2000). A review of organization regulatory strategies, pending actions, related costs and benefits. *The Science of the Total Environment*, Vol. 258, pp. 21–71.

Champ M.A. (2003). Economic and environmental impacts on ports and harbors from the convention to ban harmful marine anti-fouling systems. *Marine Pollution Bulletin*, Vol. 46, pp. 935–940.

Chantelauve G. (2003). An overview of maritime safety assessment trends in a stakeholder perspective. 14th European Safety and Reliability Conference, 15–18 June, Maastricht, Vol. 2, pp. 387–395.

Chen C.L., Liu T.K. (2013). Fill the gap: developing management strategies to control garbage pollution from fishing vessels. *Marine Policy*, Vol. 40, pp. 34–40.

Clark X., Dollar D., Micco A. (2004). Port efficiency, maritime transport costs, and bilateral trade. *Journal of Development Economics*, Vol. 75(2), pp. 417–450.

Dahlstrom A., Hewitt C., Campbell M., (2011). A review of international, regional and national biosecurity risk assessment frameworks. *Marine Policy*, Vol. 35, pp. 208–217.

Devine D. (2000). Port state jurisdiction: a judicial contribution from New Zealand. *Marine Policy*, Vol. 24, pp. 215–219.

Dyke J.M. (2005). The disappearing right to navigational freedom in the exclusive economic zone. *Marine Policy*, Vol. 29, pp. 107–121.

Dyke J.M. (2008). Canada's authority to prohibit LNG vessels from passing through Head Harbor passage to US ports. *Ocean & Coastal*, Vol. 14, pp. 45–50.

Equasis Statistics. (2005). The world merchant fleet in 2005. Statistics from Equasis.

Equasis Statistics. (2011). The world merchant fleet in 2011. Statistics from Equasis.

Gan X., Li K.X., Zheng H. (2011). Inspection policy of a port state control authority. In Proceedings of the International Forum on Shipping, Ports and Airports (IFSPA) 2010 – Integrated Transportation Logistics: From Low Cost to High Responsibility, 15–18 October 2010, Chengdu, Sichuan, China.

Garnacho E., Law R.J., Schallier R., Albaiges J. (2010). Targeting European R&D for accidental marine pollution. *Marine Policy*, Vol. 34(5), pp. 1068–1075.

Giziakis K., Bardi-Giziaki E. (2002). Assessing the risk of pollution from ship accidents. *Disaster Prevention and Management*, Vol. 11(2), pp. 109–114.

Glen D., Marlow P. (2009). Maritime statistics: a new forum for practitioners. *Maritime Policy & Management*, Vol. 36(2), 185–195.

Goss R. (2008). Social responsibility in shipping. *Marine Policy*, Vol. 32, pp. 142–146.

Goulielmos A., Tzannatos E. (1997). Management information system for the promotion of safety in shipping. *Disaster Prevention and Management*, Vol. 6(4), pp. 252–262.

Häkkinen J.M., Posti A.I. (2013). Overview of maritime accidents involving chemicals worldwide and in the Baltic Sea. *Marine Navigation and Safety of Sea Transportation: Maritime Transport and Shipping*, Vol. 15, pp. 15–25.

Hamzah B.A. (2003). International rules on decommissioning of offshore installations: some observations. *Marine Policy*, Vol. 27, pp. 339–348.

Harrald J.R., Mazzuchi T.A., Spahn J., Dorp R.V., Merrick J., Shrestha S., Grabowski M. (1998). Using system simulation to model the impact of human error in a maritime system. *Safety Science*, Vol. 30, pp. 235–247.

Hassler B. (2010). Global regimes, regional adaptation: environmental safety in Baltic Sea oil transportation, *Maritime Policy & Management* Vol. 37(5), pp. 489–503.

Hsu K.W. (2012). Ports' service attributes for ship navigation safety. *Safety Science* Vol. 50(2), 244–252.

Hsu K.Y., Chang Y.C., Chou H.P. (2008). An analysis of marine casualties of the international commercial port on the west coast of Taiwan. *Maritime Quarterly*, Vol. 17(1), pp. 45–62.

IACS. (2007). What, why and how. www.iacs.org.uk/_pdf/Class_WhatWhy&How.PDF [5 October 2007].

IMO. (1977). International Maritime Organization Convention. www.imprensa.macau. gov.mo/bo/i/92/16/out02.asp#eng [11 July 2006].

IMO. (2000). Objectives of the Organization in the 2000s, Resolution A.900 (21), February.

IMO. (2006a). *International Shipping and World Trade Facts and Figures*. IMO Publishing, London.

IMO. (2006b). *Revised Guidelines for the Identification and Designation of Particularly Sensitive Sea Areas*. IMO Publishing, London.

IMO. (2008). *Implications of the United Nations Conventions on the Law of the Sea for the International Maritime Organization*. IMO Publishing, London.

INTERCARGO. (2010). *Benchmarking Bulk Carriers: Casualty Report 2010*. INTER-CARGO.

ITOPF. (2012). Oil tanker spill statistics: 2006. www.itopf.com/stats.html [19 September 2012].

Karlsson J., Ytreberg E., Eklund B. (2010). Toxicity of anti-fouling paints for use on ships and leisure boats to non-target organisms representing three trophic levels. *Environmental Pollution*, Vol. 158(3), pp. 681–687.

Katarelos E.D., Alexopoulos A.B. (2007). The master's role in relation to the safety of the port, particularly under the concept of the ISM and the ISPS codes. In International Symposium on Maritime Safety, Security and Environmental Protection, Athens (Greece), 20 September.

Keyuan Z. (2002). Navigation of foreign ships within China's jurisdictional waters. *Maritime Policy Management*, Vol. 29(4), pp. 351–374.

Kim S.W. (2005). Formal fire safety assessment of passenger ships. Liverpool John Moore University. School of Engineering, PhD Thesis.

King J. (2005). The security of merchant shipping. *Marine Policy*, Vol. 29, pp. 235–245.

Klikauer T., Morris R. (2003). Human resources in the German maritime industries: 'back-sourcing' and ship management. *International Journal of Human Resource Management*, Vol. 14(4), pp. 544–558.

Knapp S., Franses P.H. (2007). A global view on port state control: econometric analysis of the differences across port state control regimes, *Maritime Policy & Management*, Vol. 34(5), pp. 453–482.

Knapp S., Franses P.H. (2009). Does ratification matter and do major conventions improve safety and decrease pollution in shipping? *Marine Policy*, Vol. 33, pp. 826–846.

Knapp S., Franses P.H. (2010). Comprehensive review of the maritime safety regimes: present status and recommendations for improvements. *Transport Reviews: A Transnational Transdisciplinary Journal*, Vol. 30(2), pp. 241–270.

Knudsen O. F., Hassler B. (2011). IMO legislation and its implementation: accident risk, vessel deficiencies and national administrative practices. *Marine Policy*, Vol. 35(2), pp. 201–207.

Kokotos D., Linardatos D. (2010). An application of data mining tools for the study of shipping safety in restricted waters. *Safety Science*, Vol. 49(2), pp. 192–197.

Kopacz Z., Morgas W., Urbanski J. (2001). The maritime safety system, its main components and elements. *The Journal of Navigation*, Vol. 54(2), pp. 199–211.

Li K.X., Cullinane K. (2003). An economic approach to maritime risk management and safety regulation. *Maritime Economics and Logistics*, Vol. 5, pp. 268–284.

Li K.X., Wonham J. (1999). Who is safe and who is at risk: a study of 20-year record on accident total loss in different flags. *Maritime Policy Management*, Vol. 26(2), pp. 137–144.

Li K.X., Wonham J. (2001). Maritime legislation: new areas for safety of life at sea. *Maritime Policy Management*, Vol. 28(3), pp. 225–234.

Lin B., Lin C.Y. (2006). Compliance with international emission regulations: reducing the air pollution from merchant ships. *Marine Policy*, Vol. 30, pp. 220–225.

Lindøe P.H., Engen O.A., Olsen O.E. (2011). Responses to accidents in different industrial sectors. *Safety Science*, Vol. 49(1), pp. 90–97.

Llacer F.J.M. (2003). Open registers: past, present and future. *Marine Policy*, Vol. 27, pp. 513–523.

Lois P., Wang J., Wall A., Ruxton T. (2004). Formal safety assessment of cruise ships. *Tourism Management*, Vol. 25, pp. 93–109.

Mason M. (2003). Civil liability for oil pollution damage: examining the evolving scope for environmental compensation in the international regime. *Marine Policy*, Vol. 27, pp. 1–12.

Mingorance M.C., Gómez J.I., Lozano F., Gómez A.U., González J.A., Calvilla J.M. (2009). Ballast and unballast operations in oil tankers: planktonic organisms that can travel with the ballast water. *Journal of Maritime Research*, Vol. 6(3), pp. 27–40.

Miola A., Ciuffo B., Giovine E., Marra M. (2010). Regulating air emissions from ships. The state of the art on methodologies, technologies and policy options. Joint Research Centre Reference Report, Luxembourg, 978–92.

Mitroussi K. (2004). Quality in shipping: IMO's role and problems of implementation. *Disaster and Prevention Management*, Vol. 13(1), pp. 50–58.

Mokashi A.J., Wang J., Vermar A.K. (2002). A study of reliability-centred maintenance in maritime operations. *Marine Policy*, Vol. 26, pp. 325–335.

Mullai A., Paulsson U. (2011). A grounded theory model for analysis of marine accidents. *Accident Analysis & Prevention,* Vol. 43(4), pp. 1590–1603.

Murray C.F. (2002). Any port in a storm? The right of entry for reasons of force majeure or distress in the wake of Erika and Castor. *Ohio State Law Journal*, Vol. 63, pp. 1465–1490.

Odeke A. (2005). An examination of bareboat charter registries and flag of convenience registries in international law. *Ocean Development and International Law*, Vol. 36, pp. 339–362.

Pallis A. (2006). Institutional dynamism in EU policy-making: the evolution of the EU maritime safety policy. *European Integration*, Vol. 28(2), pp. 137–157.

Paris MOU on port state control (2006). www.parismou.org/upload/doc/28th%20 Amendment.pdf [12 November 2006].

Perepelkin M., Knapp S., Perepelkin G., Pooter M. (2010). An improved methodology to measure flag performance for the shipping industry. *Marine Policy*, Vol. 34, pp. 395–405.

Plomaritou E., Plomaritou V., Giziakis K. (2011). Shipping marketing & customer orientation: the psychology & buying behaviour of charterer & shipper in tramp. *Management*, Vol. 16, pp. 57–89.

Psarros G., Skjong R., Eide M.S. (2010). Under-reporting of maritime accidents. *Accident Analysis & Prevention*, Vol. 42(2), pp. 619–625.

Ringbom H. (1999). Preventing pollution from ships: reflection on the 'adequacy' of existing rules. *Preventing Pollution from Ships*, Vol. 8(1), pp. 21–28.

Roberts J., Tsameny M., Workman T., Johnson L. (2005). The western European PSSA proposal: a 'politically sensitive sea area'. *Marine Policy*, Vol. 29, pp. 431–440.

Roberts S.E., Marlow P.B. (2002). Casualties in dry bulk shipping (1963–1996). *Marine Policy*, Vol. 26, pp. 437–450.

Robertson D.W. (2011). Criteria for recovery of economic loss under the Oil Pollution Act of 1990. Texas Journal of Oil, Gas & Energy Law, Vol. 7, pp. 241–414.

Roe M. (2009). Multi-level and polycentric governance: effective policymaking for shipping. *Maritime Policy & Management*, Vol. 36(1), pp. 39–56.

Sampson H. (2004). Romantic rhetoric, revisionist reality: the effectiveness of regulation in maritime education and training. *Journal of Vocational Education and Training*, Vol. 56(2), pp. 245–268.

Silos J.M., Piniella F., Monedero J., Walliser J. (2012). Trends in the global market for crews: a case study. *Marine Policy*, Vol. 36, pp. 845–858

Stenman C. (2005). The development of the MARPOL and EU regulations to phase out single hulled oil tankers. School of Economics and Law, Goteborg University. Master's thesis.

Talley W.K., Jin D., Powell H.K. (2005a). Determinants of crew injuries in vessel accidents. *Maritime Policy Management*, Vol. 32(3), pp. 263–278.

Talley W.K., Jin D., Powell H.K. (2005b). Post OPA-90 ship oil transfer spill prevention: the effectiveness of coast guard enforcement. *Environmental and Resource Economics*, Vol. 30, pp. 93–114.

Tan A., Khee J. (2002). The sea transport industry and the challenges of state regulation. NITAR Conference on the Seas and Security, 6–8 March, Hiroshima, Japan.

Toffoli A., Lefever J.M., Bitner-Gregersenc E., Monbaliua J. (2005). Towards the identification of warning criteria: analysis of a ship accident database. *Applied Ocean Research*, Vol. 2, pp. 281–291.

UNCTAD. (2012). *Review of Maritime Transport, 2012*. United Nations, New York and Geneva.

Vanem E., Endresen Ø., Skjong R. (2008). Cost-effectiveness criteria for marine oil spill preventive measures. *Reliability Engineering & System Safety*, Vol. 93(9), pp. 1354–1368.

Viladrich-Grau M. (2003). Monitoring policies to prevent oil spills: lessons from the theoretical literature. *Marine Policy*, Vol. 27, pp. 249–263.

Vince J., Haward M. (2009). New Zealand oceans governance: calming turbulent waters? *Marine Policy*, Vol. 33, pp. 412–418.

Wang J. (2006). Maritime risk assessment and its current status. *Quality and Reliability Engineering International*, Vol. 22, pp. 2–19.

Wonham J. (1998). Agenda 21 and sea-based pollution: opportunity or apathy? *Marine Policy*, Vol. 22(4–5), pp. 375–391.

Yercan F., Fricke D., Stone L. (2005). Developing a model on improving maritime English training for maritime transportation safety. *Educational Studies*, Vol. 31(2), pp. 213–234.

Yip T.L. (2008). Port traffic risks: a study of accidents in Hong Kong waters. *Transportation Research Part E: Logistics and Transportation Review*, Vol. 44(5), pp. 921–931.

Yu L., Das P.K., Zheng Y. (2009). A response surface approach to fatigue reliability of ship structures. *Ships and Offshore Structures*, Vol. 4(3), pp. 253–259.

3 Management tools for implementing maritime regulations

3.1 Introduction

The success of the regulatory regime described in the previous chapters is threatened due to two main risks. The first one is that the regulations introduced are excessive. The other is that a maritime regulation may be inadequately enforced in some regions. The IMO, recognizing a potential risk of excessive regulatory regime with inadequate enforcement, decided to change its strategy by targeting the worldwide implementation of regulations. Some of the practices and tools of the IMO are analysed in the first part of this chapter. In the second part, sectors with similar concerns about excessive regulations, such as high-risk industries and governments, are investigated. Lessons could be learned from other industries when comparing available practices, which may be applicable to the shipping industry.

3.2 The IMO strategic plan

The IMO developed a strategic plan in order to monitor its performance towards its aims and objectives. This strategic plan was first introduced in 2004 with Resolution A.909(22). This plan was further developed by IMO Resolutions A.944(23) and A.970(24). In this plan the IMO drafted a list of 18 performance indicators to monitor the achievement of an organization's objectives. According to this plan, the implementation of regulations is monitored through three indicators, such as the number of conventions adopted by states, the number of conventions that have entered into force and the number of states that have adopted a self-audit scheme. Currently the strategic plan has been revised for the six-year period 2012 to 2017 with IMO Resolution A.1037(27). However, the 43 performance indicators are not a measurement system capable of evaluating the success of the organization objectives. Moreover, it appears that these indicators are of equal importance, which may not always be true.

3.3 Tools that the IMO has introduced for regulation implementation

As an internal improvement, the IMO has adopted the Formal Safety Assessment (FSA) method as a valuable tool to evaluate all aspects of a proposed and an existing maritime regulation in terms of costs vs benefits and minimization of any new risk (Rosqvist and Tuominen 2004; Lois 2004; IMO 1997b). Furthermore, at a state level, the IMO encourages coastal states to exercise their authority more rigorously by inspecting foreign ships regarding their compliance with international maritime regulations and by strengthening the procedure of the PSC (Sage 2005). In addition, the IMO has introduced the ISM Code as a valuable tool to obligate ship operators to adopt maritime regulations. Many IMO circulars include a reminder for ship operators that they have an obligation to revise their management systems when such a circular is applicable to their ships. Such a wording limits the options of a ship operator to adopt the circular or to justify why he did not adopt it.

3.3.1 Formal safety assessment

The IMO, having identified problems in the willingness of some states to enforce regulations either as flag or coastal states, adopted the FSA methodology targeting the improvement of maritime regulations. The FSA method was proposed to the IMO by the UK's Maritime and Coastguard Agency (MCA) and was accepted as an essential tool to evaluate maritime regulations (Ruuda and Mikkelsen 2008; Alderton and Winchester 2002; IMO 1997a). The aim of the FSA is to provide the appropriate scientific background for the design of maritime regulations (Wang 2000). The IMO, recognizing the need for a uniform implementation of maritime regulations, promoted the FSA method as a part of the regulatory process (IMO 2002).

The FSA is a rational and systematic process for assessing the risks related to maritime safety and protection of the marine environment, as well as for evaluating the costs and benefits of the IMO's options (Knapp and Franses 2009). Under the FSA method, every new proposed regulation should be thoroughly examined by the following five steps (Lois *et al.* 2004):

1   identify any hazards;
2   conduct risk assessment;
3   find risk control options;
4   estimate costs and benefits;
5   make recommendations for decision making.

The FSA method, due to its generic form, was used in many applications to assess the effectiveness of a regulation. The application of the FSA is limited to major changes in the regulative framework, but its concept is to provide a proactive versus a reactive approach (Knapp and Franses 2009). Many FSA studies focused on the safety of bulk carriers due to their high rate of loss in the 1990s.

Although some generic studies were attempted for bulk carriers (MCA 1998), it was found that, due to the complicated nature of bulk carriers' structure, some studies were focused on specific parts of the ships. For instance, Lee *et al.* (2001) studied the hatchway watertight integrity of bulk carriers and Spyrou *et al.* (2003) assessed the standards for the construction of bulk carriers.

The FSA method was also used in other types of ships, such as cruise ships (Lois *et al.* 2004) and passenger ships (Tzannatos 2005), as well as for carrying out studies for various types of accidents, such as oil spill accidents (Ventikos and Psaraftis 2004). In more recent applications, academics have investigated the risks in various ship operations, such as navigation (Hu *et al.* 2007). The FSA studies were used to assess the cost-effectiveness of hull girder safety (Skjong and Bitner-Gregersen 2002), and to evaluate port safety (Trbojevic and Carr 2000) and offshore safety (Wang 2002). The applicability of the FSA has also been extended to coastal states (Sage 2005). Antao and Soares (2008) noted that with the development of a structured and systematic methodology, such as FSA, several studies have been conducted on its application to high-speed crafts. Eide *et al.* (2009) applied the FSA method to assess the cost-effectiveness of CO_2-reducing measures in shipping, while machinery space fire hazards in the maritime oil sector have also been examined (Ikeagwuani and John 2013).

The extensive number of studies mentioned above revealed a number of limitations when the FSA method is applied. Its generic approach assumes a generic ship model as a reference point for comparison. However, when studying a more specialized ship, this generic approach has several limitations (Chantelauve 2004). Furthermore, the risk identification is based on the existing fault-tree and event-tree analysis. The fault tree analysis begins with a known event (referred to as the top event) and describes possible combinations of events and conditions that can lead to this event. In both cases, you start by analysing what was wrong which led to an accident or what could go wrong. These approaches are sometimes restricted to more complicated studies (Kaneko 2002; Mennis *et al.* 2005).

Apart from the hazard identification stage, there was great concern with respect to the cost–benefit analysis. The cost of a regulation may affect some stakeholders more than others. This issue is not included in the FSA studies of Vanem *et al.* (2008), something that is of high importance, as is discussed in Chapter 2. In terms of safety, the FSA addresses three levels of risk: intolerable, as low as reasonably practicable (ALARP) and negligible. The use of resources applies to the ALARP region, and although this may not be the best idea, it is a rather convenient solution.

The limitations of the FSA method have slowed down its establishment in the IMO procedures. Disagreements among member states of the IMO with respect to the results of each study were enough to put aside the method. FSA studies from Japan, Greece and the UK had very different conclusions, creating regulatory confusion rather than agreement in respect of double-skin bulk carriers' efficiency (IMO 2004; Wang 2006). On the other hand, there are some who believe that the different FSA outcomes were mainly based on the lack of historical data regarding accidents and pollution incidents. For instance, Psarros *et al.* (2010) have also argued that the validity of historical data may be undermined by uncertainties, which will considerably affect the FSA studies.

A solution to the data selection issue could be the inclusion of qualitative parameters that will ensure the validity of the available data when included in FSA studies. The quality assurance of a study is a term to describe that the result could be repeatedly found by different researchers. Like in any other research method, when different data are used the results may vary significantly. An outcome of the FSA method is very likely to depend on the different data that will be selected and evaluated (Rosqvist and Tuominen 2004). The role of the stakeholders and experts in providing qualitative and quantitative information is crucial with respect to the quality of the FSA method (Rosqvist and Tuominen 2004).

Moreover, the FSA focuses on the identification of good cost–benefit outcomes and risk-reducing measures, and not on the explicit reduction of individual or societal risks. This is understandable since the goal of the IMO is to have a risk-based methodology widely accepted by the member states that may have different approaches to risk criteria or may not have risk criteria at all (Trbojevic 2006).

It should be stressed that the FSA method is not designed to assist a ship operator to improve its management or to implement a new regulation, although some shipowners have developed their own safety approaches (Wang 2006). On the contrary, it is applied by governments and non-governmental organizations working within the framework of the IMO (IMO 1997b). However, it should be considered as a milestone in safety improvement on board ships, since it introduced a rational framework for risk assessment. It is also recognized in FSA studies that a hazard could be minimized but within reasonable costs. It is a well-known concept in engineering that the ratio of safety to cost becomes meaningless after a certain point, since absolute safety cannot be achieved and minor hazards will remain. On the other hand, this concept should not be confused with the practice of reducing safety in favour of minimizing costs.

3.3.2 *International safety management code for the safety of ships and pollution prevention*

The origins of the International Safety Management Code for the Safety of Ships and Pollution Prevention (ISM Code) are based on several early studies arguing that the most common root for accidents is human error. This could easily be translated to error on board ships but also to poor management decisions of ship operators (Thai and Grewal 2006). The ship operator is free to structure and develop his organization as he feels is best. One part of this management is to develop procedures for his employees on board and ashore, in order for them to follow his managerial decisions. This management practice is already in use by other industries, such as nuclear and the offshore industry (Goulielmos *et al.* 2008). The IMO encouraged the establishment of a safety management system (SMS) in accordance with the ISM Code, which was a critical milestone for maintaining legislative control in shipping (Celik *et al.* 2010). Although the ISM Code is a maritime regulation with a limited scope, it was a step ahead for setting quality standards in the shipping industry.

The ISM Code is related to the improvement of public control and its follow-up, as well as to the improvement of contract relations among the flag states (Triantafylli and Ballas 2010). Each flag state sets its unique requirement with regard to the ISM Code implementation in the ships flying its flag. Those requirements are referred to as the minimum procedures that should be included by each ship operator. Typical evidence that these procedures are being followed is the records that are generated, such as certificates, checklists and inventories. The ISM Code applies at all levels ashore and afloat. It includes 12 paragraphs that cover a wide range of issues, as shown in Table 3.1. Every ship operator should design an SMS that will include procedures for continuous improvement in the areas of policy, planning, communication, emergency preparedness, emergency response, checking and corrective actions (Pun *et al.* 2003; IMO 1993).

The SMS should especially involve risk management along with self-checking and self-critical measures (Bhattacharya 2012). For instance, in paragraph 10 of the ISM Code, the procedures, requirements and obligations that a shipping company must have in place are mentioned to ensure the company's conformity with international regulations (Lazakis *et al.* 2010).

The effectiveness of the SMS should be evaluated through a process of audits. The audit is carried out by an experienced individual with relevant certification, and includes interviews and examination of the relevant documents. It is a requirement of the code that the internal examination of the SMS will be annual. Any procedures that were not followed or not updated in accordance with maritime regulations will be recorded as non-conformities. The academic and industrial background of an auditor may vary. Therefore, the SMS should also be examined by external auditors annually regarding the office and periodically regarding the ship (Thai and Grewal 2006; Chen 2000). The SMS is externally audited by approved organizations of the flag state, such as a classification society (Chen 2000). However, all these audits are carried out on a sample basis procedure and may fail to reveal existing management limitations. It is therefore up to the ship operator to set the quality standards of its fleet (Fafaliou *et al.* 2006).

Table 3.1 The ISM Code Paragraphs

Part A – Implementation
General
Safety and Environmental-Protection Policy
Company Responsibilities and Authority
Designated Person(s)
Master's Responsibility and Authority
Resources and Personnel
Shipboard Operations
Emergency Preparedness
Reports and Analysis of Non-Conformities, Accidents and Hazardous Occurrences
Maintenance of the Ship and Equipment
Documentation
Company Verification, Review and Evaluation

Part B – Certification and Verification
Certification and Periodical Verification
Interim Certification
Verification
Forms of Certificates

The key element of an effective SMS, as stated within the text of the ISM Code, is commitment from the top management. The choices of an FOC or a substandard classification society are two efficient tactics for a ship operator who does not wish to pursue full compliance with the Code. As all other maritime regulations, the certification of a ship and/or its operator is evidence of a flag state's compliance and non-compliance with the IMO standards. As it was clarified above, the intention of the IMO was not to develop a punishment regulatory environment. However, several courts and states used the records produced by an SMS as evidence of potential criminal liability to which the carrier, the master or the crew are exposed (Chen 2000). A similar approach has also been adopted in commercial disputes, where inadequate documentation of a ship operator could lead to claims issued by third parties, such as cargo owners (Chen 2000). It is argued that the ISM Code is an attempt to regulate human actions because they are likely to lead to claims regarding ship accidents (Talley *et al.* 2005). From this aspect, the ISM Code has been established in the shipping industry as a regulation/punishment of human omissions.

A main challenge for a ship operator is to set the baseline of his SMS with the risk to exclude essential issues. The audit process is not an effective solution. Feedback which could come from third-party inspections could provide more information. An SMS depends on the effective management of information by the crew and others, such as PSC's and classification societies' inspections. This information is used for carrying out quality ship management and maintenance by setting the foundations for a preventive maintenance regime (Goulielmos and Tzannatos 1997; Lazakis *et al.* 2010). However, relying on the many different international and national safety standards could be confusing, as they are numerous. Nevertheless, those standards provide guidance to help ship operators develop their SMS (Pun *et al.* 2003).

The skills required of managers in a ship operator's organization are significant, as the ISM Code structure and success is based on their leadership and commitment. In Chapter 7 the issue of evaluating a manager with respect to his lack of knowledge and experience is discussed extensively. The managers' beliefs and attitudes may mislead top management in a ship operator's organization about the safety standards of his ships. This issue may be more acute in small-scale ship operators. Due to financial limitations, a minor ship operator may choose managers with a more technical background rather than quality assurance knowledge. Some say that such a ship operator should be out of the maritime industry. However, this may be challenging since, as they represent a significant proportion of the market, they may experience various difficulties complying with the ISM Code requirements. A positive solution could be for a ship operator to hand over management of his fleet to a third-party ship management company (Mitroussi 2004). However, such a solution would favour major ship operators.

The training of seafarers is another important element of the ISM Code; they must be capable of operating the ship according to its requirements (Norris 2007). However, it has been argued that the training requirements may be difficult to fulfil in a modern and automatic ship with newly introduced technologies

(Goulielmos 2003). The transition from paper charts to electronic chart display and information systems (ECDIS) is a typical example of this move to new technologies. PSC officers frequently reveal that navigation officers are not very familiar with these new technologies.

However, even regarding the traditional navigation practices, training needs are frequently found by PSC authorities to be highly variable, because many ISM Code certified ships' bridge teams appear to lack the appropriate training, attitude, culture and management (Thai and Grewal 2006). Those training needs could partially be fulfilled after the Manila amendments to the STCW. The path for online training and certification is now officially open and ship operators can benefit from it. Of course, the training of ships requires experienced personnel ashore and adoption of software packages.

The shipping industry adopted the ISM Code in a generic form, something that resulted in a bureaucratic system that may not be reliable if not appropriately monitored. For instance, this bureaucratic system was supported by the increase of manpower on board ships. Consequently, the shipping industry may become one in which it is very difficult for small ship operators to run their businesses. In addition, some ship operators may have an over-reliance on following procedures but without this resulting in signficant improvement, or may adjust procedures to fit the existing culture, believing this to be satisfactory. Employees over-burdened with paperwork required by the ISM Code may prefer to take shortcuts (Thai and Grewal 2006). Therefore, such shortcuts may lower the safety standards of their ship. Furthermore, a misunderstanding of the ISM Code elements could exist in an organization. The findings of Tzannatos and Kokotos (2012) show a considerable gap between managers' and seafarers' understanding of the use of the ISM Code, resulting in a wide gap between its intended purpose and practice.

A significant limitation regarding the ISM Code implementation is the beliefs and understanding of each person with respect to the safety systems. To date, there are several theories that attempt to explain human behaviour towards those systems. There are two main schools of thought: one refers to the safety culture as established by Havold (2000, 2005), and the other to national cultures (Hofstede 1983). The safety culture approach deals with the attitude of top management. Many academics have identified that the safety priorities of a company are subject to its safety culture. The safety culture of a company is established by its top management team and progressively adopted by its employees (Havold 2000). Safety culture is difficult to accurately describe, but it consists of essential procedures, such as communications, decision making, problem solving and conflict resolution (Havold 2005). Research has also identified the role of nationality in safety culture in the shipping industry. Havold (2005) suggested that the safety culture of a shipping company is related to the nationality of its employees. A mix of nationalities is a disadvantage for a company when developing its safety culture. Literature from other industries supports this finding. The ISM Code is based on the Western point of view, which is not necessarily appreciated or understood by other nations.

3.3.3 *Quality systems*

The limited scope of the ISM Code and its generic format has led organizations to adopt other management tools. A quality system such as the ISO 9001:2008 standards set by the International Organization for Standardization (ISO) appears to be a positive solution. The scope of these standards is to help organizations ensure that they meet the needs of customers and other stakeholders while meeting statutory and regulatory requirements related to the product. Compliance with ISO is a requirement imposed by some governmental agencies on companies competing for public procurement contracts and by some major customer groups (such as automotive) on their suppliers (Kleindorfer and Saad 2005). The clauses of ISO 9001:2008 standards are shown in Table 3.2.

The ISO 9001:2008 could be considered as an extension of the ISM Code into the shipping industry, including quality of services. The adaptation of the

Table 3.2 The clauses of ISO 9001:2008 standards

1 Scope
2 Normative references
3 Terms and definitions
4 Quality management system
   4.1 General requirements
   4.2 Documentation requirements
5 Management responsibility
   5.1 Management commitment
   5.2 Customer focus
   5.3 Quality policy
   5.4 Planning
   5.5 Responsibility, authority and communication
   5.6 Management review
6 Resource management
   6.1 Provision of resources
   6.2 Human resources
   6.3 Infrastructure
   6.4 Work environment
7 Product realization
   7.1 Planning of product realization
   7.2 Customer-related processes
   7.3 Design and development
   7.4 Purchasing
   7.5 Production and service provision
   7.6 Control of measuring and monitoring devices
8 Measurement, analysis and improvement
   8.1 General
   8.2 Measurement and monitoring
   8.3 Control of non-conforming product
   8.4 Analysis of data
   8.5 Improvement

ISO quality standards in the shipping business provides invaluable benefits with regard to the technical management of the merchant fleet, and is also very useful for both improving the service quality and enhancing customer satisfaction in the market. A brief list of stakeholders that benefit from shipping services could include charterers, terminals and cargo owners in terms of speedy and safe delivery of cargo (Triantafylli and Ballas 2010). However, use of ISO 9001 in the shipping industry is on a voluntary basis. Companies that choose to follow these standards receive an ISO 9001 certification to assure their customers about the quality of the services they offer. It is an effort to convince their customers that their aim is not only regulatory compliance as per the ISM Code requirements, but it is also a customer-focused strategy.

A detailed comparison of the ISM Code with ISO 9001:2008 standards shows many similarities. Although these two tools are different in scope, some elements, such as the human resources, planning and measurement, are common. The similar structures of the ISM Code and the ISO 9001 standards has led academics, such as Celik (2009), to propose integrated quality and safety management systems (IQSMS) for shipping operations. However, in the same research a main limitation that was revealed was ensuring compliance of the ISO quality standards with the relevant maritime regulations while structuring an integrated management system in practice.

3.3.4 Port State Control

The overall ineffective flag state monitoring of their fleets led the coastal states to make more rigorous Port State Control (PSC) inspections. Historically the roots of PSC can be traced to the exercise of inspections for customs and immigration purposes (Molenaar 2007). UNCLOS 1982 clearly states that a coastal state can inspect foreign ships within its territorial water to identify their compliance with maritime regulations (Sage 2005). Based on the existing legal framework, the IMO motivates PSC inspections through specific circulars on how the inspections should be conducted and on the minimum qualifications of PSC officers (Knapp and Franses 2007a, 2007b).

Unfortunately, although ships trading even in limited geographical areas are subject to a rigorous inspection, so far the success of PSC inspections is regional and not worldwide. Therefore, the majority of ships should be in full compliance with maritime regulations if they intend to visit states such as the United States, EU or Australia.

It has been argued that PSC has insufficient quality and capacity to fully compensate for flag state defects (Knudsen and Hassler 2011). For instance, the main focus of PSC for several years has been to increase safety standards on board and prevent pollution, while other regulatory issues, such as ILO conventions about the daily life of those persons living and working on the vessel, are of lower significance (Silos *et al.* 2012). The labour standards are an issue that, after the enforcement of the Maritime Labour Convention 2006 (MLC), is expected to be resolved. The main change of MLC 2006 is that the labour standards will now be inspected by flag states and PSC. Any violation could result in penalties for the negligent ship operator. The PSC role in the regulatory implementation should be distinguished from the FSA and the ISM Code, due to its policing nature.

A typical PSC inspection consists of two main stages: the inspection and the imposition of penalties when violations of maritime regulations are found. Each inspection of the ship includes examination of safety, firefighting, navigation and marine pollution prevention equipment. Other structural items that are also examined may obstruct the welfare of seamen as well as their payment. It is up to the PSC to decide how severe a violation is and to take a series of measures to prevent the ship sailing (Li and Zheng 2008). The severity of a violation could lead to the issuance of a report listing the deficiencies which should be rectified in a specific period or even before the departure of the ship; otherwise the ship could be prohibited from sailing. A deficiency will be recorded when a PSC officer identifies a threat to the safety of a ship or its crew, to the marine environment or to the health or labour rights of seamen. In exceptional cases where immediate repairs are required, the PSC authority may allow the ship to sail to the nearest shipyard for immediate repairs (Molenaar 2007; Keselj 1999).

The results of the records are released to the flag state and public databases. Cariou *et al.* (2009) found that the factors that could lead to a detention of a ship following a PSC inspection would mainly be the age of the vessel at inspection (40 per cent), the recognized organization (31 per cent) and the place where the inspection occurs (17 per cent). In their research, they concluded that the detention rates are essentially explained by the differences in the characteristics of vessels calling in a specific country rather than by the differences in the way the inspections are done. On the other hand, Tzannatos and Kokotos (2012) remarked that the recorded deficiencies, being the result of a PSC inspector's opinion, are easily influenced by a host of subjective issues, such as the attitude of the crew, the ease of inspection and the inspector's mood.

There are some limitations of the PSC in terms of its quality, its operational costs and its effectiveness. One limitation is the variation in the PSC officers' skills (Bloor *et al.* 2006). In order for someone to become a PSC officer, he should follow a unique pathway which is beyond the relevant IMO guidelines. This pathway should include a selection of criteria regarding academic qualifications and professional experience. Then, it is necessary for the officer to receive special training regarding the maritime regulations. Although this process sounds simplified, there are a few main obstacles. Initially, there are not qualified PSC officers in all states, since ship knowledge is not at equal levels everywhere (Knapp and Franses 2007a). The scope of the technical committee created by the IMO is to increase knowledge within certain states. The training should be regular and efficient. However, this is an expensive process because of the training hours that a candidate PSC officer should regularly spend and because of the failure rate.

It is up to the PSC officer to fully appreciate and understand the fundamental role of a ship's safety. A second limitation is the integrity of the PSC officers (Bloor *et al.* 2006). Since the detention of a ship is published, it also has a negative value. There are some occasions on which ship operators and crew members are forced to pay PSC officers in order to avoid detention. Of course, in such a case it is obvious that there are deficiencies on board the ship which should be ratified. However, the use of PSC detentions as a tool to evaluate a ship is sometimes used for unethical purposes by other PSC authorities and/or charterers.

A PSC report of a ship with many deficiencies will most likely reflect a negative image of its crew. Therefore, crew members are anxious and may try to mislead authorities regarding damage to the ship and its equipment. This poor cooperation with authorities could be listed as a third limitation in promoting overall safety. The current system is focused on finding failures rather than promoting successes. The PSC deficiencies should be read as the percentage of items examined and found successful.

The port contingency of some places and insufficient manpower have led to the target factor system. The rationale of this system is that ships with few deficiencies will be inspected less frequently and less severely. The limitation of this system is that some ship characteristics, such as the flag, the classification society, the type and the age of a ship, may indicate the need for immediate inspection (Cariou *et al.* 2008; Sampson and Bloor 2007; Knapp and Franses 2007b). A major disadvantage of this system is that its factors rely on previous records, which may not represent the true condition of a ship. Statistics from previous inspections show either a high or a low probability that a ship will be found poorly managed and/or defective.

A fifth limitation is the costs of PSC inspections, which can be divided into two categories:

1   administration costs of PSC;
2   cost of rectifying deficiencies.

The administration costs are all the necessary expenses that a coastal state must bear in order to maintain a PSC administration, such as training PSC officers (Li and Zheng 2008). There are several administrative employees that support the task of PSC officers, who are included in the above expenses. Another main expense is salaries at a level that will eliminate the alleged corruption incidents. Some states have several ports with few ship visits per year. However, it is very challenging to have PSC officers at all these ports. Consequently, funding is a main challenge for many states, especially after the recession period of 2008, which left many states struggling to save their economies.

The second category of costs generates a burden for the ship operators (Molenaar 2007). Some deficiencies may be very costly due to repairs and availability of the required equipment, especially in small ports. These costs look like a reasonable punishment for poorly operated ships, since the PSC officers usually ask for repairs when a ship is found to be of a low standard. However, a careful examination of the above critical review carried out by Cariou *et al.* (2009) indicates that older ships are more likely to be found with deficiencies. This poses a commercial disadvantage to ship operators who manage older ships and especially those who cannot afford to acquire new ships. Therefore, the PSC benefits the most powerful ship operators.

Many PSCs have launched a regional cooperation known as Memorandum of Understanding (MOU) agreements. The states participate in the MOU and today nine PSC regimes exist covering most port states. These regional MOUs enforce the international legislation and act as a second line of defence against substandard shipping, where the first line of defence is the flag state itself (Perepelkin *et al.* 2010). The Paris MOU organization, which consists of 25 member states, decided to ban any ship that exceeds a specific number of detentions from its ports (Molenaar 2007). The banning rule targets not only substandard ships, but also substandard flags, since the flag is a main criterion in banning. The ban rule of the Paris MOU states that any ship with more than two or three detentions, depending on its flag, will be banned from all Paris MOU member ports.

The banning of a ship has devastating financial and reputation damages for its operator. If a ship is banned it is prohibited to sail in a large geographical area that includes the member states of Paris MOU, Canada and the Russian Federation. The detention of a ship under the above ban rule is expected to reduce its commercial value, since the detention record remains with the ship even if it changes owner or operator.

3.4 Investigation of sectors with excessive regulatory regimes

The maritime industry is overregulated because it is characterized as high risk. A maritime accident may cause catastrophic results to the marine environment and/ or to human beings. The solutions discussed above are mainly borrowed from other high-risk industries. Those practices in industries such as aviation, nuclear plants, chemicals and petrochemicals have been applied for several years, and can also be introduced to the maritime industry. Therefore, it is interesting to examine the evolution of those industries in terms of safety with respect to their regulatory environment.

Reiman and Rollenhagen (2011), by examining the safety management systems of aviation and nuclear, found that it is quite common to detect deviations from rules and regulations. They argued that in such complicated industries the fact that something deviates from a prescribed rule is not necessarily a contributor to an accident or even an abnormal event. People have the tendency to prefer their own practices rather than follow written procedures. Therefore, a major question that is worthy of investigation is why those industries have experienced fewer accidents than the shipping industry, when observance of procedures and regulations is not absolute.

From the regulatory perspective, the leading authority in the shipping industry is the IMO, which brings together many world states. Some researchers, such as Björn (2010), have argued that too much effort has been made by the IMO focusing on the implementation of the existing universal conventions, when local action that has been taken in areas where individual countries' interests are strong has not been indispensable (e.g. particularly sensitive sea areas). Some safety issues could be more effectively dealt with by using global conventions, whereas others seem to be more successfully managed at lower levels, involving only one or a small number of countries. Additionally, a main issue for states that are willing to implement regulations is the cost-effectiveness of the abatement measures (Heitmann and Khalilian 2011). Therefore, it is noteworthy to examine how governments face the risk of excessive regulation. Governments are concerned with the issue of effective regulation. Otherwise the management of a state is ineffective, providing fertile land corruption and suffering of its citizens. An effective regulation should not pose a disadvantage to small companies, but should be rigorous. Furthermore, a government should drive local companies to follow innovation and modern practices. Thus, various tactics used by governments were investigated as an alternative approach to those that exist in industries.

3.4.1 The offshore industry regulatory regime

The offshore industry is very similar to the shipping industry, due to its sea environment and the associated hazards and problems. Vinnem *et al.* (2010) have identified the organizational/regulatory factors that are important for safety in the offshore industry. The dimensions are: technology/operations, values/attitudes/skills, relationships/networks and interaction (Vinnem *et al.* 2010). The offshore industry forerunner for the shipping industry. For instance, Lindøe *et al.* (2011) noticed that in Norway there was a delay of 15–20 years from the development of enforced self-regulation in the offshore petroleum industry until the emergence of the same principles within the maritime industries, including fisheries.

It is also bound by various regulations at both local and international level. For instance, in some countries the political regime may perceive labour as cheap and disposable, while in other countries the moral and ethical obligations of governments associated with protecting people from harm at work should be a sufficiently strong motivating force to ensure the implementation of effective safety management systems that go beyond the local legislative requirements (Mearns and Yule 2008). In many states the regulations are very descriptive, including definitions of hazards. For instance, the definition of a serious occupational injury in Norway is described in the regulations (Vinnem *et al.* 2010). Compared to the maritime industry, the offshore regulatory regime is more uniform. Hayes (2012) noted that the Australian regulatory regime for offshore safety is based on the same theoretical frameworks as the equivalent regimes in Europe.

It appears that the most suitable solution that could be used in the maritime industry is related to the management systems. Safety at sea could benefit by moving from the ISM Code to more robust ISO standards, such as ISO 9001 and ISO 1400. In the offshore industry it is argued that safety should be the result of the development of new procedures where appropriate (Stacey and Sharp 2007; Mohamed Ali and Louca 2008). With regard to the human factor, academics have suggested that building a stronger safety culture among employees in the offshore industry will accomplish quality systems' goals (Conchie and Donald 2008; Mearns and Yule 2008). This practice has also been examined in the maritime industry.

Both of the available solutions place a major responsibility on an operator of an oil platform to provide evidence by means of an FSA that he has identified risks to occupational health and safety (Paterson 2011). For this to happen, the regulator must be convinced of the theoretical and practical challenges. Regarding the theoretical challenges, statistics should be used when risk assessment studies are carried out to identify potential risks and determine their consequences. In the second stage the results of these studies should by applied in practice, in order to demonstrate how this risk minimization was or would be achieved. Such requirements often demand that specialist consultants be involved. While this appeared to be useful in the post-Piper Alpha era, the understanding of the offshore risks is now believed to be mature (Paterson 2011). Therefore, instead of consultants, it is the management of the offshore industry that are obliged to carry out risk assessment studies.

The above solutions have partially been introduced in the shipping industry through the ISM Code. However, this partial enforcement may be one reason for the low achievement, as discussed in Section 3.3.2.

3.4.2 The aviation industry regulatory regime

Aviation has much in common with the maritime industry. Both are international in nature, their fleets travel worldwide carrying goods and people, with the headquarters of the company often based in one country. The aviation industry has international safety regulatory bodies with which all member states must comply (e.g. the European Aviation Safety Agency, EASA) (O'Connor *et al.* 2011). An essential part is the existence of a mechanism for national and international regulations, which is the system of aircraft registration (Odeke 2005). The regulatory framework is based on collective agreements in international bodies, such as the EU and International Civil Aviation Organisation (Brooker 2006a). Each aircraft is registered to a state and, in a similar way to ships with regard to flag states, it should also comply with that state's laws. In the aftermath of security incidents, the aviation industry is more rigorously regulated, going beyond safety standards (Zhang and Round 2008; Bailey 2002). The commercial impact of those regulations refers mainly to security controls.

The introduction of regulations in aviation generated some scepticism in the industry with respect to their efficiency. Although safety inspections are welcomed, the burden should be on essential operational practices (Brooker 2006a). It is also believed that the regulatory pressure does not necessarily include all safety factors, which in some cases remain unknown. Furthermore, Liou *et al.* (2008) noted that as a result of the regulatory pressure, SMSs have been institutionalized by most airlines, but there is no comprehensive SMS model for the aviation industry, while the structural relations among SMS still remain unknown. Brooker (2006b) concluded the following points from his study:

1   There is a risk of generating unnecessary and/or unproductive bureaucracy in safety regulation.

2   The safety regulations need to be exposed to the scrutiny of professional criticism, with all the key source material underpinning regulations being in the public domain.
3   The scope of definitions and characteristics should be as comprehensive and open as possible, and safety responsibilities should be clear, complete and comprehensive.

The EASA and other aviation regulatory bodies, such as the Federal Aviation Authority and the Civil Air Navigation Services Organization, have recognized the importance of safety culture and are engaged in research exploring, measuring and enhancing safety climate (O'Connor *et al.* 2011). The safety culture is a widespread concept in high-risk industries as it puts emphasis on management issues and human factors. When investigating safety culture in aviation, among other issues, it was found to depend on the regulator's role, safety management, training and decision making (O'Connor *et al.* 2011). In the absence of clear-cut rules, pressure from the employer can induce risk-taking behaviour among workers (Hopkins 2011). On the other hand, the same rule cannot apply for all cases, especially in complicated industries. For instance, rules governing commercial airline pilots may not be appropriate for emergency service pilots who spend much of their on-duty time awaiting call-out, or for balloon pilots who must begin work very early in the morning (Hopkins 2011). Furthermore, other studies have shown that in the field of aviation, practitioners may not have a coherent, consistent and complete framework guiding how they view and understand safety (Reiman and Rollenhagen 2011). The main findings from a study carried out by O'Connor *et al.* (2011) showed that pilots believed luck to be the most important factor in aviation safety, and employers were not perceived to be placing much importance on safety management systems and safety culture.

It is to be expected that both shipping and aviation industries would adopt similar practices in order to deal with problems of safety and operate internationally. The IMO introduced the ISM Code in the expectation of bringing the safety standards of shipping much closer to those of the aviation industry (Chen 2000). Moreover, the IMO has taken the model used in the international aviation security environment to structure its own plan for terrorist threats (Brooks and Button 2006). In terms of risk assessment techniques, the IMO adopted a proactive approach to safety, which is the FSA. Checklists are used for various procedures in aircraft (Degani and Wiener 1993), a practice that has also been adopted in the shipping industry. From the above list, it appears that in aviation a concern has been raised regarding the purpose and design of regulations, similar to the shipping industry. However, the aviation industry has not developed a method or tool to assist with this issue.

3.4.3 The nuclear industry regulatory regime

The nuclear industry has been identified as a high-risk industry, and, therefore, from its outset it was highly monitored and had strict regulations (Keller and Modarres

2005). Following the Three-Mile Island accident in 1979 and the Chernobyl accident in 1986 the nuclear power sector has introduced several safety regulations and an international scale to classify accidents (INES), which relate to notification criteria and a specific procedure (Dechy *et al.* 2012). Many probabilistic risk assessment (PRA) methods were introduced to the nuclear industry 50 years ago as an adjunct, prominent force in nuclear plant regulation (Modarres 2005). One of them is the safety management system (Trbojevic and Carr 2000) that was implemented in the shipping industry with the ISM Code. Another one is the risk assessment approach, which was transferred to shipping in the context of the FSA. In contrast to the maritime industry, it should be noted that nuclear plants are located in one state and are bound by the laws of that state. In addition, the majority of the employees in a nuclear plant will be scientists with specific knowledge, whereas in the maritime industry the standards for seamen are comparatively low.

Bureaucracy in the nuclear industry is well developed (Hess *et al.* 2005). Several activities are described in procedures that are performed by specialized and skilful personnel. With this level of organization, a nuclear plant where several crucial activities take place daily is successfully managed. The procedures are produced in a relatively centralized decision-making process and include the scope of each task as well as details of how it can be performed.

However, a number of failures in the area of safety management procedures have been identified, such as poor management oversight, poor training and deliberate procedural violations (Kettunen *et al.* 2007). In addition, the very detailed regulations encode the best engineering practice of the time they were written, while they rapidly become deficient when changes occur, e.g. with evolving technologies. In fact, it is quite probable that prescriptive regulations eventually prevent the service provider from adopting the current best practice (Bloomfield and Bishop 2010).

In the nuclear industry, nuclear plants are safely controlled with detailed procedures and clear instructions (Park *et al.* 2005). On the other hand, regulations tend to be a distillation of past experience and, as such, they can prove to be inappropriate or, at worst, to create unnecessary dangers in industries that are technically innovative (Bloomfield and Bishop 2010). Emphasis is put on how information is communicated within the organization from the top level to the bottom level. Performance-based systems are also enforced to analyse, improve and set new targets (Hess *et al.* 2005; Modarres 2005). There is theoretical support that a transition to a risk-informed, performance-based regulatory structure will provide long-term safety benefits and that it can be accomplished without significant public safety impacts during its use.

3.4.4 The process industry regulatory regime

In the process industry, regulations are seen as a source of information that completes managerial gaps. It is, therefore, important to extend their management systems in order to update that information regularly. One method introduced was the safety information management (SIM) approach (Tzou *et al.* 2004).

In the SIM concept all data generated from a company's failures are evaluated and contribute to the improvement of the management system. Those procedures are considered as part of the production development and are put in place during the lifecycle of each product (He *et al.* 2006). Emphasis, therefore, is given to placing the resources for data collection and analysis within the company in a proactive manner.

SIMs that are already used in the process industry are ISO 9001, ISO 14001 and OHSAS 18001 (Duijm *et al.* 2008; Mannan *et al.* 2007). These systems are used as quality system tools in order to extend the narrow regulatory compliance (Gillespie 1995).

The US Occupational Health and Safety Administration (www.osha.gov) publishes the Occupational Health and Safety Assessment Series, and it requirements appear here in Table 3.3 (OHSAS 18001:1999). This standard aims at supporting and helping to systematize the management of risk factors and the promotion of good working conditions (Vinodkumar and Bhasi 2011). The ISO 14000 family addresses various aspects of environmental management (Marimon *et al.* 2010). With regard to ISO 14000, the requirements of which appear in Table 3.4, it is important to point out that this is a standard establishing a reference model for implementing a company's environmental management system, defined as that part of the global management system that describes the organizational structure, planning activities, responsibilities, practices, procedures, processes and resources for preparing, applying, reviewing and maintaining the company's environmental policy (Marimon *et al.* 2009).

The difference of those systems, such as ISO 9001:2008, ISO 14001 and OHSAs 18001, is that they require additional resources for implementation and monitoring. Although sometimes they may overlap, still the scope of each system is different and this should be known by its users.

For instance the need for OHSAS 18001 certification is to reduce the accidents and, thereby, to reduce liability and improve productivity, safety and health of employees (Vinodkumar and Bhasi 2011). While OHSAS 18001 is directed at the proactive control of an occupational risk, enabling the organization to improve its safety and health-related performance, ISO 9001 is geared towards customer satisfaction (Matias and Coelho 2002). ISO 14001, on the other hand, improves the environmental performance of a company or organization.

The documentation required from these systems will produce bureaucratic challenges. It is, therefore, significant for the organization to evaluate the cost of improvement of those challenges. Since many times the certification of standards is voluntary, market research should be carried out before such a system is implemented (Kleindorfer and Saad 2005).

In the process industry there is some scepticism regarding the efficiency of compulsory safety management systems versus self-regulation. The argument has been stated long ago and it underlines the significance of each company to develop its own unique safety standards (Richards *et al.* 2000). The legal regulations, on the other hand, could be used as an additional safety technology for inherent safety (Shah *et al.* 2003).

Table 3.3 Requirements of OHSAS 18001:2007

4.1 General requirements

4.2 OH&S policy

4.3 Planning
    4.3.1 Hazard identification, risk assessment and determining controls
    4.3.2 Legal and other requirements
    4.3.3 Objectives and programmes

4.4 Implementation and operation
    4.4.1 Structure and responsibility
    4.4.2 Competence, training and awareness
    4.4.3 Communication, participation and consultation
    4.4.4 Documentation
    4.4.5 Control of documents
    4.4.6 Operational control
    4.4.7 Emergency preparedness and response

4.5 Checking
    4.5.1 Performance measurement and monitoring
    4.5.2 Evaluation of compliance
    4.5.3 Incident investigation, non-conformity, corrective action and preventive action
    4.5.4 Control of records
    4.5.5 Internal audit

4.6 Management review

Table 3.4 Requirements of ISO 14001

4.1 General requirements

4.2 Environmental policy

4.3 Planning
    4.3.1 Environmental aspects
    4.3.2 Legal and other requirements
    4.3.3 Objectives and targets
    4.3.4 Environmental management programmes

4.4 Implementation and operation
    4.4.1 Structure and responsibility
    4.4.2 Training, awareness and competence
    4.4.3 Communication
    4.4.4 Environmental management system documentation
    4.4.5 Document control
    4.4.6 Operational control
    4.4.7 Emergency preparedness and response

4.5 Checking and corrective action
    4.5.1 Monitoring and measurement
    4.5.2 Non-conformance and corrective and preventive action
    4.5.3 Records
    4.5.4 Environmental management system audit

4.6 Management review

Recognizing the importance of quality systems, the American Bureau of Shipping (ABS) proposed various SIM systems for the shipping industry, such as ISO 9000 for quality standards, ISO 14001 for environmental issues, and OHSAS 18001 for safety and health aspects (ABS 2006). Although not yet mandatory, the ABS states that shipping companies may reduce most potential accidents by adopting such systems. It is found that OHSAS 18001 certified firms have higher levels of all safety management practices and safety behaviour compared with ISO 9001 certified firms, while OHSAS 18001 has been developed to be compatible with ISO 9001 (Vinodkumar and Bhasi 2011). In addition, Celik (2009) proposed that an integrated implementation procedure of ISO 9001:2000, ISO 14001:2004 and OHSAS 18001:2007 should be in compliance with the ISM Code. Moreover, major industrial organizations suggest that quality systems, such as the Tanker Management and Safety Assessment (TMSA), may be a solution to the implementation of maritime regulations by the tankers' operators (OCIMF 2004). Weaknesses of the ISM Code have led organizations to adopting other management tools. The TMSA is being seen as a tool for reinforcing the implementation of the ISM Code, with particular emphasis on self-assessment and continuous improvement. However, it has been designed for tanker operators and, therefore, its applicability is limited.

3.5 Regulatory implementation assessment of governments

A state involved in the shipping industry also has to deal with the management of regulatory issues. On the one hand, it should keep up with modern regulatory trends, while at the same time it should protect its commercial interests. As the problem exists in other business sectors as well, a generic approach that has been adopted by many governments is to incorporate the Regulatory Implementation Assessment (RIA) into their existing policy-making processes (Staronova *et al.* 2007; Kirkpatrick *et al.* 2004).

A RIA consists of a series of steps involving an assessment of all likely economic, social and environmental impacts of various alternative policy options addressing the same problem, and a comparison of these options, in order to obtain an indication of 'the most preferred' option (Ragona *et al.* 2012). The aim is to produce effective regulations and minimize the administration costs, which are a heavy economic burden for the states.

In the European Union (EU), as well as in many other countries throughout the world, all major regulatory proposals need to be examined through a RIA before being approved and entered into force (Ragona *et al.* 2012). According to the RIA approach, issues such as costs, benefits, scope, consultation of the public sector and risk assessment of financial validity should be included in the design process of a regulation (Ballantine and Devoland 2006). Regulatory duplication has the potential to impose compliance costs. The purpose of a RIA seeks to identify and quantify those costs, with a view to determining whether government action is warranted to address regulatory duplication, while it also seeks to develop options that would reduce avoidable costs of duplication (McGregor-Lowndes and O'Connell 2013). Broader issues are included, such as the 'do nothing option' and the 'small firm impact' (Vickers 2008). The 'do nothing option' is based on the fact that sometimes a proposed regulation can generate more difficulties than the result it may produce. Difficulties of companies implementing a regulation may mean additional regulations need to be involved, so producing a vicious circle. The 'small firm impact' is also a fundamental issue, since every industry should be open to anyone who wants to be involved. However, some academics have raised arguments about RIA, pointing out some weaknesses of the process relating to the competence of staff. Lofstedt (2007) noted that RIAs are still haphazard regulations that are based on emotions, not science.

Although the IMO has introduced the FSA approach, it may be that the RIA approach should be used to address more specific issues when producing regulations. The economic burden of a small stakeholder generated by a regulation should be taken into account by regulators. Furthermore, the 'do nothing option' of regulators may work as a resistance to excess negative media coverage in the case that there is a scientific doubt about the results of a proposed regulation.

References

ABS. (2006). Guide for marine health, safety, quality and environmental management. Copyright. American Bureau of Shipping.

Alderton T., Winchester N. (2002). Flag states and safety: 1997–1999. *Maritime Policy Management*, Vol. 29(2), pp. 151–162.

Antao P., Soares C.G. (2008). Causal factors in accidents of high-speed craft and conventional ocean-going vessels. *Reliability Engineering and System Safety*, Vol. 93, pp. 1292–1304.

Bailey E.E. (2002). Aviation policy: past and present. *Southern Economic Journal*, Vol. 69(1), pp. 12–20.

Ballantine B., Devonald B. (2006). Modern regulatory impact analysis: the experience of the European Union. *Regulatory Toxicology and Pharmacology*, Vol. 44, pp. 57–68.

Bhattacharya S. (2012). The effectiveness of the ISM Code: a qualitative enquiry. *Marine Policy*, Vol. 36, 528–535.

Björn H. (2010). Global regimes, regional adaptation: environmental safety in Baltic Sea oil transportation. *Maritime Policy & Management*, Vol. 37(5), pp. 489–503.

Bloomfield R., Bishop P. (2010). Safety and assurance cases: past, present and possible future – an Adelard perspective. In *Making Systems Safer* (pp. 51–67). Springer, London.

Bloor M., Datta R., Gilinskiy Y., Horlick-Jones T. (2006). Unicorn among the cedars: on the possibility of effective 'smart regulation' of the globalized shipping industry. *Social Legal Studies*, Vol. 15, pp. 534–551.

Brooker P. (2006a). Air traffic management accident risk. Part 1: the limits of realistic modelling. *Safety Science*, Vol. 44, pp. 419–450.

Brooker P. (2006b). Air traffic management accident risk. Part 2: repairing the deficiencies of ESARR4. *Safety Science*, Vol. 44, pp. 629–655.

Brooks M., Button K.J. (2006). Market structures and shipping security. *Maritime Economics and Logistics*, Vol. 8, pp. 100–120.

Cariou P., Mejia M.Q., Wolff F.C. (2009) Evidence on target factors used for port state control inspections. *Marine Policy*, Vol. 33, pp. 847–859.

Celik M. (2009). Establishing an Integrated Process Management System (IPMS) in ship management companies. *Expert Systems with Applications*, Vol. 36(4), pp. 8152–8171.

Celik, M., Lavasani, S.M., Wang, J. (2010). A risk-based modelling approach to enhance shipping accident investigation. *Safety Science*, 48(1), 18–27.

Chantelauve G. (2004). Generic ship, specific ship? Towards risk-based approaches to maritime regulation. 7th Conference on Probabilistic Safety Assessment and Management, 14–18 June Berlin, Vol. (1–6), pp. 3250–3255.

Chen L. (2000). Legal and practical consequences of not complying with ISM code. *Maritime Policy Management*, Vol. 27(3), pp. 219–230.

Conchie S.M., Donald I.J. (2008). The functions and development of safety-specific trust and distrust. *Safety Science*, Vol. 46, pp. 92–103.

Dechy N., Dien Y., Funnemark E., Roed-Larsen S., Stoop J., Valvisto T., Arellano A.L.V. (2012). Results and lessons learned from the ESReDA's Accident Investigation Working Group: introducing article to 'Safety Science' special issue on 'Industrial Events Investigation'. *Safety Science*, Vol. 50(6), pp. 1380–1391.

Degani A., Wiener E.L. (1993). Cockpit checklists: concepts, design and use. *Human Factors*, Vol. 35, pp. 28–43.

Duijm, N.J., Fievez, C., Gerbec, M., Hauptmanns, U., Konstandinidou, M. (2008). Management of health, safety and environment in process industry. *Safety Science*, 46(6), pp. 908–920.

Eide M.S., Endresen Ø., Skjong R., Longva T., Alvik S. (2009). Cost-effectiveness assessment of CO_2 reducing measures in shipping. *Maritime Policy & Management*, Vol. 36(4), 367–384.

Fafaliou I., Lekakou M., Theotokas I. (2006). Is the European shipping industry aware of corporate social responsibility? The case of the Greek-owned short sea shipping companies. *Marine Policy*, Vol. 30, pp. 412–419.

Gillespie D.P. (1995) Comprehensive information management: EPA, OSHA and beyond. *ISA Transaction*, Vol. 34, pp. 359–368.

Goulielmos A. (2003). Complexity theory applied to management of shipping companies. *Maritime Policy Management*, Vol. 29(4), pp. 375–391.

Goulielmos A., Tzannatos E. (1997). Management information system for the promotion of safety in shipping. *Disaster Prevention and Management*, Vol. 6(4), pp. 252–262.

Goulielmos A., Mitrousi K., Gatzoli A. (2008). Marine accidents: quality vs. safety and one step further. *International Journal of Ocean Systems Management*, Vol. 1(1), pp. 45–67.

Havold J.I. (2000). Culture in maritime safety. *Maritime Policy Management*, Vol. 27(1), pp. 79–88.

Havold J.I. (2005). Safety-culture in a Norwegian shipping company. *Journal of Safety Research*, Vol. 36, pp. 441–458.

Hayes, J. (2012, January). A new policy direction in offshore safety regulation. Working paper 84, National Research Centre for OHS regulation, The Australian National University, Canberra, 2012, http://regnet. anu. edu. au/sites/default/files/WorkingPaper_84. v2. pdf.

He W., Ming X.G, Ni Q.F, Lu W.F, Lee B.H. (2006). A unified product structure management for enterprise business process integration throughout the product lifecycle. *International Journal of Production Research*, Vol. 44(9), pp. 1757–1776.

Heitmann N., Khalilian S. (2011). Accounting for carbon dioxide emissions from international shipping: burden sharing under different UNFCCC allocation options and regime scenarios. *Marine Policy*, Vol. 35, pp. 682–691.

Hess S.M., Albano A.M., Gaertner J.P. (2005). Development of a dynamical systems model of plant programmatic performance on nuclear power plant safety risk. *Reliability Engineering and System Safety*, Vol. 90, pp. 62–74.

Hopkins A. (2011). Risk-management and rule-compliance: decision-making in hazardous industries. *Safety Science*, 49(2), 110–120.

Hu S., Fang Q., Xia H., Xi Y. (2007). Formal safety assessment based on relative risks model in ship navigation. *Reliability Engineering and System Safety*, Vol. 92, pp. 369–377.

Ikeagwuani U.M., John G.A. (2013). Safety in maritime oil sector: content analysis of machinery space fire hazards. *Safety Science*, Vol. 51(1), pp. 347–353.

IMO. (1993). *International Management Code for the Safe Operation of Ships and for Pollution Prevention (International Safety Management (ISM) Code)*. Resolution A.741(18). IMO Publishing, London.

IMO. (1997a). *Guidelines to Assist Flag States in the Implementation of IMO Instruments*. IMO Publishing, London.

IMO. (1997b). *Interim Guidelines for the Application of Formal Safety Assessment (FSA) to the IMO rule-Making Process*. IMO Publishing, London.

IMO. (2002). *Bulk Carrier Safety: Report on FSA Study on Bulk Carrier Safety Submitted by Japan*. IMO Publishing, London.

IMO. (2004). *Amendments to the Annex of the Protocol of 1978 relating to the International Convention for the Prevention of Pollution from Ships, 1973 (revised annex I of MARPOL 73/78). Resolution MEPC.117(52)*. IMO Publishing, London.

Kaneko F. (2002). Methods for probabilistic safety assessment of ships. *Journal of Marine Science and Technology*, Vol. 7(1), pp. 1–16.

Keller W., Modarres M. (2005). A historical overview of probabilistic risk assessment development and its use in the nuclear power industry: a tribute to the late professor Norman Carl Rasmussen. *Reliability Engineering and System Safety*, Vol. 89, pp. 271–285.

Keselj T. (1999). Port state jurisdiction in respect of pollution from ships: the 1982 United Nations Convention on the Law of the Sea and the Memoranda of Understanding. *Ocean Development and International Law*, Vol. 30, pp. 127–160.

Kettunen J., Reiman T., Wahlstrom B. (2007). Safety management challenges and tensions in the European nuclear power industry. *Scandinavian Journal of Management*, Vol. 23, pp. 424–444.

Kirkpatrick C., Parker D., Zhang Y.F. (2004). Regulatory impact assessment in developing and transition economies: a survey of current practice. *Public Money and Management*, October, pp. 291–296.

Kleindorfer P.R., Saad G.H. (2005). Managing disruption risks in supply chains. *Production and Operations Management*, Vol. 14(1), pp. 53–68.

Knapp S., Franses P.H. (2007a). A global view on port state control: econometric analysis of the differences across port state control regimes. *Maritime Policy and Management*, Vol. 34(5), pp. 453–483.

Knapp S., Franses P.H. (2007b). Econometric analysis on the effect of port state control inspections on the probability of casualty. Can targeting of substandard ships for inspections be improved? *Marine Policy*, Vol. 31, pp. 550–563.

Knapp S., Franses P.H. (2009). Does ratification matter and do major conventions improve safety and decrease pollution in shipping? *Marine Policy*, Vol. 33, pp. 826–846.

Knudsen O.F., Hassler B. (2011). IMO legislation and its implementation: accident risk, vessel deficiencies and national administrative practices. *Marine Policy*, Vol. 35, pp. 201–207.

Lazakis I., Turan O., Aksu S. (2010). Increasing ship operational reliability through the implementation of a holistic maintenance management strategy. *Ships and Offshore Structures*, Vol. 5(4), pp. 337–357.

Lee J.O., Yeob I.C., Yang Y.S. (2001). A trial application of FSA methodology to the hatchway watertight integrity of bulk carriers. *Marine Structures*, Vol. 14, pp. 651–667.

Li K.X., Zheng H. (2008). Enforcement of law by the Port State Control (PSC). *Maritime Policy and Management*, Vol. 35(1), pp. 61–71.

Lindøe P.H., Engen O.A., Olsen O. E. (2011). Responses to accidents in different industrial sectors. *Safety Science*, 49(1), 90–97.

Liou J.J.H., Yen L., Tzeng G.H. (2008). Building an effective safety management system for airlines. *Journal of Air Transport Management*, Vol. 14, pp. 20–26.

Lofstedt R.E. (2007). The 'Plateau-ing' of the European better regulation agenda: an analysis of activities carried out by the Barroso commission. *Journal of Risk Research*, Vol. 10(4), pp. 423–447.

Lois P., Wang J., Wall A., Ruxton T. (2004). Formal safety assessment of cruise ships. *Tourism Management*, Vol. 25, pp. 93–109.

Mannan M.S., West H.H., Berwanger P.C. (2007). Lessons learned from recent incidents: facility siting, atmospheric venting, and operator information systems. *Journal of Loss Prevention in the Process Industries*, Vol. 20, pp. 644–650.

Marimon F., Heras I., Casadesus M. (2009). ISO 9000 and ISO 14000 standards: a projection model for the decline phase. *Total Quality Management*, Vol. 20(1), pp. 1–21.

Marimon F., Casadesús M., Heras I. (2010). Certification intensity level of the leading nations in ISO 9000 and ISO 14000 standards. *International Journal of Quality & Reliability Management*, Vol. 27(9), pp. 1002–1020.

Matias J.C.O., Coelho D.A. (2002). The integration of the standards systems of quality management. *International Journal of Production Research*, Vol. 40(15), pp. 3857–3866.

MCA (1998). MCA research project 442 bulk carrier formal safety assessment preparatory work. Report No: 305B213/3 www.mcga.gov.uk/c4mca/research_project_442.pdf [20 May 2006].

McGregor-Lowndes M., O'Connell A. (2013). Regulatory impact assessment of potential duplication of governance and reporting standards for charities. www.coag.gov.au/node/492.

Mearns K., Yule S. (2008). The role of national culture in determining safety performance: challenges for the global oil and gas industry. *Safety Science*, doi:10.1016/j.ssci.2008.01.008.

Mennis E., Lagoudis I.N., Nikitakos N., Platis A. (2005). Improving formal safety assessment in shipping transportation. 11th International Congress of the International Maritime Association of the Mediterranean, 26–30 September, Vol. 1–2, pp. 1565–1571.

Mitroussi K. (2004). The role of organisational characteristics of ship owing firms in the use of third party ship management. *Marine Policy*, Vol. 28, pp. 325–333.

Modarres M. (2005). Technology-neutral nuclear power plant regulation: implications of a safety goals driven performance-based regulation. *Nuclear Engineering and Technology*, Vol. 37(3), pp. 221–230.

Mohamed Ali R.M., Louca L.A. (2008). Performance based design of blast resistant offshore topsides, Part I: Philosophy. *Journal of Constructional Steel Research*, Vol. 64, pp. 1030–1045.

Molenaar E.J. (2007). Port state jurisdiction: toward comprehensive, mandatory and global coverage. *Ocean Development and International Law*, Vol. 38(1), pp. 225–257.

Norris A. (2007). AIS Implementation-Success or Failure? *The Journal of Navigation*, Vol. 60, pp. 1–10.

OCIMF. (2004). Tanker management and self assessment: A best practice guide for ship operators. OCIMF, June.

O'Connor P., O'Dea A., Kennedy Q., Buttrey S.E. (2011). Measuring safety climate in aviation: a review and recommendations for the future. *Safety Science*, 49(2), pp. 128–138.

Odeke A. (2005). An examination of bareboat charter registries and flag of convenience registries in international law. *Ocean Development and International Law*, Vol. 36, pp. 339–362.

Park J., Jeong K., Jung W. (2005). Identifying cognitive complexity factors affecting the complexity of procedural steps in emergency operating procedures of a nuclear power plant. *Reliability Engineering and System Safety*, Vol. 89, pp. 121–136.

Paterson J. (2011). Significance of regulatory orientation in occupational health and safety offshore, *Boston College Environmental Affairs Law Review*, Vol. 38, p. 369.

Perepelkin M., Knapp S., Perepelkin G., Pooter M. (2010). An improved methodology to measure flag performance for the shipping industry. *Marine Policy*, Vol. 34, pp. 395–405.

Psarros G., Skjong R., Eide M.S. (2010). Under-reporting of maritime accidents. *Accident Analysis & Prevention*, Vol. 42(2), pp. 619–625.

Pun K.F., Richard C.M., Winston Y., Lewis G. (2003). Safety management system registration in the shipping industry. *International Journal of Quality and Reliability Management*, Vol. 20(6), pp. 704–721.

Ragona M., Mazzocchi M., Rose M. (2012, April). Regulatory impact assessment of food safety policies: a preliminary study on alternative EU interventions on dioxins. In 86th Annual Conference, 16–18 April 2012, Warwick University, Coventry, UK (No. 135093). Agricultural Economics Society.

Reiman T., Rollenhagen C. (2011). Human and organizational biases affecting the management of safety. *Reliability Engineering & System Safety*, 96(10), 1263–1274.

Richards J.P., Glegg G.A., Cullinane S. (2000). Environmental regulation: industry and the marine environment. *Journal of Environmental Management*, Vol. 58, pp. 119–134.

Rosqvist T., Tuominen R. (2004). Qualification of formal safety assessment: an exploratory study. *Safety Science*, Vol. 42(2), pp. 99–120.

Ruuda S., Mikkelsen A. (2008). Risk-based rules for crane safety systems. *Reliability Engineering and System Safety*, Vol. 93, pp. 1369–1376.

Sage B. (2005). Identification of 'high risk ships' in coastal waters. *Marine Policy*, Vol. 29, pp. 349–355.

Sampson H., Bloor M. (2007). When Jack gets out of the box: the problems of regulating a global industry. *Sociology*, Vol. 41, pp. 551–569.

Shah S., Fischer U., Hungerbuhler K. (2003). A hierarchical approach for the evaluation of chemical process aspects from the perspective of inherent safety. *Trans IChemE*, Vol. 81 (part B), pp. 430–433.

Silos J.M., Piniella F., Monedero J., Walliser J. (2012). Trends in the global market for crews: a case study. *Marine Policy*, Vol. 36, pp. 845–858.

Skjong R., Bitner-Gregersen E.M. (2002). Cost effectiveness of hull girder safety. Proceedings of OMAE, Offshore Mechanics and Arctic Engineering Oslo, Norway, 23–28 June.

Spyrou K.J., Papanikolaou A.D., Samouelidis M., Servis D., Papadogianni S. (2003). Risk assessment of double-skin bulk barriers: WP6 of the international formal safety assessment study of bulk carriers. www.naval.ntua.gr/~sdl/Publications/Other/fsa_ntua. pdf [26 May 2006].

Stacey A., Sharp J.V. (2007). Safety factor requirements for the offshore industry. *Engineering Failure Analysis*, Vol. 14, pp. 442–458.

Staronova K., Pavel J., Katarina Krapez K. (2007). Piloting regulatory impact assessment: a comparative analysis of the Czech Republic, Slovakia and Slovenia. *Impact Assessment and Project Appraisal*, Vol. 25(4), pp. 271–280.

Talley W.K., Jin D., Powell H.K. (2005). Determinants of crew injuries in vessel accidents. *Maritime Policy Management*, Vol. 32(3), pp. 263–278.

Thai I.V., Grewal D., (2006). The Maritime Safety Management System (MSMS): a survey of the international shipping community. *Maritime Economics and Logistics*, Vol. 8, pp. 287–310.

Trbojevic V.M., Carr B.J. (2000) Risk based methodology for safety improvements in ports. *Journal of Hazardous Materials*, Vol. 71, pp. 467–480.

Triantafylli A., Ballas A. (2010). Management control systems and performance: evidence from the Greek shipping industry. *Maritime Policy & Management*, Vol. 37(6), pp. 625–660.

Tzannatos E. (2005). Technical reliability of the Greek coastal passenger fleet. *Marine Policy*, Vol. 29, pp. 85–92.

Tzannatos E., Kokotos D. (2012). Analysis of accidents in Greek shipping during the pre- and post-ISM period. *Marine Policy*, Vol. 36, 528–535.

Tzou T.L., Hankinson G., Edwards D., Chung P. (2004). Evaluating safety information management performance: a key to preventing disaster: Bhopal and its effects on process. Safety International Conference on the 20th Anniversary of the Bhopal Gas Tragedy at Indian Institute of Technology, Kanpur, India, 1–3 December.

Vanem E., Endresen Ø., Skjong R. (2008). Cost-effectiveness criteria for marine oil spill preventive measures. *Reliability Engineering and System Safety*, Vol. 93, pp. 1354–1368.

Ventikos N.P., Psaraftis H.N. (2004). Spill accident modeling: a critical survey of the event-decision network in the context of IMO's formal safety assessment. *Journal of Hazardous Materials*, Vol. 107, pp. 59–66.

Vickers, I. (2008). Better regulation and enterprise: the case of environmental health risk regulation in Britain. *Policy Studies*, Vol. 29(2), pp. 215–232.

Vinnem J.E., Hestad J.A., Kvaløy J.T., Skogdalen J. E. (2010). Analysis of root causes of major hazard precursors (hydrocarbon leaks) in the Norwegian offshore petroleum industry. *Reliability Engineering & System Safety*, Vol. 95(11), pp. 1142–1153.

Vinodkumar M.N., Bhasi M. (2011). A study on the impact of management system certification on safety management. *Safety Science*, Vol. 49(3), pp. 498–507.

Wang J. (2000). A subjective modelling tool applied to formal ship safety assessment. *Ocean Engineering*, Vol. 27, pp. 1019–1035.

Wang J. (2002). Offshore safety case approach and formal safety assessment of ships. *Journal of Safety Research*, Vol. 33, pp. 81–115.

Wang J. (2006). Maritime risk assessment and its current status. *Quality and Reliability Engineering International*, Vol. 22, pp. 2–19.

Zhang Y., Round D.K. (2008) China's airline deregulation since 1997 and the driving forces behind the 2002 airline consolidations. *Journal of Air Transport Management*, Vol. 14, pp. 130–142.

4 Evaluating the implementation performance of a maritime regulation

4.1 Introduction

The previous chapters reveal that many world states have difficulties meeting the international agreements of the IMO without the involvement of all the stakeholders of the shipping industry. Furthermore, the shipping industry is unfamiliar with effective management systems that can assist its stakeholders to monitor their regulatory implementation performance. Consequently, a stakeholder may be exposed to uncertainty about his regulatory implementation performance. In this chapter a discussion is carried out focusing on the benefits and costs that a regulation may create for a stakeholder. It is suggested that excessive and unnecessary regulations may lead certain stakeholders to seek for more lax regulatory regimes, where they can run their business. In addition, a performance management system is developed to measure the profit of a stakeholder as a result of his adequate regulatory implementation. The use of such a system will highlight to a stakeholder the fact that he may find some positive commercial advantages by implementing a specific maritime regulation. These issues will be discussed in the sections below and will introduce techniques that already exist in other business sectors.

4.2 Measurement of the regulatory implementation in the shipping industry

Till now the burden of regulatory implementation has been falling on states. Apart from regulating, their most significant contribution to the industry is the punishment of violators and/or substandard players. The introduction of the FSA demonstrated the need for a rational regulation which would take into account the cost generated to a ship. However, contrary to the regulatory benefits, the cost is not equally distributed among industrial stakeholders. According to some authors, this is a key element for regulatory success that has been overlooked by regulators (Aven and Korte 2003; Chantelauve 2003; Karahalios *et al.* 2011).

A substandard player has an economic disadvantage against its competitors. The fear of PSC detentions was a successful tool that put those players at significant economic disadvantage. Moreover, due to the variety of regulations in the shipping industry, it may be very difficult for new players or specific groups of stakeholders to cope. Therefore, the fundamental issues of a regulation should target two main principles:

1   fair play for new entrants;
2   reasonable distribution of costs and benefits for stakeholders.

A newly introduced regulation should be considered as a measure that leads the stakeholders of the maritime industry to be innovative or excellent in their business. The protection of safety at sea and in the maritime environment is within the scope of many fields of science, and this should be the approach followed when a regulation is introduced in the maritime industry.

The maritime industry should be convinced of the results of each regulation before it agrees to comply with it. Fewer regulations are believed to be better; however, this should be measured at two levels:

1   the overall regulatory performance of the industry;
2   the regulation implementation performance of each stakeholder.

The concept of performance measurement of an organization has already been successfully introduced in the business world.

4.2.1 Measurement of the stakeholders' commercial interactions

To design a performance management system, someone should initially establish the scope of its existence as well as its user. This scope has been clearly identified in this book and is the implementation success of a developed maritime regulation. The supreme organization that has the overall responsibility for the implementation of the regulations is the IMO. Therefore, the measurement system has been designed with the assumption that it will be used by the IMO.

As has been shown in the literature, there is a greater probability that a regulation will be implemented adequately and in a logical time period if the benefits and costs generated are equally distributed among the industry's stakeholders. By measuring the benefits and costs of each stakeholder, it is then possible to evaluate the possibility that this regulation will be implemented successfully. The evaluation result is stated as the performance of the regulation.

A main limitation in designing a performance management system is the size of the industry and the number stakeholders affected by maritime regulations, which is high. Thus, it is necessary to limit the number of stakeholders studied. The approach used suggests that stakeholders can be grouped according to their interests and from every group a representative stakeholder is chosen for the development of the performance tool. Hence, a representative sample of all main stakeholders can be studied.

4.2.2　Measuring a stakeholder

The establishment of a performance system for various stakeholders poses some challenges that need careful consideration. A main challenge is that some stakeholders are non-profit organizations. Therefore, their structure, aims and operational priorities are significantly different from those of the commercial stakeholders, (e.g. labour unions vs shipowners). Besides the regulatory performance of stakeholders, it is necessary for the performance management system to be applicable both to smaller and larger organizations. This concept will allow the measurement of challenges of smaller stakeholders. The new players are expected to be among the smaller stakeholders, so the commercial restrictions due to the regulatory regime will give an advantage to the existing and larger stakeholders. The measurement system should measure the regulatory impact on various common business sectors that could be used as reference points.

4.2.3　Performance management systems: the balanced scorecard

One of the main contributions of quality standards, such as ISO 9001, is the self-assessment requirement of a company. To facilitate such an assessment, a company must establish key performance indicators (KPIs). Then, it is easier for the company to measure its performance with respect to those KPIs, which should be simple and shared among a company's departments and occasionally among its employees. A critical issue is that the KPIs should be capable of measuring many different aspects of a company, such as human resources, knowledge, finance and infrastructure. The goal of these standards is customer satisfaction.

However, the principle of measurement with KPIs could be applicable to other business activities as well, in order to evaluate costs and managerial challenges. A performance management system should include KPIs already established in the business world. The implementation of maritime regulations is an activity that could be measured in a similar way. In this case, the aim is to make a cost–benefit analysis of a stakeholder intending to implement a maritime regulation.

A valuable method that can be used to investigate the costs and benefits of maritime regulations is the BSC that was established by Kaplan and Norton (1996a, 1996b). The BSC is the most recognized and utilized contemporary performance measurement system. The main concept in BSC is that the measurement of achieving a specific goal can be done by monitoring the multiple perspectives of the strategy at the same time, as shown in Figure 4.1. Focusing on only one perspective can lead a company to fail in its goal, because there are many other non-financial aspects that should be monitored by the company.

The early experiences of companies using the BSC have demonstrated that it meets several managerial needs, since both financial and non-financial indicators are included in the measurement tool. The BSC has been used broadly as a

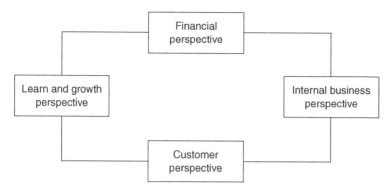

Figure 4.1 The perspectives of a balanced scorecard.

management tool in a variety of industries. It is extensively discussed in this book because, compared to other performance measurement methods, it has a broad applicability in many business sectors (Punniyamoorthy and Murali 2008; Shafia *et al.* 2011). Several applications of the BSC can be found in the literature dealing with management issues in a variety of industries. With respect to organizational issues, a list of notable research may include Park *et al.* (2005), Franco-Santos and Bourne (2005) and Solano *et al.* (2003).

Successful BSC applications have been demonstrated in the safety management process as well (Chung *et al.* 2006; Kettunen and Kantola 2005). More applications of the BSC have also been seen in general applications, such as in evaluating the value that IT adds to the process of project information management in construction (Stewart and Mohamed 2003), healthcare organization evaluation (Chan 2006), assessing public relations and communications performance (Fleisher and Mahaffy 1997) and assessing corporate strategies and environmental forces (Sohn *et al.* 2003). It has also been used as an alternative option to the existing total quality management systems, such as ISO (Watkins and Arrington 2007; Wagner 2007). As a competitor to ISO standards, it has been successfully tested in public organizations. It can be argued, therefore, that the BSC is qualified as a method that can apply to different organizations despite their scope, whether they are public or commercial, and their size.

In terms of regulations, the BSC has already been tested with respect to its regulatory compliance. Some of these studies have focused on the self-regulated approach (Mearns and Havold 2003; Kettunen and Kantola 2005). Those studies demonstrated that the use of the BSC in a private organization can indicate regulatory failures and the reasons behind those failures may be various, for example resource or knowledge.

The BSC approach has recently been used by many companies to monitor their regulatory compliance (Stevens 2006; Huang 2007; Garcia-Valderrama *et al.* 2008; Pedersen and Neergaard 2008; (Osmundsen *et al.* 2008). Additionally, various governments and administrations have used the BSC to monitor a variety of regulatory issues or their overall performance (Phillips and Phillips 2007; Ramos *et al.* 2007; Farneti and Guthrie 2008; Lee 2008).

In the maritime industry, the BSC has so far been used in offshore health-and-safety studies (Mearns and Havold 2003). Wu and Liu (2010) developed a system of BSCs that enables managers to gain a greater understanding of the practical effect of ISO certification. Havold and Nesset (2009) proposed the BSC as a benchmarking tool to measure aspects of the safety culture of an organization, which relates closely to ISO 9001:2008 and the ISM Code and organizational learning. Perepelkin *et al.* (2010) have established a system for measuring the performance of flag states by developing a methodology which can be applied on a regional or global level and to other areas of legislative interest (e.g. recognized organizations, documentation of compliance companies).

The BSC has been designed as a tool to measure the achievement of a goal. The founders of this method (Kaplan and Norton 1996a, 1996b) suggested that the achievement of a goal goes beyond financial perspectives. Although significant, the financial numbers may not clarify the potential threat in achieving a predetermined goal. It also constitutes a simple way of passing to each part of the company a simplistic idea of their contribution to the goal. Therefore, it is easy for each department in an organization, or even for an individual, to self-evaluate his/her performance with respect to the company's policies and aims (McAdam and O'Neill 1999; Mearns and Havold 2003).

In the original version of BSC by Kaplan and Norton, the setting of a goal needs measurement of four performance perspectives: (1) financial, (2) learning and growth; (3) customer; and (4) internal business (Kaplan and Norton 1996a, 1996b). Then, it is necessary to set indicators that will describe needs to be measured, while a scorecard is then drafted stating clearly what is monitored as well as the results of each department and/or individuals. Some scholars have wrongly argued that these four perspectives have a narrow scope. On the contrary, the founders of the BSC have clarified through the extensive literature that the perspective may be modified as necessary in order to fit different situations.

It is also of high importance for the BSC to be distributed as close to the bottom of an organization as is practicable (Kaplan and Norton 2005; Mearns and Havold 2003). It is broadly acceptable nowadays that the success of a company is greatly dependent on those employees who are at lower management levels, and therefore closer to customers. This approach of distribution of the BSC is called 'cascade'. Although impracticable, in some cases it would be beneficial for each employee to have his own BSC. It is also a matter of ethics, since the performance of each employee can then be pragmatic, clear and rational.

Following the above brief overview of BSC, it appears that it has some advantages over other performance tools. Those advantages could be its simplicity and its successful application to business and governmental organizations. By adopting the same scorecards for a company, it is possible to develop a common performance management system in terms of different perspectives and departments. Then the performance of various sources can be measured in a common space. Therefore, the BSC is supported in this book as a strategic tool that is capable of monitoring the regulatory performance of the shipping industry.

4.3 General principles for designing a BSC

A successful application of the BSC could be used for measuring the performance of stakeholders in the shipping industry and, consequently, the industry itself through overall comparisons. The BSC could be used as a tool to draft a list of significant items that should be gradually followed by any stakeholder, in order for them to achieve an effective implementation. This list should include some vital functions of a company, such as the implementation procedure, the cost assessment, the availability of resources and the monitoring.

4.3.1 The size of a BSC

The architects of the BSC method (Kaplan and Norton 1996a, 1996b) suggested that a company should not use an excessive number of measures in their BSCs. An upper limit of 25 measures per BSC may assist managers to keep a focus on their company's goal. This approach should be followed when developing a stakeholder's scorecard. In a typical BSC, each perspective will include certain indicators and the measures for each indicator. However, as it is believed by the author, when few measures are used, the indicators could simply be overwritten. Therefore, this will reduce the terminology needs and further explanations when it has to be applied in the business world.

4.3.2 Proposed measures

An exhaustive literature has already produced several measures to evaluate the four perspectives introduced by Kaplan and Norton (1996a, 1996b; 2000; 2004). Although some of them are very specific for some industries – e.g. manufacturing lead time, material stock-out – there are some basic measures that have been accepted through surveys and research as appropriate for use in order to measure the costs and benefits generated to a stakeholder of the shipping industry while implementing a maritime regulation.

Starting from the financial perspective, four indicators have been chosen: *profit, revenues, cost* and *use of asset*. The profit could be considered as the paramount indicator for any organization. This can be affected by a maritime regulation, especially when it is enforced in awkward times for the shipping industry, such as during a recession. Another separate indicator that can be used is the revenue, which refers to smaller financial gains that can be obtained by an organization from a maritime regulation without deterministic effects on the profit. The cost generated by a maritime regulation is another indicator. This indicator refers to the money spent on a permanent basis on the ship's operation. Of course, another important indicator is the use of assets, which describes the resources, such as cash flow, for the initial implementation. The choice of the above indicators is to measure the initial and permanent costs generated by a regulation.

The other important perspective described in BSC is the *customer satisfaction perspective*. The scope of incorporating such a perspective is to identify what customers expect from an organization. A key indicator is the *productivity*, which is defined differently for each stakeholder in the shipping industry. The *productivity* is defined as the operational efficiency that can be achieved from a regulation's implementation. The *competitiveness* is another important indicator, which can be defined as the commercial advantage that can be achieved from a regulation's implementation. Another chosen indicator is the *quality*, measuring the increased quality level that can be achieved from a regulation's implementation. Finally, the *reputation* is the improved image of the organization that can be achieved from a regulation's implementation.

In modern times, the generation of knowledge is exponent. The organizations or companies that were left behind in this evolution will very soon realize that they have severe management failures. This is the reason for adopting the learning and growth perspective. A paramount indicator is the *human capital* that describes the required skills, talent and knowledge that a company's employees should possess in order to implement a new regulation. A second indicator is the *information capital*, which contains the required databases, information systems, networks and technology infrastructure of a company. However, despite the human power and IT technologies, the company's culture and leadership, the alignment of its people with its strategic goals and its employees' ability to share knowledge need to be measured. Those items fall in the scope of the *organizational capital* indicator. Eventually, a company or an organization needs to be innovative, and this is something that is measured with the *innovation* indicator, defined here as the ability of people to produce new practices.

4.3.3 *Internal business measures*

As per the ISM Code, a company should establish management practices in order to eliminate the risk of accidents at sea and/or marine pollution. It is therefore a regulatory requirement that the ship operators will exercise their authority to avoid occurrence of such an incident. Failure to comply will result in commercial damages proportional to the damage caused, such as pollution, loss of life, wreck, etc. However, any incident will also affect the stakeholders who, at that particular time, had a relationship with the ship involved, such as insurers, states and classification societies.

The shipping industry has been considered as high risk due to the threats to which ships and crew members are exposed. The consequent impacts of shipping accidents vary in scope, including loss of life, extensive marine pollution, damage to the ship or its cargo. Therefore, it is very important for a stakeholder to develop a risk management system in order to verify that his company can deal with such a threat if it occurs. The concept of crisis management is well known in the shipping industry, since it is used in various shipboard contingency plans, as it is proposed by the IMO.

The IMO, recognizing that a main threat in the shipping industry is oil pollution, which could be the outcome of many situations, issued a guideline for the Shipboard Oil Pollution Emergency Plan (SOPEP). The SOPEP is a manual which, according to Regulation 37 of Annex I of MARPOL, states that every ship of 400 tons gross tonnage or more and every oil tanker of 150 tons gross tonnage or more must carry an approved oil pollution plan in case a pollution incident occurs or is likely to occur (IMO 2004). Further requirements include issues such as reporting to authorities and cooperation. According to this plan, a list of situations that could put a ship at risk includes:

1 fire/explosion
2 collision (with fixed or moving object)
3 ship grounded/stranded
4 excessive list
5 hull failure
6 ship submerged/foundered/wrecked
7 hazardous vapour release.

The execution of the SOPEP plan in the event of an emergency principally depends on the actions of the captain. It also provides guidance as to the actions to be taken for the safety of the crew. However, despite the experience of the master and his crew, many reasons, such as stress, may force the seamen to be confused and act in a different way. The SOPEP manual fulfils part of the ISM Code requirements, where ship management companies have to document the following actions:

1 provide for safe practices in ship operation and a safe working environment;
2 assess all identified risks to their ships, personnel and the environment and establish appropriate safeguards;
3 continuously improve safety management skills of personnel ashore and aboard ships, including preparing for emergencies related both to safety and environmental protection.

The *internal business* measures are based on three main sources. The first one is the crisis management proposed by Watkins and Bazerman (2003; 2004), which deals with identification, assessment and management (Kramer 2005; Pollard and Hotho 2006). Based on their approach, the drafting of an emergency response plan should include a combination of the existing emergency plans usually drafted for minor or unique cases. Then the responsibilities of individuals are clearly drafted. In the event of an incident, communication methods should be activated using specific means. The success of a plan will greatly depend on the frequency of regular drills that will identify any additional needs for backup resources. As this concept of Watkins and Bazerman (2003; 2004) refers mainly to business and organizational failures, it includes a post-crisis review stage, although in the shipping industry this may not exist for the violated parties in an accident.

The second source is the IMO resolution for contingency planning for ships (IMO 1997), which is the nearest approach of crisis management in the shipping industry. Under this approach, a risk analysis is a compulsory request for the identification of hazards. Then appropriate, response tasks should be established to mitigate those hazards. Those tasks are based on the availability and functionality of the resources and communication lines. Each response plan should be examined in conjunction with other plans, as the existence of one threat may activate more than one plan. For the IMO an essential element for success is the continuous training of personnel ashore and on board followed by frequent review and update.

The third source that is used is the ABS guidance notes on the investigation of marine incidents (ABS 2005). After an incident investigation, a stakeholder will have to demonstrate that he took prudent measures in the risk analysis of the identified hazards and the implementation of countermeasures. A primary evidence of this process will be the correct documentation. Records should also exist to evidence the training standards and review the existing emergency plans.

Although different in scope, the above emergency plans are based on some common elements, which are identified as: risk analysis, planning, training and review. To maintain a simple but robust performance management, it is suggested that those elements should be indicators of the internal business perspective, since failure to partially implement a maritime regulation may have devastating results for the organization of a stakeholder.

4.3.4 BSC measures and their objectives

The indicators are mainly used to show areas that require special attention, as identified from an organization or a company. Then it is necessary to establish measures for each indicator in order to monitor the progress in fulfilling each perspective. It goes without argument that each measure should have a unique objective and be clear in its purpose. According to Niven (2002), 'The objectives should act as a bridge from the high level strategy to the specific performance measures that are used to determine the progress towards overall goals.' Therefore, each measure should be self-defined by including its objective.

4.3.5 The concept of measurement quantity in a BSC

Starting from the financial perspective, the four indicators can be measured in terms of the money added to or deducted from each of them. Precisely, the profit will indicate the increase in revenues from new services and products. The revenue could be measured as an increase of the existing revenues, while the cost could be measured as the amount of money reduced directly and/or indirectly. The easiest approach to monitor the use of assets indicator is to keep the generated expenditure cash flow to a minimum. The above indicators will be negatively affected when poor planning of an organization or a company leads to last-minute solutions to implement a maritime regulation.

The indicators of the *customer perspective* can be measured in terms of market share growth. The productivity will increase with the addition of new services and products sales, while the competitiveness will increase when new customers are acquired by an organization or a company showing commercial advantage. A key indicator is the *quality*, which can be measured by the number of the management deficiencies as recorded by third-party inspections. Eventually, the reputation of an organization and/or a company could be measured by the number of claims and/or disputes due to poor services. When an organization or a company is in full compliance with the maritime regulations, it should be expected to have positive results in the indicators described above.

The *learning and growth perspective* is hard to measure with respect to a maritime regulation, but not impossible. Starting with *human capital* as an indicator, it should be ensured in an organization or a company that its employees have high skills, talent and knowledge sufficient to fulfil the regulatory gaps, such as backup personnel requirements. Therefore, there should be no exceptional need for vacancies after a newly introduced maritime regulation. The *information capital* should also be sufficient to cope with current and future regulations. Any unexpected need for the adoption of additional information systems, networks and technology infrastructure may be due to insufficient management. The *organizational capital* can simply be measured by human errors, and particularly those related to poor leadership, employees' ability to share knowledge and failure of employees to understand the strategic goals of top management. The innovation in the shipping industry usually comes from other industries and/or major organizations. It should be beneficial for an organization and/or company at least to be able to adopt those practices in a reasonable time frame.

The *internal business perspective* is easier to measure as it reflects not only failures but also the time needed for a process. Failures will easily be identified by third-party inspections or incidents. However, since these failures may be rare, it is also worth measuring the skills of employees to complete each stage of risk analysis, planning, training and review. The ratio of money to hours could be a measurement of quantity, which will indicate the cost of people involved in each state and the duration of such involvement. For instance, a project with several top managers that lasts several days will have a higher ratio than a project completed faster by lower-level employees.

4.3.6 *The link of perspectives and their measures*

The proposed scorecards could be used for the evaluation of an organization or a company with regard to its management system. After all, compliance with maritime regulations is an essential part of management. As shown in Figure 4.2, each perspective could be used to assess different levels of management represented as tiers.

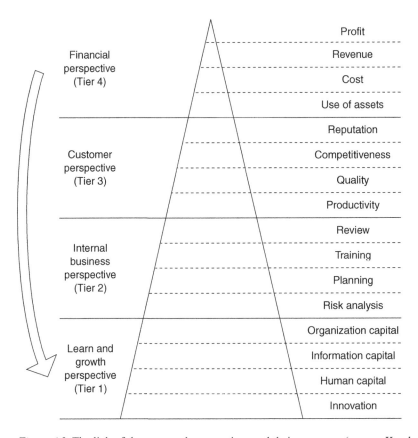

Figure 4.2 The link of the proposed perspectives and their measures (source: Karahalios 2009).

As regards the foundation of a company, regardless of its size and structure, its employees should each contribute with his/her unique skills. The educational background and working experience of each individual will be a part of the entire knowledge that the company has. In addition, the technological changes demand personnel that can easily adapt to those changes. The *organization capital* is the ability of the management structure to get the most out of its personnel's skills and to innovate. When innovation is missing, the company will be outdated. The *learning and growth perspective* at Tier 1 in Figure 4.2 is used to measure all of these issues.

As was stated in this chapter, a failure to comply with one of the numerous maritime regulations could have devastating commercial results for an organization. Consequently, an organization should frequently carry out risk analysis studies to identify potential threats from the maritime regulations. Those risks will be minimized by careful planning and training. However, every action should be followed by monitoring and periodic review for its rational choice.

The process that appears in Tier 2 in the *internal business perspective* represents the procedure of implementing a regulation.

The results of the rational selection of people and the risk analysis studies should appear in the next level, which is Tier 3. Tier 3 is the *customer perspective*, which indicates the results of a regulation in business practices. A customer expects a company to fulfil its contractual obligations, which could be summarized by productivity and quality of services. When a customer is satisfied with both issues, they may become a loyal customer (Yang *et al.* 2003), increasing the company's market share. As a result, the competition and reputation will improve significantly.

Tier 4 is the *financial perspective*, which indicates the economic achievements or losses from the implementation of a regulation. After a company's establishment in the market, its next care should be to maximize its profitability. This could be achieved by sacrificing the quality of products and services in order to reduce costs. On the other hand, the maximization of the *use of assets*, proper investment and budget control could increase profitability.

Tier 4 is not the end of the process but the end of a cyclic process. One part of the investment strategy should be research and development, in order to improve the skills of existing personnel. Alternatively, the recruitment of new personnel could be a part of a long-term investment. The adoption of new technologies and equipment should also be evaluated for their contribution to the company's goals.

4.4 Ranking priorities

In addition to the adoption of the BSC, it is useful to pursue a procedure of weighting its perspectives. When a stakeholder sets his BSCs for regulatory compliance, he must evaluate what is more important for his organization. At this stage he should evaluate the weights of his divisions and the BSC perspectives. Starting with the divisions, the role of each division in the required goal should be evaluated. For instance, a company with eight divisions may eventually find that, for a given maritime regulation, two of them will be involved more than the others. The implementation success will depend more heavily on the efforts of these two divisions.

Perspectives should be weighted as well. The BSC approach advocates that the four perspectives should be monitored. However, according to the structure of an organization and the market position of a stakeholder, the perspectives not to be treated as equal to each other. In the real world, although the four perspectives of a regulation need to be met by each stakeholder, they may be of different priorities. The size of an organization, its financial exposure at the time, the available personnel and the know-how will be critical factors for the determination of a company's or an organization's priorities. For instance, the financial perspective will have different weight in a large company with more capital. On the other hand, a small firm may struggle to survive and even minor expenses may put its survival at risk.

Many managers argue that measuring everything in money is a very good business tactic. However, the significance of some issues may not be measured in money, such as the skills and experience of personnel. It may be extremely difficult to measure the contribution of an employee to the financial performance of a company relying on his experience. Even in terms of money, an expense that occurs when a company runs its business in a profitable market cannot be compared with the value of the same expense for the same company in a recession period. Another challenge may be the fact that data may not exist when a decision needs to be made. In other words, an unexpected event may need an urgent solution using data that may not exist at all.

It has been argued that industrial people with a proven track record of successful management skills could make a judgement of significant accuracy when data are not available (Gigerenzer 2007). However, when such a tactic is adopted, it should be structured in an organized way. The divisions of a company, the perspectives and the indicators should be weighted for their significant contribution to a given problem. Then, by completing a detailed ranking, it is possible to map a strategy for achieving the desired goal. Therefore, it is appropriate to provide the means of ranking the four proposed BSC perspectives for their priorities. There are some available methods with regard to the weighting elements of a given problem, such as the technique for order of preference by similarity to ideal solution (TOPSIS) and the analytic hierarchy process (AHP; Berrah *et al.* 2004). However, the AHP has some advantages compared to other methods because of its simplicity and its ability to rank parts of a multi-criteria problem in a hierarchical structure (Chan 2006).

The AHP established by Saaty (1990) is a method that can solve multi-criteria decision problems by setting priorities, as shown in Figure 4.3. The best decision can be made when qualitative and quantitative aspects of a decision need to be included (Saaty 1990, 2003). The application of the AHP to a complex problem consists of the following four steps (Cheng *et al.* 1999):

1   Break down the complex problem into a number of small elements and structure them in a hierarchy.

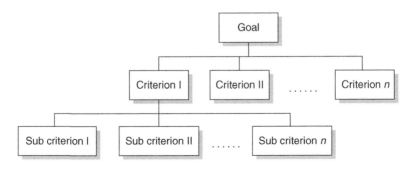

Figure 4.3 An example of a hierarchical structure.

2   Make pairwise comparisons among the elements.
3   Estimate the relative weights of the elements.
4   Aggregate these relative weights and synthesize them for the final measurement of given decision alternatives.

4.5 Collecting qualitative data: the Delphi method

The AHP and BSC can be used independently or combined with each other as appropriate tools for a stakeholder in order for him to evaluate the performance of his organization with respect to the implementation of maritime regulations. However, a main issue that could appear in the application of such tools is the lack of reliable data, when there is no relevant feedback from past events. The introduction of a new maritime regulation could be such a case. When the ISM Code was introduced, very few stakeholders had experience of such management systems.

The AHP has been discussed in previous sections as a valid method for decision making and ranking of certain criteria in terms of their weights. However, the weight of these criteria can only be determined with regard to certain data. In the case where data are unavailable or limited, it may be appropriate to consult with experts who, with their high levels of experience, can provide a form of data. An alternative or combined technique is the Delphi method, which is faster and less expensive than other weight-assigning methods.

The name 'Delphi' derives from the Oracle of Delphi. The Delphi method is based on the assumption that a group of judgements is more valid than individual judgements. The Delphi concept may be viewed as one of the spinoffs of defence research. 'Project Delphi' was the name given to an Air Force-sponsored Rand Corporation study, starting in the early 1950s, concerning the use of expert opinion. The data collected with this method provide some degree of objectivity in pulling evidence from various sources (Sii and Wang 2003). Other researchers (Chang and Wang 2006) mentioned that this method has the following advantages:

1   decreases the time of questionnaire survey;
2   avoids distorting the individual expert opinion;
3   clearly expresses the semantic structure of predicted items;
4   considers the fuzzy nature during the interview process.

The Delphi method has been used in several applications where there was a need for expert judgement, such as in evaluating decision-making systems (Sii and Wang 2003; Khorramshahgol and Moustakis 1998). One if its main contributions is the identification of priorities through expert judgement when data are insufficient for statistical models. Those cases may include changes in a business sector where interactions are complicated (Chang *et al.* 2007). However, in the classical Delphi a statistical aggregation of group response is used for a quantitative analysis and interpretation of data (Skulmoski *et al.* 2007; Chen and Chen 2005).

The process of the Delphi method is executed in several rounds. Initially, a panel of experts is formed and the ideas are circulated. Some degree of the initial disagreement is expected to be reduced after several rounds. Anonymity is a key issue, since it could affect the opinion of some panel experts. This would be more complicated when the panel members are senior managers of the same company, where alliances and sympathies may exist.

Sii and Wang (2003) described the Delphi method as a procedure of the following five steps:

1   select the anonymous experts;
2   conduct the first round of a questionnaire survey;
3   conduct the second round of a questionnaire survey;
4   conduct the third round of a questionnaire survey;
5   integrate expert opinions to reach a consensus.

Steps 3 and 4 are normally repeated until a consensus is reached on a particular topic. The results of the literature review and the experts' interviews can then be used to identify all common views of the survey and simplify Step 2, replacing the traditional open-style survey. The simplification of the above process produces the modified Delphi method. In this case, the individuals that will draft the first round of the survey should have some expertise in the area. Otherwise, important issues may be excluded from the initial survey and, therefore, not be further discussed. If one of the excluded issues is later found to be critical, the decision made may have devastating results.

Starting from a blank page and noting any ideas could be an alternative solution to the above issue. With this approach, a blank page is given to each member of the panel where he/she lists the initial points for discussion. Although this approach is more liberal, it could be a long process and occasionally time would not be available.

4.6 Linguistic terms: fuzzy set theory

Sometimes the data are unavailable or the numbers are insufficient to use the AHP and Delphi methods. In such a situation, linguistic terms may be used to facilitate the decision-making process. The logic is that for some cases people would prefer to provide a word when evaluating something rather than a number. Ma *et al.* (2007) highlighted the following issues when using linguistic terms:

1   Experts need to select linguistic terms for presenting their opinions according to their preference. It is not demanded that all experts use the same linguistic terms.
2   It is not required that all linguistic terms are placed symmetrically and have a total order. Therefore, experts and decision makers have a more independent right to present their opinions.

3   Each linguistic term should be treated as a whole and only its determinacy and consistency should be a cause for concern.

The use of linguistic terms could be useful when adopted in a formal way. This could be achieved by applying the fuzzy set theory developed by Zadeh (1965) in order to deal with linguistic difficulties while collecting data. The simple form of the fuzzy numbers is the triangular one. A triangular fuzzy number $\tilde{M}$ can be defined by a triplet (a, b, c), as shown in Figure 4.4.

The meaning of this fuzzy number is that a linguistic term such as 'likely' will be in a range from a to c, with most probable value b. To simplify the above, someone may describe the temperature of water as hot when the temperature varies from 40 to 45 °C, when another person may use the same term when the temperature varies from 38 to 47 °C. Although both individuals use the same term, their understanding is slightly different.

The adoption of fuzzy sets in everyday decision making may be challenging for untrained managers. However, when people are asked to describe or give a judgement by using linguistic terms, they may use these terms in a different context to what they understand.

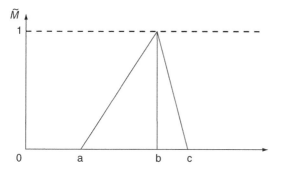

Figure 4.4 A triangular fuzzy number $\tilde{M}$.

4.7 Hierarchical scorecards

The complicated business world needs advanced decision-making tools. To this end, the above tools have been combined to provide more applicable solutions. Sohn *et al.* (2003) proposed a calculation of weights for the BSC measures, where the relative weights for each performance measured can be calculated using the AHP. The AHP and BSC approach were combined to evaluate the performance of the IT department in the manufacturing industry in Taiwan (Lee *et al.* 2008). Chang *et al.* (2007) used the Delphi method to define the evaluating criteria of an AHP matrix used to select an optimal-performing machine in terms of precision, and establish a hierarchical framework. The Delphi method was also applied to provide a framework for evaluating the impact of implementing a customer relationship management (CRM) based on the BSC (Shafia *et al.*

2011). Wu and Chen (2012) used the Delphi method and the BSC in order to evaluate and compare the performance of enterprises with ISO accreditation.

The above decision-making tools could be combined with each other in order to eliminate their limitations. Such an effort introduced the hierarchical scorecards with applicability in measuring the implementation performance of a maritime regulation in the shipping industry and its stakeholders (Karahalios *et al.* 2011). The combination of these tools provides the following framework:

1   Use BSCs to measure the commercial performance of a representative stakeholder.
2   Adopt the AHP to rank the contribution of representative stakeholders in the regulatory process.
3   Use the AHP to rank the perspectives of each representative stakeholder.
4   Use the Delphi method to collect data for a panel of experts.
5   Use the fuzzy sets to evaluate linguistic experts.

The studies carried out with the adoption of this methodology showed that the implementation success of maritime regulations is based on the stakeholders' balances between costs and benefits. These balances can be measured as for the benefit of maritime regulators and businesspeople. Following the above process, an industrial tool capable of evaluating the implementation performance of the shipping industry in terms of compliance with a maritime regulation has been designed.

References

ABS. (2005). Guidance notes on the investigation of marine incidents. American Bureau of Shipping, June.

Aven T., Korte J. (2003). On the use of risk and decision analysis to support decision-making. *Reliability Engineering and System Safety*, Vol. 79, pp. 289–299.

Berrah L., Mauris G., Vernadat F. (2004). Information aggregation in industrial performance measurement: rationales, issues and definitions. *International Journal of Production Research*, Vol. 42(20), pp. 4271–4293.

Chan Y.C.L. (2006). An analytic hierarchy framework for evaluating balanced scorecards of healthcare organizations. *Canadian Journal of Administrative Sciences*, Vol. 23(2), pp. 85–104.

Chang C.W., Wu C.R., Lin C.T., Chen H.C. (2007). An application of the AHP and sensitivity analysis for selecting the best slicing machine. *Computers and Industrial Engineering*, Vol. 52, pp. 296–307.

Chang P.C., Wang Y.W. (2006). Fuzzy Delphi and back-propagation model for sales forecasting in PCB industry. *Expert Systems with Applications*, Vol. 30, pp. 715–726.

Chantelauve G. (2003). An overview of maritime safety assessment trends in a stakeholder perspective. 14th European Safety and Reliability Conference, 15–18 June, Maastricht, Vol. 2, pp. 387–395.

Chen S.J., Chen S.M. (2005). Aggregating fuzzy opinions in the heterogeneous group decision-making environment. *Cybernetics and Systems: An International Journal*, Vol. 36, pp. 309–338.

Cheng A.C., Yang B.K., Hwang C. (1999). Evaluating attack helicopters by AHP based on linguistic variable weight. *European Journal of Operational Research*, Vol. 116, pp. 423–435.

Chung L.H., Gibbons P.T., Schochw H.P. (2006). The management of information and managers in subsidiaries of multinational corporations. *British Journal of Management*, Vol. 17, pp. 153–165.

Farneti F., Guthrie J. (2008). Italian and Australian local governments: balanced scorecard practices. A research note. *Journal of Human Resource Costing and Accounting*, Vol. 12(1), pp. 4–13.

Fleisher C.S., Mahaffy D. (1997). A balanced scorecard approach to public relations management assessment. *Public Relations Review*, Vol. 23(2), pp. 117–142.

Franco-Santos M., Bourne M. (2005). An examination of the literature relating to issues affecting how companies manage through measures. *Production Planning and Control*, Vol. 16(2), pp. 114–124.

Garcia-Valderrama T., Mulero-Mendigorri E., Revuelta-Bordoy D. (2008). A balanced scorecard framework for R&D. *European Journal of Innovation Management*, Vol. 11(2), pp. 241–281.

Gigerenzer G. (2007). *Gut Feelings: the Intelligence of the Unconscious*. Allen Lane, London.

Havold J.I., Nesset E. (2009). From safety culture to safety orientation: validation and simplification of a safety orientation scale using a sample of seafarers working for Norwegian ship owners. *Safety Science*, Vol. 47(3), pp. 305–326.

Huang H.C. (2007). Designing a knowledge-based system for strategic planning: a balanced scorecard perspective. *Expert Systems with Applications*, doi:10.1016/j. eswa.2007.09.046.

IMO. (1997). Guidelines for a structure of an integrated system of contingency planning for shipboard emergencies adopted by the Organization by resolution A.852(20). IMO, November.

IMO. (2004). Amendments to the annex of the protocol of 1978 relating to the international convention for the prevention of pollution from ships, 1973 (revised annex I of MARPOL 73/78). Resolution MEPC.117(52). IMO Publishing, London.

Kaplan R.S., Norton D.P. (1996a). Linking the balanced scorecard to strategy. *California Management Review*, Vol. 39(1), pp. 55–79.

Kaplan R.S., Norton D.P. (1996b). Using the balanced scorecard as a strategic management system. *Harvard Business Review*, January–February, pp. 75–85.

Kaplan R.S, Norton D.P. (2000). Having problem with your strategy? Then map it. *Harvard Business Review*, Vol. 78(5), pp. 167–176.

Kaplan R.S, Norton D.P. (2004). Measuring the strategic readiness of intangible assets. *Harvard Business Review*, Vol. 82(1), pp. 52–63.

Kaplan R.S, Norton D.P. (2005). The office of strategy management. *Harvard Business Review*, October, pp. 72–80.

Karahalios H., Yang Z.L., Wang J. (2011) A study of the implementation of maritime safety regulations by a ship operator. In *Advances in Safety, Reliability and Risk Management*, ed. Berenguer, Grall and Guedes Soares, Proceeding of 2011, Annual European Safety and Reliability Conference (ESREL), Troyes, France, 18–22 September, pp. 2863–2869.

Kettunen J., Kantola I. (2005). Management information system based on the balanced scorecard. *Campus-Wide Information Systems*, Vol. 22(5), pp. 263–274.

Khorramshahgol R., Moustakis V.S. (1988). Delphic hierarchy process (DHP): a methodology for priority setting derived from the Delphi method and analytical hierarchy process. *European Journal of Operational Research*, Vol. 37, pp. 347–354.

Kramer R.M. (2005). A failure to communicate: 9/11 and the tragedy of the informational commons. *International Public Management Journal*, Vol. 8(3), pp. 397–416.

Lee, A.H., Chen, W.C., Chang, C.J. (2008). A fuzzy AHP and BSC approach for evaluating performance of IT department in the manufacturing industry in Taiwan. *Expert Systems with Applications*, 34(1), pp. 96–107.

Lee J. (2008). Preparing performance information in the public sector: an Australian perspective. *Financial Accountability and Management*, Vol. 24(2), pp. 117–149.

McAdam R., O'Neill E. (1999). Taking a critical perspective to the European business excellence model using a balanced scorecard approach: a case study in the service sector. *Managing Service Quality*, Vol. 9(3), pp. 191–197.

Ma J., Ruan D., Xu Y., Zhang G. (2007). A fuzzy-set approach to treat determinacy and consistency of linguistic terms in multi-criteria decision making. *International Journal of Approximate Reasoning*, Vol. 44, pp. 165–181.

Mearns K., Havold J.I. (2003). Occupational health and safety and the balanced scorecard. *The TQM Magazine*, Vol. 15(6), pp. 408–423.

Niven P.R. (2002). *Balanced Scorecard Step by Step: Maximizing Performance and Maintaining Results*. John Wiley and Sons, Inc., New York.

Osmundsen P., Aven T., Vinnem J.E. (2008). Safety, economic incentives and insurance in the Norwegian petroleum industry. *Reliability Engineering and System Safety*, Vol. 93, pp. 137–143.

Park J., Jeong K., Jung W. (2005). Identifying cognitive complexity factors affecting the complexity of procedural steps in emergency operating procedures of a nuclear power plant. *Reliability Engineering and System Safety*, Vol. 89, pp. 121–136.

Pedersen E.R., Neergaard P. (2008). From periphery to center: how CSR is integrated in mainstream performance management frameworks. *Measuring Business Excellence*, Vol. 12(1), pp. 4–12.

Perepelkin M., Knapp S., Perepelkin G., Pooter M. (2010). An improved methodology to measure flag performance for the shipping industry. *Marine Policy*, Vol. 34, pp. 395–405.

Phillips J.K., Phillips D.M. (2007). Development of variant definitions for stakeholder groups with regard to the performance of public transit in the United States. *The Electronic Journal of Business Research Methods*, Vol. 5(2), pp. 61–70.

Pollard D., Hotho S. (2006). Crises, scenarios and the strategic management process. *Management Decision*, Vol. 44(6), pp. 721–736.

Punniyamoorthy M., Murali R. (2008). Balanced score for the balanced scorecard: a benchmarking tool. *Benchmarking: An International Journal*, Vol. 15, pp. 420–443.

Ramos T.B., Alves I., Subtil R., Melo J.J. (2007). Environmental performance policy indicators for the public sector: the case of the defense sector. *Journal of Environmental Management*, Vol. 82, pp. 410–432.

Saaty T.L. (1990). An exposition of the AHP in reply to the paper 'remarks on the analytic hierarchy process'. *Management Science*, Vol. 36(3), pp. 259–268.

Saaty T.L. (2003). Decision-making with the AHP: why is the principal eigenvector necessary. *European Journal of Operational Research*, Vol. 145, pp. 85–91.

Shafia M.A., Mazdeh M.M., Vahedi M., Pournader M. (2011). Applying fuzzy balanced scorecard for evaluating the CRM performance. *Industrial Management & Data Systems*, Vol. 111(7), pp. 1105–1135.

Sii H.S., Wang J. (2003). A design–decision support framework for evaluation of design options/proposals using a composite structure methodology based on the approximate reasoning approach and the evidential reasoning method. *Proceedings of the I MECH E Part E Journal of Process Mechanical Engineering*, Vol. 217(1), pp. 59–76.

Skulmoski G.J., Hartman F.T., Krahn J. (2007). The Delphi method for graduate research. *Journal of Information Technology Education*, Vol. 6, pp. 1–21.

Sohn M.H., Youb T., Lee S.L., Lee H. (2003) Corporate strategies, environmental forces, and performance measures: a weighting decision support system using the k-nearest neighbor technique. *Expert Systems with Applications*, Vol. 25, pp. 279–292.

Solano J., Ovalles M.P., Rojas T., Padua A.G., Morales L.M. (2003). Integration of systemic quality and the balanced scorecard. *Information Systems Management*, winter, pp. 66–80.

Stevens S.T. (2006). Applying CMMI and Strategy to ATE Development. Systems Readiness Technology Conference, IEEE, pp. 813–818.

Stewart R.A, Mohamed S. (2003). Evaluating the value IT adds to the process of project information management in construction. *Automation in Construction*, Vol. 12, pp. 407–417.

Wagner M. (2007). Integration of environmental management with other managerial functions of the firm: empirical effects on drivers of economic performance. *Long Range Planning*, Vol. 40, pp. 611–628.

Watkins A.L., Arrington C.E. (2007). Accounting, new public management and American politics: theoretical insights into the national performance review. *Critical Perspectives on Accounting*, Vol. 18, pp. 33–58.

Watkins M.D., Bazerman M.H. (2003). Predictable surprises: the disasters you should have seen coming. *Harvard Business Review*, Vol. 81(3), pp. 72–80.

Watkins M.D., Bazerman M.H. (2004). *Predictable Surprises: The Disasters You Should Have Seen Coming and How to Prevent Them*. Harvard Business School Press, Boston, MA.

Wu, S.I., Chen, J.H. (2012). The performance evaluation and comparison based on enterprises passed or not passed with ISO accreditation: an appliance of BSC and ABC methods. *International Journal of Quality & Reliability Management*, 29(3), pp. 295–319.

Wu, S.I., Liu S.Y. (2010). The performance measurement perspectives and causal relationship for ISO-certified companies: a case of opto-electronic industry. *International Journal of Quality & Reliability Management*, Vol. 27(1), pp. 27–47.

Yang Z., Peterson R. T., Cai S. (2003). Services quality dimensions of internet retailing: an exploratory analysis. *Journal of Services Marketing*, Vol. 17(7), pp. 685–700.

Zadeh L. (1965). Fuzzy sets. *Information and Control*, Vol. 8, pp. 338–353.

5 The role of stakeholders in the implementation of maritime regulations

5.1 Introduction

Lindøe *et al.* (2011) examined responses to accidents occurring in different industrial sectors. Their findings showed that the relationship between power and trust among the regulating agencies and the industrial actors influences the pattern of interaction. As it was discussed in Chapters 2 and 3, the same principle also applies in the shipping industry because the different private stakeholders expect regulatory compliance from their customers as part of their commercial interaction. Despite the fact that the authority of some stakeholders could be relatively minor, if challenged, it could create costs for a stakeholder such as claims, delays, ship arrest and prosecutions.

For a better understanding of the above concept, the various stages of cargo transportation at sea should be examined. In a very simplistic scenario a ship operator hires out the volume of his ship for a certain period of time for transportation of a cargo. The person or corporation who will pay for this service will be a cargo owner or, more frequently, a charter (Tsai *et al.* 2009). In some cases a shipbroker may also be involved in order to bring together, in a series of negotiations, the two parties who hopefully will reach an agreement (Hetherington 1991). The contract that binds this agreement is known as 'charter party' and its duration could be for one voyage – then called a voyage charter party. A very common practice is the charter to be for a predetermined period of time; this kind of charter is called a time charter party and usually lasts for one year. In this case, the ship operator has the responsibility to satisfy the needs of his customer, who is the cargo owner and/or charterer.

However, the industry does not work in such a simplistic way as several parties are involved in the above operation. These parties expect the ship operator to comply with certain requirements that could be stated in an agreement between the ship operator and the other interested party, which includes various private contractors that receive services from a ship operator (e.g. port corporation). This category could be broad since all the parties are bound by various agreements with the ship operators and, to some degree, they expect something as consumers of their services. Such agreements exist among the shipowner and his ship operator and the master, the crew, the classification society, port agents, suppliers, repairers and insurers (Maclachlan 2004). The following sections examine in detail the commercial and regulatory authority of these parties. A violation of a maritime regulation may prove to be extremely costly for a ship operator, as it will be a breach of a commercial contractual condition.

As an alternative, the requirements of cargo transportation could be examined under the light of statutory law. For instance, each ship is obligated to comply with the laws of any coastal state whose territorial waters it is sailing in. What is more, a ship operator is expected to comply with the requirements of a small yet important group of regulatory bodies, such as flag states, coastal states and classification societies, or else the ship operator and his employees would be liable for penalties and occasionally criminal sentences. However, a ship operator is free to select the geographical regions where he will run his business, and may choose areas where law enforcement is less severe.

5.2 Commercial structure and authority of stakeholders

The shipping industry consists of several stakeholders, such as organizations and companies, with each one being unique due to the specialization of the services it offers. In fact, this uniqueness of each stakeholder raises an issue concerning their potential authority over other stakeholders, which emerges from the fact that a stakeholder has the freedom to choose companies that comply with his requirements in order to run his business. The decision of a group of stakeholders to run their business with companies that follow certain criteria, such as ISO standards, constitutes a great force for the market. An example in the shipping industry is the decision of insurance companies not to insure ships that do not comply with the ISM Code, something that enhanced its implementation by the ship operators. This process is termed as the authority of each stakeholder.

When examining the authority of each stakeholder there are two noteworthy issues that should be very carefully reviewed: the duration and the power of this authority. The duration of a group of stakeholders could be defined as the period of time that this authority stands in terms of market demands. Since it is difficult to find identical market cycles in the history of the shipping industry, every period should be considered as unique. To simplify the above, one could read the supply and demand curves for sea services. In recent years, China and India have carried out reforms that may have contributed to their rapid growth (Hsieh and Klenow 2009), which has driven demand for ship services. Since the number of ships could not increase instantly, ship operators found themselves in an advantageous commercial position in the shipping market, as initially the freights increased. However, the costs also increased and they had to hire any available ship, regardless of its standards. Therefore, if someone would like to define the authority among ship operators and cargo owners, he would certainly rank the ship operators higher in terms of their commercial power. However, the global financial crisis of 2008 decreased the demand for ship services. Consequently, the ship operators found themselves possessing expensive ships in an exceptionally poor market with low freights. This period would definitely devalue the commercial authority of the ship operators in the shipping industry.

Referring now to the power of the authority of a group of stakeholders, we could define it with regard to the number of stakeholders affected by the actions of such a group in the chain of the shipping industry. Some stakeholders could take a decision that may affect more than one group of stakeholders. For example, the Paris MOU is an international effort to identify substandard ships and take corrective actions with respect to environmental protection and safety at sea. Many states, such as the EU, Canada and Russian Federation, have joined this campaign, which enforces quality control across ships, ship operators, charterers, flag states, crew members and classification societies worldwide. In the event that any of the mentioned stakeholders was found to systematically violate the international agreements he would be penalized, while a mere violation by crew members and stakeholders could result in prosecutions. Therefore, it is easy to identify that the authority of these port states is higher than all the other stakeholders.

5.3 Representative stakeholders within the shipping industry

The shipping industry is a complicated network composed of various stakeholders. In 1998 the MCA proposed that the stakeholders in the bulk carrier sector be grouped according to their interests, as shown in Table 5.1. In order to estimate how costs and benefits of a regulation are distributed in the industry, one can use a sample of representative stakeholders from every group. For instance, Karahalios *et al.* (2011) selected three representative stakeholders in their case study: the UK flag state, the United States as a coastal state and the ABS as a classification society.

Table 5.1 The stakeholders of the bulk carrier sector

---

1 Owners and operators
2 Staff and support (master, crew, crew agency, trade unions, families)
3 Hardware (ship designers, ship builders, ship repairers, equipment makers, port commercial (supply) services)
4 Regulatory bodies (IMO, international regulators, port state, flag state, port authority)
5 Non-governmental bodies and pressure groups (classification societies, professional bodies, trade associations, training establishments, environmental groups)
6 Cargo groups (cargo owner, charterer(s), terminal operators, stevedores)
7 Insurance group (hull & machinery underwriters, cargo underwriters, P&I)
8 Response services (rescue and emergency services, salvors, coastal state)
9 Media
10 Service group (legal services, marine consultancy and surveying services, general insurance)
11 Upstream and downstream group (commercially or geographically dependant region or states, other trading nations, suppliers, consumers)

Source: MCA research project.

The representative stakeholders discussed in this chapter are:

1 Flag state
2 Coastal state
3 Classification society
4 P&I Club
5 Ship operator
6 Underwriter
7 Marine consultant
8 Ship builder
9 Cargo owner
10 Crew members

The media and consumers groups of stakeholders were excluded from this sample of representative stakeholders as they do not directly participate in the sea trade. In addition, the P&I club is distinguished from the group of underwriters because it has different interests and so it should be studied separately. A P&I club is likely to be exposed to higher financial responsibilities due to the third-party liability cover that it offers, while the underwriters generally have financial responsibility to the value of the insured property (Aase 2007; Goss 2003). The third party liabilities in the case of pollution may include financial losses of large groups of people.

The authority and power that some stakeholders possess can be used to force other stakeholders to enhance the regulatory process due to the fear of commercial isolation. A key issue in this approach is to estimate the weighting in the regulatory process of each stakeholder. Korte *et al.* (2002) argued that the current regulatory system poses a regulatory authority level among the stakeholders. They also suggested that the stakeholders are not exposed to hazards at the same level. For this reason, they constructed a graph presenting the distance of stakeholders from a potential hazard in terms of physical distance and time, as shown in Figure 5.1. The stakeholders are posted on the vertical axis according to their level of authority, with the highest level being at the top, while they are posted on the horizontal axis with regard to their distance from the hazard, with the right side being closer to the hazard.

5.3.1 Flag state

The flag state is at the top of Figure 5.1 as it has the direct authority over and responsibility for the ships flying its flags. This authority is exercised directly over the ships; substandard ships found through inspections are penalized. There are also restrictions regarding the crew training and certification. Consequently, the seamen of some states with insufficient training standards may not be allowed to work in some flag states (UK P&I 1996). A further authority can be exercised over classification societies by restricting them from issuing statutory certification on behalf of the flag state. A classification society does not have the

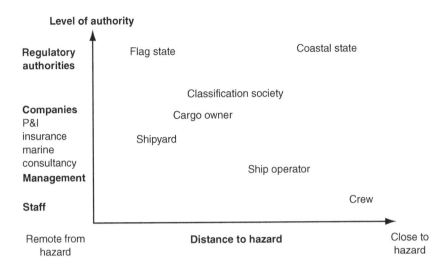

Figure 5.1 The representative stakeholders and their distance from a hazard (source: Karahalios 2009).

luxury of losing its commercial relationship with a major flag state since this is a major source of income.

Although the flag state seems to be very powerful, in the case of an accident it is usually at the greatest physical distance from the ship (with the exception of its ships when involved in coastal trade in the same state). Therefore, apart from reputation damage, no other significant harm could threaten the flag state of a substandard ship. Of course, the effort of other states with the means of PSC is working to this direction but the results are minor when compared to reactions to accidents on the scale of the *Exxon Valdez*. On the other hand, as the case of FOCs has shown, an extremely rigorous flag state may cause a loss of income if many ship operators register their ships elsewhere. What is more, apart from the economic burden, such a loss would also reduce the state's negotiating power in the IMO.

5.3.2 Coastal state

The coastal state can exercise authority over foreign ships in its territory and EEZ. This authority has commercial implications for violating parties. Starting from substandard ships, which are restricted from their ports, PSC records regarding stakeholders who benefited from those ships are forming valuable databases. Consequently, there is damage caused to the reputation of flag states, classification societies, cargo owners and ship operators who make profits by allowing the existence of those substandard ships. Such reputation damage will push prudent ship operators away from these stakeholders. However, substandard ships could restrict their operations to ports in other regions. It is for this reason that such commercial pressure is more rigorously exercised by states that have the means, yet at the same time are large exporters of commodities (e.g. Australia and the United States).

The ISPS Code revealed that a poorly managed ship could eventually pose a threat to international trade. For effective and efficient management of security in maritime transportation, activities are monitored to ensure they are completed as planned, and any significant deviations are corrected (Yilmazel and Asyali 2005). The coastal states can be damaged not only by an unexpected event, but also intentionally by a terrorist act. Therefore, the risks that a coastal state faces are increasing in a changing geopolitical environment. Of course, it is essential to add that domestic trade with coastal state ships generates additional hazards for a state's natural resources.

5.3.3 Classification society

In terms of authority, the classification society is in a lower position compared to states, and in a middle position regarding its distance to hazards. The role of classification societies is extremely important in the implementation of maritime regulations. According to SOLAS Ch II-1, Reg 3-1, ships shall be designed, con-structed and maintained in compliance with the structural, mechanical and elec-trical requirements of a classification society which is recognized by a flag state. Fees apply for any of these services, therefore providing the funding for the existence of classification societies. A classification society may refuse to provide a ship with a certificate. However, the position of a major ship operator may provide him with some kind of immunity towards such risks since he has bargaining power. Furthermore, the position of classification societies has been heavily criticized because they are paid for their services by the owners/ managers of the ships they monitor for regulatory compliance. The PSC deten-tion records reveal that even ships registered with IACS members do not neces-sarily reach high standards (Cariou and Wolff 2011).

5.3.4 Protection and indemnity club

The protection and indemnity (P&I) clubs usually suffer financial damage because of their insured ships' violations of the IMO regulations, usually due to cargo mishandling. The IMO has published plenty of regulations regarding cargo operations for the majority of cargoes. The inappropriate stowage, carriage and/ or cargo operations may lead a ship to become unseaworthy (Zobel 2012). In this case, a P&I club could put significant commercial pressure on its insured ships by withdrawing the insurance coverage. Therefore, although the physical distance from the hazard is great, the level of authority is high. On the other hand, from the commercial point of view, a few substandard ships may be tolerated as an insurance risk for a P&I. The philosophy of risk assessment is accepting the fact that an extreme accident is very rare. The role of a P&I club is the mutual protection of ship operators against such risks.

5.3.5 *Ship operator*

The ship operator is a major beneficiary in the shipping industry and is the recipient of negative publicity and heavy criticism in the case of an accident. His regulatory responsibility is significant as he mans and maintains his ships according to the requirements of the ISM Code. However, as is shown Figure 5.1, public opinion is sometimes misled due to the fact that he is physically closer to a potential accident. In other words, he is one of the few stakeholders that will stand before an authority and defend his actions and/or omissions in the case of an accident.

The *Bourbon Dolphin* is a recent case revealing that the responsibility of a ship operator is extended to the monitoring of maritime regulatory compliance in construction stages (Lyng *et al.* 2008). The loss of that offshore supply vessel showed managerial defects regarding adequate training and stability issues. The ship operators argued that ship stability issues are beyond their control. However, this defence was rejected by the commission.

5.3.6 *Underwriter*

The underwriters suffer financial losses mainly due to structural damage or even ship loss. SOLAS is a text mainly describing how a ship should be designed and equipped in order to be ready for a sea voyage. An unseaworthy ship could be the result of inappropriate design, operation and/or maintenance, something that indicates deviation from maritime regulations. Similarly to P&I clubs, an underwriter could put significant commercial pressure on its insured ships when they are found to be substandard in third-party inspections. Therefore, although the physical distance from the hazard is very long, its regulatory authority is high.

5.3.7 *Marine consultant*

Ship operators occasionally seek cooperation with advisors, such as lawyers and technicians, that will guide them to recruit, manage and save money in a way that should not be in conflict with the maritime regulations. The introduction of the ISM and ISPS Code constitutes a notable example. A great number of ship operators had limited experience regarding the requirements of such codes and, consequently, they hired marine consultants. Similarly, in the cases that new equipment was placed on board, technicians were often asked to provide training. There are numerous cases in which marine consultants assist ship operators to implement maritime regulations. Therefore, since they guide them through regulatory process, they have some authority over ship operators. On the other hand, such services would be unlikely to make them responsible for a substandard ship.

5.3.8 *Ship builder*

A ship builder is involved at the earliest stage of a ship's life, ensuring that the ship is built according to the applicable maritime regulations. His role in the regulatory process is considered to be of high importance and so is strictly monitored by the ship operator and classification society of the ship. The results appear immediately after the ship's construction, when the ship is first launched into the sea. Any stability and/or mechanical failure will appear at that critical moment and, consequently, loss of reputation and commercial damages will follow. As the *Bourbon Dolphin* case showed, the trend is for the responsibility of the construction stage of a ship to remain with the ship operator.

5.3.9 Cargo owner

The cargo owner is also a great beneficiary of ship services. Although he is not a regulator, he has an interest in safety at sea since an accident could damage or lose the cargo. Therefore, his physical distance is close to the accident. The value of some cargoes could exceed the value of the ship, while sometimes their loss could produce marine pollution. In this case the media would point to the cargo owner, resulting in the loss of his reputation, as happened in the case of the *Exxon Valdez*. On the other hand, such accidents do not occur very often. In the case that there is high demand for cargo transportation and the number of available ships is relatively small, the hiring of ships of lower standards would be a tempting choice. In addition, an older ship will always be offered at a lower price than a new one of the same type and size. Recognizing such practices, the PSC authorities are issuing reports where, among others, they rate the charterers and cargo owners which hire defective ships. This tactic eventually puts commercial pressure on ship operators for continuous improvement.

5.3.10 Crew members

The crew members have no significant authority; they follow everyone's instructions. An odd practice has been adopted by the regulators in the shipping industry, which differs from the other high-risk industries discussed in Chapter 3. This practice is to put pressure on the ship operator to monitor the performance and training of his crew, when few efforts have been made concerning the educational standards of seamen. Therefore, the commercial authority that is exercised over crew members is merely to keep their jobs. This is an excessive burden for professionals that work in a hazardous environment. A further challenge is that seamen change ships and management companies very often, and they experience different working environments each time. Such an allocation may create an attitude where a seaman would deal with safety issues only as long as he is on board.

5.4 Implementation generates benefits and costs for a stakeholder

The IMO's efforts will be proven fruitful when international ships operate according to unilateral standards. Through shipping history it appears that a regulation implemented all over the world would be more easily enforced provided appropriate stakeholders strive to move in this direction. The discussion in this chapter is developed to address the need for a new strategy targeting the effective implementation of a maritime regulation based on the assumption that some stakeholders could fail to implement a regulation due to lack of resources. In order to examine this argument, it is necessary to adopt the viewpoint of the IMO. This viewpoint is chosen because the IMO is the highest worldwide authority that is responsible for introducing regulations and monitoring their implementation. From this viewpoint, every stakeholder is considered as a partner of the IMO with regard to the implementation process.

Every time a new regulation is enforced it challenges the organizational structure of a prudent ship manager. The terms 'benefits' and 'costs' are used in a broad sense instead of the old-fashioned financial values 'revenues' and 'expenses', reflecting the needs of modern shipping businesses. Therefore, the term *benefits* should include not only the direct contribution to safety and/or marine pollution prevention, but also the commercial advantages. A rigorously regulated ship is expected to be technically reliable, faster and economical. On the other hand, the term *costs* should include short- and long-term acquisition and maintenance of resources, including lack of knowledge, inadequate access to technologies and lack of human recourses. The enforcement of a regulation may include parameters, such as safety culture, that may apply to different states and may not be measurable. As a result of an excessive burden, a stakeholder may choose to disregard a regulation because he cannot identify and/or evaluate the long-term benefits that he may achieve by implementing that particular regulation.

The successful implementation of an existing and/or a newly introduced maritime regulation could be evaluated through a cost–benefit analysis for all the relevant stakeholders. If the benefits and costs of a newly introduced regulation are reasonably distributed among the industry's stakeholders, then they will be more motivated to implement it. This balance can be achieved by reducing the costs of implementation to an affordable level for the shipping industry. The competitive advantages that a stakeholder may gain can be identified and evaluated. The advantage of this approach is that the evaluation of costs and benefits of a regulation can be achieved and consequently it facilitates a direct comparison among them. As a result, there is a greater probability that the regulation will be implemented adequately and in a reasonably short period.

Any failure to effectively implement a maritime regulation may have adverse effects in terms of safety, pollution and business damage for the violated party. Consequently, all the requirements of a regulation should be completely implemented since partial implementation of a regulation may generate the grounds for possible accidents. Therefore, the efforts of a stakeholder should always be self-assessed until they are perfect. If the regulatory requirements' targets are very hard to achieve, it may be an indication that some of these requirements need to be revised.

A list of significant items should be gradually followed by any stakeholder in order to achieve effective implementation. This list should include fundamental issues for a company, such as implementation procedures, cost assessment, availability of resources and monitoring. Moreover, there is much evidence that accidents are more likely to occur due to deficiencies of management systems (ABS 2005). It should be stressed that stakeholders in the shipping industry have different needs and goals, and so a successful strategy should be able to identify and evaluate those needs. As it is argued in this chapter, the excessive burden that some stakeholders suffer due to a regulation could have a negative effect on its implementation.

5.5 The commercial interactions of stakeholders analysed with BSC

The implementation of a maritime regulation will eventually fall upon the stakeholders, generating some benefits and costs for them. An interesting question at this point is whether there is a proportional distribution of this burden among the stakeholders with regard to the magnitude of their benefits. The principles of small firms introduced in RIA should reasonably apply in the shipping industry as well.

Chapter 4 examines the availability of decision-making models and how these could be used as tools in order to measure the regulatory implementation performance of representative stakeholders and, consequently, of the shipping industry. A stakeholder can measure his regulatory implementation performance by focusing on the four perspectives of BSC mentioned in Chapter 4.

The benefits and costs to a stakeholder can be found in the initial four perspectives of the BSC method: financial, internal business, learning and growth and customer. However, a generic BSC for the complicated shipping industry may not be effective. Consequently, a structure of many scorecards should be produced in order to identify the contribution and performance of every stakeholder in the maritime regulation implementation process. Every stakeholder's BSC should be addressed with appropriate perspectives and measures. It should be stressed that every representative stakeholder is unique, and so different measures should be applied in each case. For instance, the learning and growth perspective measures should be common to all stakeholders, since they reflect principles of successful management. However, the financial perspective measures address the main sources of income and expenses of each stakeholder, and this is something that may vary. What is more, the customer perspective measures are developed on the basis of the stakeholder analysis, in order to identify the regulatory link among the stakeholders. The stakeholders with a high level of authority are considered to be the customers of those stakeholders with a lower authority level. As regards the internal business perspective measures, they are common to all the stakeholders since they consist of fundamental issues of risk assessment and analysis.

When trying to define the appropriate measures, what should be mostly taken into account is the fact that the stakeholders in the shipping industry are a variety of non-profit organizations, private companies and groups of people. The literature review is used to address the measures of each representative stakeholder according to its unique needs and obligations. In this section there is a discussion carried out on how BSC could be used as a tool in order to measure costs and benefits of representative stakeholders and, consequently, of the shipping industry.

5.5.1 Flag state

The financial survival of a flag state will come from the increasing revenues from its registered ships (Odeke 2005), which will consist of taxes and additional administration charges, such as issuing of certificates and endorsements. The revenues may grow by increasing the number of ships with new registries, while, at the same time, the flag state should not have registration losses from the existing fleet. What is more, the administration costs, such as headquarters and employees for bureaucratic purposes, should always be maintained at a low level (Tenold 2003). Some new maritime regulations may need immediate cash expenditures, especially if they are ignored until the deadline for enforcement. A well-organized administration should be in a position to foresee such needs.

Ship operators should be considered as direct customers of a flag state. However, many other stakeholders, such as coastal states, could be added to this list due to PSC restrictions that they may apply as a result of poor performance of their fleet. All of them have something in common; the expectation that a flag state will increase the operation efficiency of its fleet. By following high standards, a flag state could establish a fleet with ships that are safer, faster and, consequently, more competitive. Of course, high standards are expected to increase the quality of the flag state's fleet (Corres and Pallis 2008). Such quality standards may result in better ship management practices and profitable ships. Therefore, an improvement in fleet records should be the evidence to customers of a rational administration.

The learning and growth perspective includes the know-how that a flag state should have in order to maintain its competitiveness. When a flag state has an effective organizational structure, it will not need to hire additional employees in the case of the introduction of a new maritime regulation. Additionally, the existing personnel will be more productive if they are provided with IT applications. The up-to-date and skilful personnel should be able to introduce new ship standards, decreasing the number of accidents.

The flag state should have the ability to carry out risk analysis studies for existing and potential threats to its ships (Qin *et al.* 2011). Reviewing the key elements of such studies, the state should maintain an updated database that should be used by experts in order to assess hazards and develop plans. Particular attention should be paid to hazards that could be generated from the introduced regulations. Training regarding the implementation of a regulation should be kept within reasonable time frames, while periodic reviews should indicate whether the existing internal business process is effective.

5.5.2 Coastal state

A main financial source for a coastal state is the revenue from its commercial ports. A disastrous event that could create interruptions in the flow of cargo through ports, such as Hurricane Katrina, can devastate a regional economy and environment for months or even years after its occurrence. In order for the ports to be competitive, they should develop new port facilities (Becker *et al.* 2012). The maritime regulations should intervene in these issues by restricting port facilities and unreasonable commercial planning. MARPOL requires that port facilities be of a generic form; in the GISIS database there are several cases of these requirements being violated. In addition, they should be enforced at minimum costs to facilities, administration and services. The need for immediate cash expenditure to meet regulations' requirements is also a major issue for states with financial difficulties.

The productivity of ports is a major issue for customer satisfaction. Ship operators and cargo owners should be considered as their main customers. A port's competitiveness can be affected by the delays caused by bureaucratic paperwork as a result of regulatory implementation (Sequeira and Djankov 2010). The enforcement of the ISPS Code is a typical example revealing problems of all these cases (Mazaheri and Ekwall 2009). The quality standards of the coastal state ports should always be improved, contributing to regional safety standards.

The learning and growth perspective should measure the needs of a coastal state to hire additional employees, as well as to purchase additional IT applications when a maritime regulation is introduced. One of the achievements of a well-organized state would be the avoidance of damage to its natural resources (Molenaar 2007). Such damage could affect other industries of the state, such as tourism and fishing industries, in a way that could devastate its national economy. The introduction of new standards that will facilitate ports' operation should be considered as a strong indication of successful growth of knowledge management.

With regards to the internal business perspective, a coastal state should establish procedures in order to avoid unpleasant outcomes from inappropriate regulatory implementation. The type and size of ships entering ports or sailing through their territorial zone could be an area in which to carry out risk assessment studies (Yip 2008). In addition, the depreciation of the environment should also be evaluated. New regulations should not require excessive efforts to develop plans or heavy training schedules. Last but not least, regarding the states with several ports, the review process could be simplified as they belong to a similar regime.

5.5.3 Classification society

A classification society has revenues from the existing ships of its class (Boisson 1994). Many of the classification societies have thousands of ships and so, in order to monitor their standards in an effective way, they maintain a huge network of inspectors. Such networks generate costs due to facilities, administration and other supporting services. Many times the class surveyors are required to inspect ships, with payment taking place later. When there is a deadline for the implementation of a maritime regulation, as in the case of ISPS Code and MLC 2006, an increased cash expenditure is necessary. This constant need for expenditure should be balanced by income, either increasing the market share with more ships or providing new services. However, the introduction of a new maritime regulation will provide new services in many fields such as planning, designing, training, certification and inspection.

The customers of a classification society are both the flag states and the ship operators (Pérez *et al.* 2012). A classification society should be able to prove to a state that it is trustworthy to provide services on its behalf and at the same time to acquire more contracts with ship operators. The pragmatic need to increase the quality standards in the shipping industry by monitoring ships' regulatory performance appears to be a link between regulators and ship operators. The improvement in ships' accidents should appear in its safety records.

The learning and growth perspective is paramount for a classification society. An excessive network of surveyors distributed worldwide should be monitored by other equally skilled employees that will guide them on any new regulations. Of course, it goes without saying that an excessive network of people would create a significant burden in financial terms. However, the purchase of additional IT applications is unavoidable in order to make this network functional. The reduction of its fleet incidents could contribute to the reputation of the class. Moreover, the need for classification societies to share this knowledge, especially through training, is a positive contribution to their income as well.

In terms of internal business, the classification society may be the stakeholder who provides the greatest assistance in the shipping industry. Their knowledge and experience is updated daily through their network of inspectors. The *Nicholas H* (1995) revealed the significance of a well-trained classification surveyor. This network should be able to examine each maritime regulation and provide guidance and assistance to ship operators, flag states and the IMO. Therefore, in order to achieve this it should have organized people who would be ready to provide accurate feedback and training internally to its staff. The risk of a misinformed inspector making an inaccurate assessment could damage the reputation of a classification society. However, revisions of the initial guidelines should not be excessive, otherwise they will cause confusion among ship managers and operators.

5.5.4 *P&I club*

The revenues for a P&I club are mainly the premiums from ship operators for the risks that they cover (Li *et al.* 2009). Those risks are covered by maritime regulations and so a plethora of maritime regulations will provide a defensive line against claims. For instance, the records generated by the safety management system of a ship operator could provide evidence of poor management with respect to a claim for damages raised by a third party. For a P&I club, regulatory compliance should not affect administration costs nor the need for immediate cash expenditure, as they pose financial instability.

Customer satisfaction could be shown when the P&I acquire more insurance contracts. In other words, an increase in market share could be an indication of improvement in competitiveness. The competition within the P&I industry has increased significantly. For instance, the Japan P&I Club experienced high completion with three other clubs that established branches in Japan for ocean-going vessels (Japan P&I Club 2006). On the other hand, the insured parties should feel that the P&I will provide them with services of high quality when required (e.g. legal disputes), while an overall reduction of accidents would be attractive for the insured members.

Learning from past experience is vital for the growth of a P&I club. For example, the sharing of knowledge from previous accidents through newly introduced ship operation standards can improve safety at sea. Consequently, a reduction of claims can improve the financial position of the club. Moreover, the correct implementation of existing and introduced maritime regulations can simplify the structure of the organization, which will require fewer employees operating fewer software applications.

With respect to the internal business perspective, the P&I club deals with a great variety of incidents. Exposure to minor claims could also be as devastating as a major catastrophe, such as oil pollution. Therefore, the club should carry out risk assessment studies in order to be prepared for the magnitude and the frequency of claims that could be raised from a maritime regulation. A supplier of P&I insurance requires specific technical expertise to assess the risks involved, a large network of agents to handle the claims and, above all, in the light of the frequency and intensity of the claims, a minimum scale to ensure that the claims to be covered follow a predictable pattern (Zhu 2008). The planning to minimize such financial exposure should include education as well as clear instructions to the employees and especially to the legal advisors. The financial risks that a P&I club is exposed to include existing and new threats from financial claims, which are already covered by existing regulations (Mason 2003), and this is something that results in frequent revision of the internal business process.

5.5.5 *Underwriter*

The underwriter is a stakeholder who, similarly to the P&I club, undertakes the risk to cover structural damage and loss of ships. Therefore, there is a direct benefit when a maritime regulation improves ships' construction and/or management. In addition, this will improve the financial position of the underwriter, since revenues will increase from new risks identified. Less frequent damage to ships will reduce the amounts of money paid for claims. Safer ships could reduce administration costs as they will produce fewer bureaucratic issues. The need for immediate cash expenditure to meet regulations' requirements should be considered as a minimum requirement.

The customer satisfaction perspective could be measured by the market share, which would increase with the acquisition of more insurance contracts. The competitiveness of an underwriter will increase when quality services are improved. Otherwise, significant cost changes, such as a measure to increase competition among insurance carriers, can initiate financial crises (Ruhil and Teske 2003). As regards the maritime regulation quality, a quick response to the regulatory environment is significant. Insurance firms invest customer premiums into asset portfolios to generate income over time, and they purchase reinsurance to dilute the underwriting risks of primary insurers. Consequently, a monitoring of accidents' frequency will ensure increasing customer satisfaction with regard to financial stability (Ruhil and Teske 2003).

As regards the learning and growth perspective, an underwriter would always need to minimize an organization's structure with fewer but more effective employees that do not need expensive hardware and software infrastructure. Insurance information systems should provide the opportunities for fast and easy modification and extension of its functions in order to support new products and changes in legislation (Bartusevics *et al.* 2012). The immediate result of such an effective organization would be the reduction in the number of claims. Ideally, their role would be extended to the introduction of new ship operation standards in the IMO, fulfilling at the same time their role as a non-government organization.

An underwriter should be able to establish effective internal procedures, which would help to foresee hazard from maritime regulations by using the incident database. The need of the insurance industry for a more scientific and technical approach in accepting risk in insurance and reinsurance coverage as well as the need for reliable and accurate information about risk made companies start dealing with professional insurance risk modelling (Njegomir and Ćirić 2012). The effective redesign of its existing policies should also follow its employees, who should be trained for any new changes. The effectiveness of such internal procedures should also be reviewed in order to minimize costs and time for the adoption of regime changes.

5.5.6 Ship builder

The financial perspective from a shipyard largely depends on its ability to comply with changes in maritime regulations, and especially those affecting a ship's design. Its revenues will increase from new ship building orders, if it has the capacity and knowledge to execute them. Regarding the contribution of productivity, it has been calculated that an increase of 10 per cent in productivity in a simple gross margin calculation (represented by a 10 per cent reduction in labour costs) could lead to a reduction of 3 per cent in total cost and an increase of around 34 per cent in profits (Scott 1995). For instance, as a result of the single-hull tanker phase-out there was an increase in shipyard capacity to construct crude oil tankers (Ellison and Corbet 2006). The income of a shipbuilder also depends on ship repairs; sometimes it is an opportunity to comply with new regulations, such as to fit new equipment. Therefore, monitoring regulatory changes should not affect administration costs, since its employees are already numerous. Any need for immediate cash expenditure to meet regulations' requirements constitutes a financial impact.

The customer satisfaction perspective could be initially measured by the increase in the number of ship buildings and repairs. In addition, studies have shown that the true cost of ownership can be reduced if due consideration is given during the design phase (Sanders and Gued 2012). However, those contracts should be cost-effective, at least regionally, in order to remain competitive. Every new market entrant is likely to have to gain market share at the expense of established specialist builders (Scott 1995). Additionally, due to the complicated task required, the shipyard's quality standards should be exceptionally high, while it should be able to prove that it contributes to the ship's design reliability.

A shipyard is a huge worksite with numerous employees of various skills. The know-how from past experience and new knowledge acquired from innovation and research should contribute to maintaining a steady number of employees. The purchase of IT and new equipment could also contribute to this. Jia and Jinke (2011) highlighted the fact that IT technologies have a profound impact on promotion of enterprise management modernization, building a modern enterprise system, enhancing market competitiveness and increasing economic benefits. The success of such innovation could minimize the number of claims related to delay or malfunctions. Eventually, a shipyard should be able to lead the industry by going to more specialized areas. Therefore, the above tasks should have, as a result, the introduction of new ship design standards.

With regard to the internal business perspective, any new regulation should not produce new hazards to a well-managed shipyard. Barlas (2012) has identified a list of existing hazards such as: carelessness of the workers, insufficient safety training and education, unawareness of costs of accidents, erroneous series of human operations and inadequate work-site environment. Its ability to carry out a risk assessment for a new regulation should be proven daily, as the hazards on a work-site are numerous. Plans should be put in place, with detailed procedures and organizational charts; training should be a part of such internal procedures, especially when the implementation of a new regulation is expected. The affect on workload for revising this internal business process should be an indication of good-quality planning.

5.5.7 Cargo owner

The cargo owner is one of the major beneficiaries of shipping services. His profits increase through faster and safer transportation of cargoes. Technical reliability is an issue that results from the majority of maritime regulations. Unsafe ships could cause damage or even loss of his cargoes. When a ship is poorly managed it could increase minor losses of cargo, such as pilferage. A change in the regulatory environment may produce an unstable market. For instance, the prohibition of single-hull tankers in the EU excluded a great number of available oil tankers (Ellison and Corbet 2006). Consequently, such a change could affect immediate cash expenditures in order to hire double-hull oil tankers.

A cargo owner with a great reputation and credibility will increase his market value. The image of a cargo owner depends on the number of years of experience in the market. For his customers, this means that he is a reliable partner transporting cargoes of high quality, free of any damage that could cause them problems. As per SOLAS chapter VI:

> The shipper shall provide the master or his representative with appropriate information on the cargo sufficiently in advance of loading to enable the precautions which may be necessary for proper stowage and safe carriage of the cargo to be put into effect.

A good indication would also be the small number of accidents or disputes caused by cargoes' characteristics and/or inappropriate instructions passed to ship managers. It is worth mentioning that the reputation damage and, consequently, the economic damage of cargo owners involved in major pollution accidents are very important.

The experience of a cargo owner will appear in the learning and growth perspective. A steady number of qualified employees supported by the appropriate infrastructure and technologies would be the evidence of an organization which is maximizing its past experience. Therefore, an effective organization would cause a reduction in the number and quantity of cargo losses. Ideally, a cargo owner should educate other stakeholders by introducing new cargo transport standards or by improving the existing ones. For instance, in the chemical industry, cargo owner associations have forced chemical tanker operators to maintain standards at reliable levels due to the potentially extraordinary catastrophic effects of chemical tanker accidents (Celik 2010).

The internal business perspective should include procedures for minimizing losses using any kind of information related to the cargoes transported. The variety of knowledge coming from accidents and laboratory experiments should allow accumulation of a significant amount of knowledge associated with all cargo transportation stages. For instance, the BC Code requires laboratory tests in order to detect physical characteristics of certain cargoes. The identification of hazards should be followed by careful planning; it is essential to state what kind of information should be provided to ship operators. Training of internal staff to share this knowledge with other stakeholders is vital. The existing internal procedures regarding cargo claims could provide the review framework of the internal business process.

5.5.8 Marine consultant

In order for someone to be a successful marine consultant, it is a prerequisite that he has advanced knowledge of new trends as, after a short period of time, his revenues from the existing consultancy services will fall as the knowledge becomes outdated. The international rules and regulations also affect the possibility for the patenting of new products and, therefore, the innovator's ability to make profit generated by an innovation (Kroneberg 2000). The shipping industry is evolving rapidly and the financial position of a consultant could improve by providing new consultancy services. As for larger organizations, profitability will be affected by administration costs. When changes occur, as for example a new regulation's implementation, the consultant should not need immediate cash expenditures in order to be educated or equipped.

When a marine consultant provides a sufficient number of services in his field, he can improve customer satisfaction. Prompt delivery and prompt response to customers' concerns and inquiries are important means of reducing dissatisfaction and increasing customer satisfaction (Yang *et al.* 2003). His reputation and credibility will be affected by rational and cost-effective advice. Quality of services should improve constantly due to the technological and regulatory changes occurring over the years. In addition, the fact that more and more people are being educated over time indicates that more competitors are being added. Furthermore, the number of failures should also be compared to their costs, even if both their high frequency and their costs will affect his customers.

In the case of a marine consultant, the learning and growth perspective may be the most significant one, as it affects his future income. It is worth mentioning here that new-to-the-world projects were found to be more profitable (Brentani 2001). His structure should remain compact but also flexible in order for him to adapt to new trends and to lead his customers. Employees in such a structure should be extremely valuable as they maximize available technologies and IT applications. One the other hand, incorrect opinions and services will lead to claims, while very frequent or very expensive claims could be an indication of knowledge gaps. Ideally, a marine consultant should have a key role in the shipping industry by producing new ship standards.

As it was stated above, the key for a successful business path would be to provide services before there is an urgent demand in the shipping industry. The internal business process should include hazard identification and potential problems from the implementation of a new regulation. A new business plan on how to approach existing and potential customers should be developed in order for services to be appropriately provided. However, Brentani (2001) mentioned that despite extensive documentation on how to achieve success, new product development remains a high-risk venture. Such services require that the employees are better trained and educated than potential customers. A constant monitoring of such planning and its execution could reveal organizational gaps and applicable solutions.

5.5.9 Ship operator

The ship operator is the most well known stakeholder in the shipping industry. His income mainly depends on maximizing the cargo capacity of his ships. However, a ship operator can make a significant capital gain when he sells his ships on the second-hand market, once the freight rates have reached their maximum level (Scarsi 2007). Pires (2001) argued that the value of ship building output could be considered as equal to the acquisition cost in the international market. Consequently, the expansion of a ship operator's fleet depends on the reduction of the capital cost of a ship, something that could be achieved in recession periods. However, a maritime regulation may increase the capital value of his existing ships, as happened with double-hull oil tankers (Glen 2010). To date, the changes into the shipping industry increase administration costs, as closer monitoring of ships includes frequent inspections and constant communications. The need for immediate cash expenditure in order to meet the regulations' requirements usually appears in balance sheets.

The customers of a ship operator are numerous, but the most important ones are the cargo owners with whom he has to sign valuable contracts (Kavussanos 1996). A good reputation and credibility will be the main advertising tool used to establish permanent or long-term business relationships in the transportation market. Quality of services should mainly include fast, safe and economic carriage of goods. Therefore, any complaint or financial claims would be a reason to query a business relationship with cargo owners.

The learning and growth perspective tends to be a major issue for ship operators because the severe penalties and criminalization enforced in the shipping industry do not allow inadequate knowledge on board or ashore (Anthony 2006). A specific number of employees and seamen should prove to be sufficient in order to avoid accidents. However, although there are not many regulatory restrictions, a ship operator takes the risk by dealing with them alone. The purchase of IT applications has solved many issues, such as communications or cargo-related calculations. A proper report of near misses is an effective tool so as to avoid fleet incidents. The term 'ship standards' usually refers to technological equipment. There could be some managerial practices that facilitate the organization of the company.

As the *Bourbon Dolphin* revealed, the internal business perspective is of utmost importance for the ship operator. He is obligated to carry out risk assessment for any new and existing hazard on board his ships (Soares and Teixeira 2001). This requires skilful managers that will develop careful plans for daily on board operations. Such plans could also bring legal liabilities for those who developed them. Therefore, effective training should be provided, especially to crew members, while its results should be re-evaluated frequently.

5.5.10 Crew members

The crew members are choosing a very promising career due to the good salaries on offer (Silos *et al.* 2012). However, the working conditions on board a ship are an issue that cannot be measured in terms of money. The introduction of MLC 2006 is an attempt to improve these working conditions. A larger number of crew required on a ship will distribute the workload, improving their working conditions. Constant training for seamen is an issue that is time consuming and expensive, whether it takes place on board or ashore in training centres. Some of these expenses could be shared by a ship operator when long-term contracts exist.

The main customer for seamen is the ship operator. The customer's satisfaction will secure their career path even if this is controlled through a manning agent. Therefore, the good quality of seamen is something that increases availability of skilful crew members (Silos *et al.* 2012). Reputation and credibility preoccupies seamen not only with regard to themselves individually, but also with regard to their co-workers. Due to the small number of crew members and the nature of work on a ship, each seaman should possess certain quality standards.

A competent seaman is also worried about his personal learning and growth perspective. As is required in STCW 95, where the career path of officers includes training and sea service, a seaman's knowledge can be improved through years of sailing. New technologies are frequently introduced and so crew members need to improve their IT skills. Crew members should protect their customers (ship operators and states) by avoiding accidents due to human error, while, ideally, they should participate in the implementation or suggestion of new ship standards and practices.

In terms of internal business, crew members should be competent to identify hazards on board and able to carry out risk assessment studies. Their opinions should be used when a ship operator develops plans to improve safety. Although some may argue that seamen are not experts to provide such judgements, it should be understood that people who live on a ship for several months could report issues that go unnoticed by the ship operator. Effective training is something that most of the time is carried out on board and that should be focused on particular issues that exist on each ship. The review of the internal business process is mandatory through the ISM Code (Objective 1.2.2). Therefore, it is a good opportunity that constitutes an essential tool for management improvement.

5.6 The weighting of representative stakeholders in maritime regulatory process

As it has been shown in previous sections, some stakeholders have higher burdens in the regulatory process. It is, therefore, necessary to evaluate this burden. A hierarchy for evaluating maritime regulations' performance from the industry point of view could be designed with regard to the particular position of each stakeholder. Eventually, this hierarchy should be completed with the weighting of each stakeholder's perspectives. It is expected that, due to the different aim of each stakeholder, the common perspectives will be prioritized by each one of them in a different way.

The BSCs can be set as a hierarchy of priorities in a complex problem. In order to design a hierarchy one must set the appropriate levels, which will simplify the solution of the perceived problem (Forman and Gass 2001). These levels consist of an overall goal in Level 1, criteria that will lead to the goal in Level 2 and sub-criteria in Level 3. Level 4 is also added in this hierarchy, containing measures for the sub-criteria. The goal is the estimation of a maritime regulation success in the shipping industry. Level 2 is the representative stakeholders' performance. It is obvious that a stakeholder's willingness to contribute positively to any new maritime regulation's enforcement greatly depends on the balance of its benefits towards its costs. Therefore, a comparison among representative stakeholders could provide a clear picture of what will be the impact on other stakeholders. It should be highlighted that the performance of any stakeholder can be evaluated by using the four perspectives of its BSC at Level 3. Every stakeholder's perspective must be addressed with its measures at Level 4. A hierarchy is designed in Figure 5.2, in order to illustrate this process.

By ranking the stakeholders' implementation performance in Level 2 (Figure 5.2) of the hierarchy, their relevant weights in the maritime regulation implementation process can be estimated. However, for a closer analysis of the commercial needs of each stakeholder, the next reasonable step is to rank the scorecard perspectives and measures according to their weights of importance. By ranking the elements of Level 3 in terms of their importance, it is possible to identify which perspectives are more important for a stakeholder. The ranking in

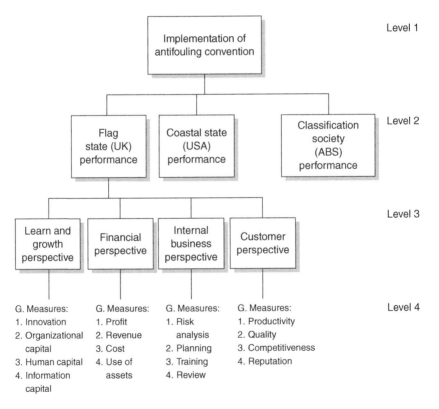

Figure 5.2 The hierarchy diagram for estimating maritime regulations performance from the industry point of view (source: Karahalios 2011).

Level 4, besides the measures for a stakeholder, can also show the weight of each measure. The significance of measures' weights is important for the evaluation of their parent perspectives. However, this calculation will reveal that the overall contribution of a measure to the implementation performance of a stakeholder would be minimal. Although in this book the AHP is preferred for the reasons explained in previous chapters, the ranking could be carried out with any multi-criteria decision-making method. To demonstrate the significance of this commercial interaction of stakeholders, the research results of Karahalios *et al.* (2011) will be presented and analyzed below.

The findings from the above studies regarding the commercial authority that stakeholders have in the implementation of a maritime regulation were revaluated in a survey carried in 2009 by Karahalios *et al.* (2011). A group of experts were chosen in this study, each having a reasonable mixture of academic qualifications, professional qualifications and industry experience. A survey was conducted through research questionnaires in which industrial experts provided valuable feedback with regard to the regulatory authority of the representative stakeholders. Then, using an AHP, the weighting of each stakeholder was evaluated. The results of this survey with respect to the weighting of stakeholders are shown in Figure 5.3. According to the experts, it appears that the most important stakeholder in the regulatory process is the flag state, followed by the coastal state and the classification society. The results verify the stakeholders' analysis of Kørte *et al.* (2002), where both the flag and the coastal state are more important than the classification society in the regulatory implementation process. The weight distribution shows that all stakeholders contribute to the regulatory standards in the shipping industry.

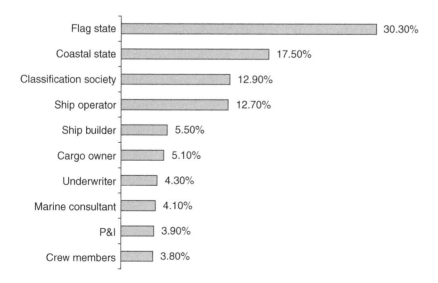

Figure 5.3 The weighting of stakeholders in the implementation of maritime regulations.

The weight of the flag state is significantly higher than that of the coastal state, despite the fact that PSC efforts are more rigorous than in the past. This position shows that, within the industry, the flag state is expected to lead safety at sea. The classification societies have a fundamental role in regulatory compliance from the design stage of a ship. This position of the classification society as an intermediate between the states and the ship operator is the reason that it is ranked third in the list. The ship operator is listed fourth in the list since he has a significant role in maintaining his ships' safety by complying with maritime regulations.

The list is completed with the remaining private stakeholders who, although they have significant commercial benefits, have lesser needs for regulatory compliance. Among them, the cargo owners appear sixth in the list. The role of cargo owners in selecting substandard ships has been criticized in the past due to the fact that they hire them due to lower costs, maximizing in this way their profits. Therefore, this commercial power of cargo owners is not considered as a powerful tool towards enhancing safety of ships. On the other hand, oil and chemical industries have shown remarkable efforts to improve safety.

The crew members are listed last in the ranking order with a relatively small weight. The position of crew members is that they follow orders from their managers, but they are the first line of defence in ships' safety. In contrast, in other high-risk industries the quality of employees is considered as the highest priority. For instance, in nuclear and aviation the skills of the personnel relating to education, training and safety culture are closely monitored.

The next level of the analysis is carried out for perspectives in Level 3 of the hierarchy. Figure 5.4 shows that, as regards a flag state, the financial perspective

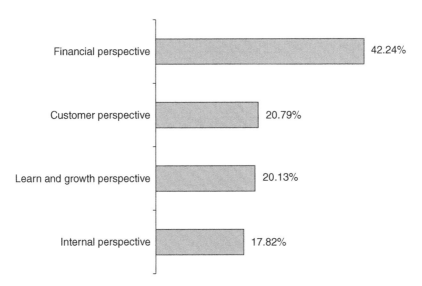

Figure 5.4 The ranking of the flag state perspectives for their burden in the regulatory process.

leads the decision-making process. Although someone may argue that the protection of the environment, citizens and labour should be a top priority, it appears that funding has the highest weight. Such a finding is not far away from the flag of convenience practices that have been identified. The customer and learning and growth perspectives have similar weights. An interesting point is that the internal business is ranked last.

Figure 5.5 shows that for a coastal state the customer perspective appears to be the most important one. This is easily justified as it is exposed to threats and the consequences of accidents will remain for long periods. The financial perspective is the second most important, since the cost related to the implementation of a maritime regulation will be deducted from other valuable services of the state. Although someone may argue that the protection of the environment, citizens and labour should be a top priority, it appears that funding has the highest weight. Such a finding is not far away from the FOC practices that have been identified earlier. The internal and learning and growth perspectives have similar weights.

The ranking within the classification society (Figure 5.6) prioritizes the customer satisfaction before the financial perspective. It has also a higher weight for learning and growth, since innovation is part of its business planning. An outdated or misinformed classification society cannot stand in the shipping industry. The financial perspective is the second highest perspective, since a profitable classification society is more likely to grow and expand. The third highest perspective is the learning and growth perspective, since innovation is the most significant area for a classification society. Internal business perspective is ranked last due the historically proven ability of classification societies to carry out studies.

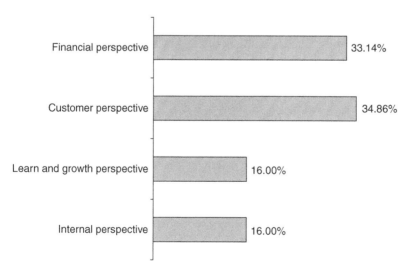

Figure 5.5 The ranking of the coastal state perspectives for their burden in the regulatory process.

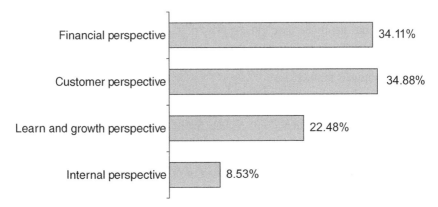

Figure 5.6 The ranking of the classification society perspectives for their burden in the regulatory process.

A further interesting point is to normalize and calculate the overall priority of the stakeholders' perspectives. With this approach it is possible for someone to understand which are the dominant perspectives in the shipping industry. The overall priority results calculated by Karahalios *et al.* (2011) are shown in Figure 5.7. Each perspective of each stakeholder shown in Figure 5.7 is a weighted value. For example, the value of 12.8 per cent for the financial perspective of the flag state is equal to 42.4 per cent (Figure 5.4), normalized with the 30.3 per cent value which is the weight of the flag state (Figure 5.3).

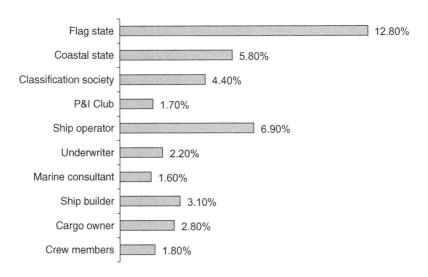

Figure 5.7 Overall priority of stakeholders' financial perspectives.

When examining its overall priorities, it appears that the expected cost for key stakeholders like states, ship operators and classification societies are significantly higher than others. In Figure 5.7 the overall priority of stakeholders' financial perspectives shows those differences. For many other stakeholders their financial performance is very low-weighted. This is an indication of the fact that the economic damages of these organizations are not very highly prioritized. From this analysis it is clear that the stakeholders may be more concerned about the severe impact on their economic responsibilities rather than about the difficulties of complying with regulations such as implementation procedures and human resources.

The customer perspective produces lower weights than the financial perspectives, although they are ranked second. As it appears again in Figure 5.8 the four dominant stakeholders appear in the first places. This is an indication that if the commercial businesses are hard to replace, it is expected that this will generate unwillingness for the affected stakeholders to implement a maritime regulation. It should also be noticed that the customer perspective for a flag state and a ship operator has higher weight than the financial perspective for many other stakeholders. It should be stressed that the stakeholders individually may have different priorities. For instance, in the case of the classification society, the customer perspective has higher weight than the financial perspective.

By examining the weights of the learning and growth perspective (Figure 5.9), it appears that the dominant stakeholders are ranked higher again. Moreover, the weight of a flag state is higher than the weight of other stakeholders in financial and customer perspectives. An explanation here could be the inability of a flag state to innovate or follow technological advantages, so being constrained to regulatory implementation.

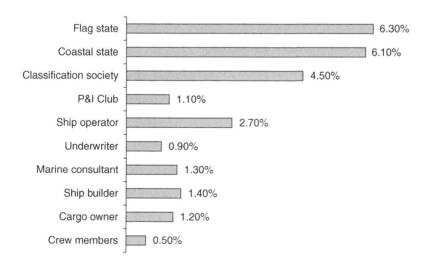

Figure 5.8 Overall priority of stakeholders' customer satisfaction perspectives.

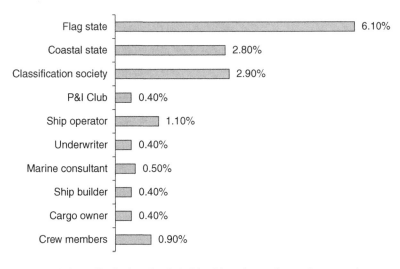

Figure 5.9 Overall priority of stakeholders' learning and growth perspectives.

The lower-ranked perspective is the internal perspective. Figure 5.10 shows the overall priority of stakeholders' internal business perspectives. The majority of the stakeholders have very small weights. This is an indication that a maritime regulation will have a minor effect on them. On the other hand, the flag state and the ship operator are leading the list. This is a reasonable example, since, if they cannot operate through a new regulation, this will have a severe impact on the implementation process.

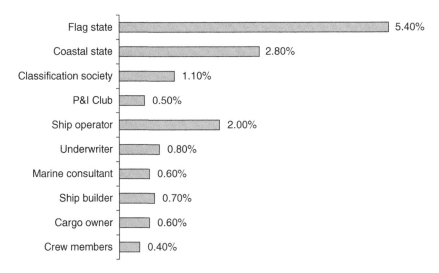

Figure 5.10 Overall priority of stakeholders' internal business perspectives.

5.7 Evaluation of the industry's performance: the case of the Marine Antifouling Convention

The calculated weights of the previous sections may be used to design a tool capable of evaluating the implementation performance of a maritime regulation. In order for the proposed tool to be functional, it should be designed in a straightforward way for a stakeholder. Hence, a stakeholder will be able to easily calculate his implementation performance. To design this tool, the initial BSCs should be updated by including the weights of their perspectives and measures. Therefore, every time a measure of a BSC is estimated, it will be possible to calculate its effect on the regulatory process.

The maritime regulation that was chosen to be investigated in the study of Karahalios *et al.* (2011) for its implications in the shipping industry was the Antifouling Convention requirements introduced by the IMO. The measures' ratings in the BSCs were developed on the basis of the previous studies and analysis (Champ 2000; 2003; Chambers *et al.* 2006; MCA 2007; ABS 2007). The challenges to the selected stakeholders resulting from these studies were evaluated by the authors while, for numerical purposes, the BCS's rates were listed in Table 5.2. These studies were carried out focusing on various implications of the antifouling coatings, such as costs and pollution.

Sometimes, due to lack of time, the regulators need to make a quick decision without having reliable data. Therefore, the feedback will be entered in the system as values of the measures in the same scale, e.g. 0–10. By adopting this approach, the input of the system will be the relative success of each measure in terms of achievement. Then, by using the weights of the parent perspectives, it will be possible to calculate the performance of each stakeholder and, consequently, of the industry. It is expected that, due to the size of the hierarchy, a large number of calculations will be carried out, something that could be solved with the adoption of the appropriate software. One option is the *Nautilus* performance management tool designed by the author.

Each BSC of a stakeholder is filled in with values from 0 to 10 for each measure by reference to Table 5.3. An example of a BSC is shown in Table 5.4, which is the BSC of the UK flag state completed for the Antifouling Convention. Each measure rate represents the performance achievement of a stakeholder for that measure. For instance, in Table 5.4 the measure rate for profit is 1. This

Table 5.2 Studies and analyses of antifouling coatings implications

Champ (2000)	USA difficulties
Champ (2003)	USA difficulties
Chambers *et al.* (2006)	UK difficulties
MCA (2007)	UK flag ships obligations
EU (2003)	EU flag ships obligations
ABS (2007)	ABS antifouling requirements
ABS (2006)	ABS inspection procedures

Source: Karahalios *et al.* (2011).

value is given because the sources of Table 5.4 have evidenced that the implementation of the Antifouling Convention will not really offer any profit to the UK flag state.

From the studies below, it appears that, regarding the financial perspective, when the UK flag state implements the Antifouling Convention, this perspective will not improve significantly. Profits and revenues are not expected to increase, due to the addition of new ships. A cost regarding studies and training will appear, but it will not be significantly high. On the other hand, due to the deadline, there will be no need for additional cash.

From the customer perspective, productivity of the fleet will not significantly be affected by the new antifouling technologies. Quality of the fleet will improve slightly but since there are no effective solutions introduced, the pollution of the marine environment may not be significantly improved. However, in terms of competitiveness, the UK flag state shows its customers that it is a leading nation

Table 5.3 An example of measures' rates

Rate	Definition
9–10	Very high performance
7–8	High performance
4–6	Medium performance
2–3	Low performance
0–1	Very low performance

Table 5.4 Implementation performance of the UK flag state

Perspective	Measure	Value
Financial	Profit	1
	Revenue	1
	Cost	2
	Use of assets	4
Customer	Productivity	2
	Competitiveness	7
	Quality	3
	Reputation	7
Internal business	Human capital	3
	Information capital	4
	Organization capital	4
	Innovation	4
Learning and growth	Risk analysis	5
	Planning	5
	Training	5
	Review	6

Source: Karahalios *et al.* (2011).

with regard to the regulatory management and that it is prepared in advance for future issues. In addition, its reputation is also significantly improved, since, towards its customers, it appears as a state that respects the marine environment and that is concerned about the performance of its ships. Therefore, the second most important perspective, on average, is achieving a medium performance.

The learning and growth perspective also seems to have a medium perform-ance. The know-how that a flag state should have in order to maintain its com-petitiveness is improving, due to the fact that studies should be carried out and, consequently, new knowledge is acquired. From the existing studies it does not appear that the implementation of the antifouling convention will generate the need to hire additional employees. The updated and skilful personnel have demonstrated their ability to innovate and produce new ship standards. However, excessive effort is not required compared to other regulations. The proactive contribution of such an organization to its fleet's environmental protection would be the decreasing number of incidents and accidents.

The flag state should have the ability to carry out risk analysis studies for existing and potential threats to its ships. While reviewing the key elements of such studies, the state should maintain an updated database that can be used by experts to assess hazards and develop plans. A particular effort should be made with regard to hazards that could be generated from the introduced regulations. Training regarding the implementation of a regulation should be kept within reasonable time frames. Periodic reviews should indicate whether the existing internal business process is effective.

In Table 5.4 the measures with rates of less than 5 indicate where the UK flag state faced difficulties during the implementation of the Antifouling Convention requirements. The value 5 is chosen because it represents 50 per cent of the desired goal, which is represented by the value 10. However, these values provide a better picture if they are combined with the information provided earlier regarding the weight of perspective for a flag state. For instance, the per-formance of the UK flag state is of lower significance because its perspectives with the higher weights have measures with small values. More precisely, the values of the financial and customer perspectives rates of the UK flag state have the higher weights but the lower measurement values. In contrast, the internal business perspective with average measure rates equal to 5.75 slightly increased the UK flag state performance due to its small weight.

It should be stressed that other flag states with less knowledge and resources may achieve much lower rates. Therefore, this is an indication that the Antifoul-ing Convention may cause significant implementation difficulties to flag states with developing economies.

5.8 Evaluation of a regulation from the industrial point of view

As can be seen in Table 5.5, the perspective rates for the three chosen stake-holders lie between 2 and 6.25. This low contribution of the three most important stakeholders means that even if all the other stakeholders achieve a value of 10

Table 5.5 The performance of stakeholders

Flag state	Financial	2
	Customer	4.75
	Learn and growth	3.75
	Internal business	5.75
Coastal state	Financial	3
	Customer	5
	Learn and growth	3.5
	Internal business	5.25
Classification society	Financial	6.25
	Customer	5.75
	Learn and growth	6.25
	Internal business	4

Source: Karahalios *et al.* (2011).

to their measures, the overall performance will not be more than 6.467, because their total weight is 0.393. By reference to experts' judgements (Table 5.3) this is a medium performance.

With regard to the UK as a typical coastal state, the customer perspective is the leading issue in decision making. This is a reasonable finding, since the income of such a state will depend on the protection of its natural resources and the business sectors using them. The financial perspective is ranked second, with a significant weight. Eventually, internal business appears last in the list after the learning and growth perspective. This could be because a state is traditionally organized, exercising authority through procedures.

After the flag state, it is interesting to compare its performance with the chosen coastal state, which is the United States. Overall, it appears that the states have many similarities regarding their performances. As it can be seen from Table 5.5, the perspective rates for the three chosen stakeholders lie between 2 and 6.25. These values are in the range from low to medium performance (Table 5.3). The financial perspective appears to have a low performance, as it is not expected to increase the revenues or reduce the costs for the state. The customer perspective appears to have a medium performance, since the quality standards from ships entering its ports are expected to be higher. As regards the third perspective, which is learning and growth, a low performance could be rated due to the fact that, compared to other maritime regulations, it is not contributing significantly to new knowledge for the UK administration with respect to handling maritime regulations. In terms of internal business, the performance could be high, because the existing procedures should be revised so as to include PSC officers' training but also monitoring of the marine environment.

The ABS, as a representative classification society, appears to have a better performance than states. In terms of the financial perspective, its performance could be high, since many ships will require guidance, inspection and certification to prove that they comply with the Antifouling Convention. These services are increasing the revenues of a classification society. In terms of the customer satisfaction perspective, a medium performance could be achieved because, as in the case of a new regulation, some ships may be found with deficiencies. Moreover, the learning and growth perspective will have a high performance, as some significant work should be carried out in order to prepare guidelines with possible interpretations of the regulations. With respect to the internal business perspective, it does not perform better than medium, since the identification of hazards is more related to environmental issues and available products in the market.

The antifouling issue has been studied since 1980 by many states and researchers (Champ 2000). The costs of banning harmful antifouling coatings from the industry are also well known to the IMO member states and scientists. The proposed method provides an explanation of why states had a very slow reaction even though the public was exposed to high health risks. In addition, it gives evidence of the limitations in the implementation of the Antifouling Convention, since the states that have not rectified the convention are at great economic advantage.

5.9 Benchmarking

The proposed process can be used as a monitoring tool for the implementation performance of the shipping industry or a stakeholder. When such a hierarchical analysis of the regulation implementation process is carried out, it is possible – when data are available – to provide a benchmark for the industry as well as for each stakeholder. The above estimations were based on previous studies and findings. However, a regulatory update of the produced scorecards could show the implementation progress of the Antifouling Convention or any other maritime regulation. This assessment could be used in two ways:

1 Identify problems to specific stakeholders.
2 Identify areas in the regulation that may need revision.

In the first case, when a stakeholder appears to have a problem improving, it means that a risk is associated with this stakeholder. The examination of the benefits and costs that could be generated by the convention make it possible to understand which stakeholders may need additional assistance by identifying where they fail or have vulnerabilities. In the second case, when a stakeholder, despite his efforts, cannot improve his performance, it may be an indication that some requirements of the regulation are too challenging to be met by the industry and their revision may be necessary.

References

Aase K. (2007). Equilibrium in marine mutual insurance markets with convex operating costs. *Journal of Risk and Insurance*, Vol. 74(1), pp. 239–268.
ABS. (2005). Guidance notes on the investigation of marine incidents. American Bureau of Shipping, June.

ABS. (2006). Guide for marine health, safety, quality and environmental management. American Bureau of Shipping.

ABS. (2007). Guidance notes on the inspection, maintenance and application of marine coating systems. American Bureau of Shipping.

Anthony O. (2006). Criminalization of seafarers for accidental discharge of oil: is there justification in international law for criminal sanction for negligent or accidental pollution of the sea? *Journal of Maritime Law and Commerce*, Vol. 37, pp. 219–243.

Barlas B. (2012). Occupational fatalities in shipyards: an analysis in turkey. *Brodogradnja*, Vol. 63(1), pp. 35–41.

Bartusevics A., Kotovs V., Novickis L. (2012). A method for the effective configuration of reuse-oriented software release and its application in the field of insurance. *Information Technology and Management Science*, Vol. 15(1), pp. 111–115.

Becker A., Inoue S., Fischer M., Schwegler B. (2012). Climate change impacts on international seaports: knowledge, perceptions, and planning efforts among port administrators. *Climatic Change*, Vol. 110(1–2), pp. 5–29.

Boisson P. (1994). Classification societies and safety at sea: back to basics to prepare for the future. *Marine Policy*, Vol. 18(5), pp. 363–377.

Brentani U. (2001). Innovative versus incremental new business services: different keys for achieving success. *Journal of Product Innovation Management*, Vol. 18(3), pp. 169–187.

Cariou P., Wolff F.C. (2011). Do Port State Control inspections influence flag- and class-hopping phenomena in shipping? *Journal of Transport Economics and Policy*, Vol. 45(2), pp. 155–177.

Celik, M. (2010). Enhancement of occupational health and safety requirements in chemical tanker operations: The case of cargo explosion. *Safety Science*, 48(2), pp. 195–203.

Chambers L.D., Stokes K.R., Walsh F.C., Wood R.J.K. (2006). Modern approaches to marine antifouling coatings. *Surface and Coatings Technology*, Vol. 201, pp. 3642–3652.

Champ M.A. (2000). A review of organizational regulatory strategies, pending actions, related costs and benefits. *The Science of the Total Environment*, Vol. 258, pp. 21–71.

Champ M.A. (2003). Economic and environmental impacts on ports and harbors from the Convention to Ban Harmful Marine Anti-Fouling Systems. *Marine Pollution Bulletin*, Vol. 46, pp. 935–940.

Corres A.J.E., Pallis A.A. (2008). Flag state performance: an empirical analysis. *WMU Journal of Maritime Affairs*, Vol. 7(1), pp. 241–261.

Ellison J., Corbet T. (2006). Modeling the effects of the single-hull tanker phase-out on the world oil tanker market. In Proceedings of the System Dynamics Conference. 23–27 July, Nijmegen, the Netherlands.

Forman E.H., Gass S.I. (2001). The analytic hierarchy process: an exposition. *Operations Research*, Vol. 49(4), pp. 469–486.

Glen, D. (2010). Modelling the impact of double hull technology on oil spill numbers. *Maritime Policy & Management*, Vol. 37(5), pp. 475–487.

Glen D., Reid S. (2010). Tanker cost elasticities revisited. *Maritime Policy Management*, Vol. 37(6), pp. 585–600.

Goss R. (2003). Maritime insurance and economic welfare. *Maritime Policy and Management*, Vol. 30(4), pp. 357–362.

Hetherington S. (1991). Fixing or unfixing a charter party. *Australian and New Zealand Maritime Law Journal*, Vol. 8, pp. 12–18.

Hsieh C.T., Klenow P.J. (2009). Misallocation and manufacturing TFP in China and India. *The Quarterly Journal of Economics*, Vol. 124(4), pp. 1403–1448.

Japan P&I Club. (2006). Annual Report 2006.

Jia C., Jinke Y. (2011). Research on the informatization of shipbuilding industry based on the investigation on Wuchang Shipyard. In *Proceedings of the 7th International Conference on Innovation & Management*, pp. 1532–1536.

Karahalios H., Yang Z.L., Williams V., Wang J. (2011) A proposed system of hierarchical scorecards to assess the implementation of maritime regulations. *Safety Science*, Vol. 49, pp. 450–462.

Kavussanos M.G. (1996). Comparisons of volatility in the dry-cargo ship sector: spot versus time charters, and smaller versus larger vessels. *Journal of Transport Economics and Policy*, Vol. 30, pp. 67–82.

Børte J., Aven T., Rosness R. (2002). On the use of risk analysis in different decision settings. European Safety and Reliability Conference (ESREL) 2002, Lyon, pp. 175–181.

Kroneberg A. (2000). Innovation in shipping by using scenarios. PhD Thesis, Tapir, Trondheim.

Li K., Liu J., Yan J. (2009). Valuation of information-sharing in marine mutual insurance. *Risk and Decision Analysis*, Vol. 2(2), pp. 65–74.

Lindøe P.H., Engen O.A., Olsen O.E. (2011). Responses to accidents in different industrial sectors. *Safety Science*, Vol. 49(1), pp. 90–97.

Lyng, I., Andreassen, D., Fiksdal, G.A.H. (2008). Official Norwegian reports: the loss of the 'Bourbon Dolphin' on 12 April 2007 (Vol. 8). Technical report NOU.

Maclachlan M. (2004). *The Shipmaster's Business Companion*. The Nautical Institute, London.

Mason M. (2003). Civil liability for oil pollution damage: examining the evolving scope for environmental compensation in the international regime. *Marine Policy*, Vol. 27, pp. 1–12.

Mazaheri A., Ekwall D. (2009). Impacts of the ISPS code on port activities: a case study on Swedish ports. *World Review of Intermodal Transportation Research*, Vol. 2(4), pp. 326–342.

MCA. (2007). Anti fouling systems. www.mcga.gov.uk/c4mca/mcga-environmental/ mcga-dqs_qual_eq_environmental_quality/ds-eq-afs.htm#ir [10 March 2007].

Molenaar, E.J. (2007). Port state jurisdiction: toward comprehensive, mandatory and global coverage. *Ocean Development & International Law*, Vol. 38(1–2), pp. 225–257.

Njegomir V., Ćirić J. (2012). Risk modeling in the insurance industry. *Strategic Management*, Vol. 17(1), pp. 53–60.

Odeke A. (2005). An examination of bareboat charter registries and flag of convenience registries in international law. *Ocean development and International Law*, Vol. 36, pp. 339–362.

Pérez R., Lamas M., Carral L.M. (2012). Classification and damage stability of flotel ships. *Journal of Maritime Research*, Vol. 1, pp. 33–38.

Pires Jr F.C. (2001). Shipbuilding and shipping industries: net economic benefit cross-transfers. *Maritime Policy & Management*, Vol. 28(2), pp. 157–174.

Qin T.R., Hu Q., Mo J.Y., Wu H., Chen X., Shi C. (2011). Research on the risk assessment of man overboard in the performance of Flag Vessel Fleet (FVF). *International Journal on Marine Navigation and Safety of Sea Transportation*, Vol. 5 (1), pp. 125–130.

Ruhil A.V., Teske P. (2003). Institutions, bureaucratic decisions, and policy outcomes: state insurance solvency regulation. *Policy Studies Journal*, Vol. 31(3), pp. 353–372.

Sanders P., Gued Y. (2012). *Ownership Cost Drivers in Ship Design & Construction*. BMT Design & Technology, Melbourne.

Scarsi R. (2007). The bulk shipping business: market cycles and shipowners' biases. *Maritime Policy & Management*, Vol. 34(6), pp. 577–590.

Scott P.W. (1995). *Marketing Strategy for Merchant Shipbuilders*. A and P Appledore International (United Kingdom).

Sequeira S., Djankov S. (2010). An empirical study of corruption in ports. Available at SSRN 1592733.

Silos, J.M., Piniella, F., Monedero, J., Walliser, J. (2012). Trends in the global market for crews: a case study. *Marine Policy*, 36, 845–858.

Soares C.G., Teixeira A.P. (2001). Risk assessment in maritime transportation. *Reliability Engineering & System Safety*, Vol. 74(3), pp. 299–309.

Tenold S. (2003). A most convenient flag: the basis for the expansion of the Singapore fleet, 1969–82. *Maritime Policy & Management*, Vol. 30(3), pp. 255–268.

Tsai M.T., Regan A., Saphores J.D. (2009). Freight transportation derivatives contracts: state of the art and future developments. *Transportation Journal*, Vol. 48, pp. 7–19.

UK P&I (1996). The Human Factor A report on manning. UK P&I Club.

Yang Z., Peterson R.T., Cai S. (2003). Services quality dimensions of internet retailing: an exploratory analysis. *Journal of Services Marketing*, Vol. 17(7), pp. 685–700.

Yilmazel M., Asyali E. (2005). An analysis of port state control inspections related to the ISPS Code. In Proceedings of the IAMU, 6th AGA conference.

Yip T.L. (2008). Port traffic risks: a study of accidents in Hong Kong waters. *Transportation Research Part E: Logistics and Transportation Review*, Vol. 44(5), pp. 921–931.

Zhu L. (2008). Compensation issues under the Bunkers Convention. *WMU Journal of Maritime Affairs*, Vol. 7(1), pp. 303–316.

Zobel H.B. (2012). The unseaworthy instant. *St. John's Law Review*, Vol. 45(2), pp. 2–11.

6 Implementation of maritime regulations by a ship operator

6.1 Introduction

After a long period of prosperity, the sea trade, which was following an upward trend, moved into a financial recession. The global crisis of September 2008 accelerated the shipping recession. This situation led people who operate ships to a long race for business survival. Fears were expressed that this economic impact would force some ship operators to reduce costs related to the safety of their ships. A ship operator faces the option to lower his quality standards in order to reduce costs. However, such a decision may not have been wise, as there are always better ways to reduce management expenses. The scope of this chapter is to examine alternative methods that ship managers may use so to achieve an effective management and reduce costs by effective regulatory implementation.

6.2 Ship operation: aims and challenges

Ship operation constitutes a key role in the shipping industry. The aim of a ship operator is not different from that of any other company in the business world, which is to ensure that his business is profitable. Profit is generated by hiring a ship's space for a certain period provided that the same ship will maintain its technical characteristics for the period of hire. Profit will necessitate the long-term business survival of the company, especially during depressed market cycles. It should be emphasized that a reasonably stable regulatory environment is an advantage for a ship operator. Therefore, the issues of employment, ship's maintenance and daily business are priorities of utmost importance for a ship operator.

A ship operator faces many challenges during his commercial activities. The ship operator makes a profit by hiring the space of each ship that he operates, in order to transfer cargo for a voyage or a specific period. Various regulated issues, such as speed, seaworthiness, effective equipment and manning are of primary importance for the ship operator. Furthermore, ships visit ports of different states on a regular basis and, consequently, they are subject to different regulatory regimes. In addition, some states have extended their jurisdiction through their EEZ. Hence, a ship sailing in the area of an EEZ, even if it does not intend to call a port of that state, may have to comply with some restrictions. It should be stressed that the coastal states will expect a ship entering their territory to comply with their unique requirements. Therefore, it could be argued that the voyage track is also regulated.

Ship operators must run their ships under a complex maritime regulatory regime, which consists of regulations posted by flag states, coastal states and the IMO. Every ship that a company operates must comply with the legislation of its flag state, the IMO and the coastal states that it visits. The issue is more complicated when a company is managing several ships registered in different flags, and, consequently, it has to comply with all different administrations. Ships must also comply with the regulations of the coastal states whose ports they call. Hence, it is very important for a ship operator to be informed of all maritime regulations and be able to comply with them.

A ship operator targets the increase of profit through the management of its ships. Of course such an aim is not necessarily motivated by greed, but is a business strategy. A prudent ship manager will reinvest an amount of its profit in order to improve its company. Furthermore, at a time where excessive profit is generated an amount of money could be saved for recession periods. One way to increase the profit is by increasing the revenues of a company. In a period of normal demand for ships' services, this will be achieved by obtaining well-paid contracts due to the good quality of services provided by the fleet. Another way of maximizing profit is to reduce costs. Of course, this is not an easy option, as it is almost certain that every unnecessary cost will have an impact on the operation of the company. For instance, there is a great deal of concern regarding the amount of money that may be saved by reducing the safety of a ship. Such cost saving may include training or providing a ship with safety equipment of low quality. The use of a company's assets may be proved to be very profitable. The price of a vessel greatly depends on market fluctuations (Scarsi 2007). Therefore, the purchase of a ship in a recession period will probably be a bargain, while the sale of the same ship in a period with high demand for ships could multiply its value and, consequently, provide an abundance of money for its owners.

The ship operator makes a profit by hiring the space of each ship that he operates in order to transfer cargo for a voyage or a specific period (Li and Cullinane 2003). From a commercial perspective, the ship operator has contractual obligations in a charter party similarly to the carrier. Therefore, a ship operator is required from a carrier to maintain his ship to a good standard in order to transport cargo safely. The carrier is obliged to provide a ship constructed, equipped, supplied and staffed according to the international regulations on the design and operation of vessels, in order for it to execute the voyage safely and to overcome those risks it could meet during the charter, known as ordinary perils of the sea (Plomaritou *et al.* 2010). Furthermore, the acquisition of a ship requires lots of capital. Such cost requirements can discourage potential entrants; in that respect, the high costs favour substantial scale economies that, in their turn, limit the number of firms that can profitably enter an industry (Triantafylli and Ballas 2010).

The services provided by a ship are the loading of goods, their safe transport and their discharge at the designated destination in the same condition as when they were loaded Therefore, a ship must maintain some technical characteristics during this operation (Yang *et al.* 2011). Furthermore, crew members employed on board should be able to perform a variety of duties related to cargo operations, maintenance and navigation. Of course, in order to succeed in a contract, the ship should be competitive in terms of quality and cost, since many similar ships will probably be available for the same charter. This relationship is not easy to determine since newer ships will be more expensive than older ones of the same size. Older ships have the advantage that the purchase loan would have been repaid and, therefore, its costs can be squeezed. On the other hand, maintenance failures that may damage the cargo or delay its delivery are more likely to occur to a ship of a certain age. Eventually, a key criterion for the selection of a ship will be the reputation of its ship managers. This will be found in the history of the company that owns the ship along with evidence that it has successfully performed similar operations in the past.

So far it has been described how a ship should perform in order to increase the profit of the company. However, a company still needs to attend to its future and set goals. A paramount issue will be the need for skilful employees, on board and ashore, that will carry out the above tasks. A company's employees should possess certain skills, talents and knowledge. A prudent ship manager should create a friendly environment that will form the desired skills of its employees through continuous training and learning. It should be highlighted that it is a long process to create a skilful employee, although there is no guarantee that he/she will stay in the firm forever. However, even with these losses, developing managers through this process could be invaluable. In the era of computer and satellite communications a company should establish databases, information systems, networks, and technology infrastructure that will improve communications and monitoring of its ships. Furthermore, the company should promote safety culture to its employees (Havold and Nesset 2009). This can be achieved by strong leadership, its people's alignment with its strategic goals and its employees' ability to share knowledge. A company, despite its size, should be innovative as far as practicable. It is not necessary for innovations to be narrowed to technological improvements, but they could be broadened to include the ability of people to produce new practices.

All the above tasks are linked together through an internal business process. This process could be briefly described as a four-step procedure. Initially, an appraisal should be carried out for any new operation. Issues such as a ship's suitability, expenses, costs and risks should be carefully considered. Of course, the ability of ashore personnel to support the operation should not be underestimated or exaggerated. Planning should be executed with care and in a self-corrective manner if mistakes or omissions have been found in the initial appraisal. It may be found that some of the employees need further guidance or training with respect to certain requirements of the operation. After the completion of the operation it is possible that some unexpected issues will arise.

Therefore, it is of vital importance that these issues are at least discussed at top management and improvements suggested, as it is likely that similar issues may happen during another operation. Additionally, a company should always target the improvement at any level.

All of the above result in a very important question: how can they become reality in an extremely complicated industry in which lack of time and cost reduction are daily concerns for a ship operator? The answer is very clear: major issues can change with minimum suffering. The difficult part is to monitor and measure the changes and their effects. Initially, it should be recognized that each company has established a management system which may not be written at all. Additionally, every ship operator has in his mind goals for the near future.

6.3 Literature survey in the implementation of maritime regulations by ship operators

The position of a ship operator could be examined from two points of view. First, the statutory, where he has to comply with regulations in order to protect the marine environment, enhance safety at sea and contribute to a secure environment; and second, the one regarding the maintenance of a profitable organization.

A ship operator is obligated to implement every new and existing maritime regulation ratified by his flag state. However, if the compliance costs are excessive, he may try to discharge his obligation even when there is strong evidence that the regulation is for the benefit of the shipping trade, the environment and/or safety at sea. Such a move should not be heavily criticized, since the aim of a ship operator is not different from that of any other company in the business world, which is to ensure that his business will remain competitive and profitable. Ship operators are always searching for ways to minimize their unit cost in all possible areas (Progoulaki and Theotokas 2010). Evidence of ship operators trying to minimize regulatory costs can be traced in the past. In the late 1960s economic globalization led many shipowners to move away from their national jurisdictions and choose to transfer the registry of their ships to countries such as Panama, Liberia and Cyprus (Bhattacharya 2012). The more lax regulatory standards required by such states were found by shipowners to be less costly. For this reason, Knudsen and Hassler (2011) argued, some ship operators manage vessels with deficiencies because of poor implementation.

A main business threat for a ship operator who caused an accident and/or pollution, due to his failure to implement a maritime regulation, could be the economic damages. From a commercial perspective, the ship operator has contractual obligations in a charter party similar to the carrier.

A further challenge for the ship operator is that the shipping industry suffers from a very negative public opinion. However, various stakeholders were very often ready to lower IMO standards if this meant an increase in the profit margin. In this context, the shipping industry created negative externalities, which contributed to the creation of a poor public image (Fafaliou *et al.* 2006).

Consequently, in the case of an accident, the public will press governments and authorities for immediate justice against the ship operator (Sampson 2004; Chantelauve 2003). The involvement of a ship operator's ship in an accident may result in a poor reputation for his company, severe financial consequences, loss of lives and even prison convictions for his employees (Chen 2000). Under this approach, the responsibility of companies is to comply with the rules while they are pursuing their basic goal, which is to create profits for their shareholders. These companies apply a standard level of operation and conformance to requirements of regulations and conventions that constitute the regulatory framework of world shipping, no matter what the costs of this conformance (Fafaliou *et al.* 2006).

In order for a ship operator to successfully run his business, he must find the appropriate human resources to fulfil positions on board his ships and ashore. Availability and quality of human resources are the cornerstones for a rational management system of a company. However, due to changes in crew labour resources, it is common for ships to be manned by crew members from the Far East when their company is based in Europe. A ship registered under an open registry may have limited restrictions regarding manning, such as crew nationality and manpower. As a result, many companies operate their ships with cheap labour from developing countries, overlooking their lack of skills (Klikauer and Morris 2003). However, despite the systemic wage differential separating the two tiers, highly paid national seafarers are not yet fully supplanted by lower-paid third-party nation ones (Tsamourgelis 2009). This phenomenon clashes with the typical theoretical model of cost minimization or profit maximization. Therefore, it could be an indication that a high number of ship operators give emphasis to their human resources. Human errors, technical and mechanical failures and environmental factors are commonly underlined factors leading to shipping accidents (Celik *et al.* 2010).

Adequate human resources should also be used ashore, in order for them to implement regulations and provide guidance and assistance to crew members on ships. The demand for human resources ashore is sometimes generated by regulations so as to cover specific positions, such as 'Designated Person Ashore' and 'Company Security Officer' required by the ISM Code (IMO 2012) and the International Code for the Security of Ships and of Port Facilities (ISPS Code; IMO 2002), respectively. Personnel training has been identified as a source of competitive advantage for a ship operator (Triantafylli and Ballas 2010).

6.4 Ship operation and customer satisfaction

Customer satisfaction is a long-term task which is hard to achieve but easy to fail at. Nevertheless, its meaning is quite simple, since failure of this goal will lead a company out of business and they will perhaps be sued if it causes damage to its customers. A prudent ship operator should be able to identify the stakeholders that may jeopardize his business from both commercial and regulatory aspects. Therefore, customer satisfaction should include all these organizations and people whose requirements will risk the smooth operation of a ship manager's business if he fails to satisfy them. Generally speaking, the customers could be divided into two categories: private and government. Additionally, it should be noted that, depending on the market, the authority level of each group of stakeholders may significantly vary. Therefore, the ship operator should be able to determine the weight of each customer he has to satisfy.

The private stakeholders include all those people that provide or expect services by the ship operator, and these agreements are usually stated in the form of a contract. The cargo owner and charterer are of vital importance for a ship manager, as they provide his company with cash flow. However, a ship needs approval from many other stakeholders in order to be considered fit for duty. Shipyards contribute to the maintenance schedule of a ship, and therefore good cooperation will probably benefit the ship operator. In order for a shipyard to achieve customer satisfaction, it has to fulfil the terms and conditions from the side of the ship operator. A clear plan in a certain timeframe as well as payments as they have been agreed should be the minimum that a prudent ship manager should consider. Furthermore, good cooperation with a list of other stakeholders, such as suppliers of bunkers, consultants, technicians, insurers, etc. will benefit a prudent ship operator. Although the point of view that even providers should be seen as customers for a ship operator sounds exaggerated, there are two major things that should be considered. First, the cost for a ship operator if during an operation an expected service is ceased or delayed, e.g. bunkers delay; and second, another issue will be the reputation that he builds with some providers with whom he often cooperates, e.g. the manufacturer of the main engine.

The other category involves government organizations, such as port administrations and flag states. Although these organizations are not commercially connected with ship operators, the authority that they have towards them is of outmost importance. This authority is enforced by the regulations that are imposed by each state to each ship that is registered to its flag. Any state has the right to exercise control over every foreign ship that visits its ports or sails in its territorial waters. The significance of these government organizations is that they have the authority to obstruct or cease the operation if they are dissatisfied with the performance of a ship in terms of safety, environmental respect and common criminal failures. Consequently, the states should be seen as customers, since they can put at risk the business of a ship operator.

The facts that the shipping industry should be open to new entries as well as the fact that there should be some kind of protection to small firms constitute two of the RIA practices. However, the same problems regarding the high cost of ships appear in both cases. A common practice for a new player would be to go into the second-hand market and acquire a relatively old ship, which is expected to have more equipment failures. Of course, such failures, which are the reason for its lower price, could be dealt with by close monitoring, especially by crew members. As it was shown in Chapter 5, crew members are also concerned about their safety, reputation and knowledge acquisition. Skilful seamen will seek to be employed by companies with modern ships and resources, where all these can be found. Therefore, some variation of the skills should also be expected in older ships. This is a circle that leads to PSC deficiencies, which are translated into violations of maritime regulations. Referring to what was discussed with regard to the commercial pressure that this new player will suffer, he may choose to exit the industry or not to enter it at all, creating, therefore, a great advantage for the older players. In a similar way, the small player will probably face the same challenges as a new player. Then, after a point, such as a recession period, in conjunction with a plethora of regulatory requirements he may choose to exit the industry in favour of the major players. An intermediate solution for this issue is third-party management, as has been explained by Mitroussi (2004). The above relationships is graphically displayed in Figure 6.1.

The '2012 Review of Maritime Transport' published by the United Nations Conference on Trade and Development (UNCTAD) reveals that world seaborne trade grew by 4 per cent in 2011, taking the total volume of goods loaded worldwide to 8.7 billion tons. At the same time, the world fleet continued to expand during 2011, reaching more than 1.5 billion deadweight tons in January 2012, an increase of over 37 per cent in the last four years. The above figures show how important the sea trade is for the wealth of nations. On the other hand, they show the new competition regime for stakeholders of the shipping industry.

From the literature review, it is clear that the interest of a ship operator to implement a maritime regulation is related to his commercial gains, as is that of any other stakeholder. Therefore, it is necessary to couple these commercial gains with the implementation performance of a maritime regulation. A ship operator normally implements a regulation through a main process, which consists of the following targets:

1 monitoring of the regulation implementation performance of his organization;
2 monitoring of the regulation implementation performance of each division;
3 application of a self-assessment tool with regard to his implementation performance.

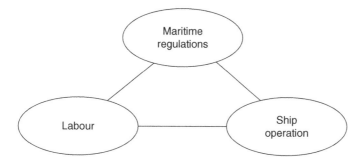

Figure 6.1 Ship operation and regulatory implementation.

6.5 The divisions of a ship operator

A ship operator is running his daily business in a complicated and regulatory environment. The organizational structure of a ship operator may consist of various divisions, each having specific activities. However, the organization of each ship operator may be unique. Therefore, the divisions' activities are verified by the literature review as shown in Table 6.1 (Chu and Liang 2001; Lyridis 2005; Panayides 2003; Panayides and Cullicane 2002; Jensen and Randoy 2002; 2006; Karahalios *et al.* 2011a). Although the managing director and the ship are not divisions, they have been added to the proposed list because they are essential parts of a ship operator's organization.

As has already been mentioned, a ship operator is running his daily business in a complicated and regulatory environment. Therefore, his organizational structure may consist of various divisions. A ship operator's company can be divided into divisions with specific activities. Each ship operator uses a different structure. Therefore, the chosen model is based on a typical medium-sized company of a ship operator in Greece.

Figure 6.2 contains a diagram which shows the management structure of a ship operator. It should be emphasized that such a structure is not typical, as in smaller companies one person may be in charge of more than one activity, e.g. technical and purchase management. On the other hand, ship operators may have chosen to assign more employees the activity of forming a department.

Besides the above issue, a managing director, who will lead and be in charge of the overall management, is going to appear in any ship operator firm. He will have to make important commercial decisions, such as ship purchases and scrapping.

Table 6.1 A typical organizational structure of a ship operator by divisions and their activities

Division	Activities
1 Managing director	Overall management, hiring employees, ships purchase and scrapping
2 Operation Department	Operation and performance of a ship in accordance with its commercial and legal obligations
3 Technical Department	Operation, performance and maintenance of the engineering and technical systems of a ship, dry-docking and repairs
4 ISM Department	Safety management, implementation of safety and pollution regulations
5 ISPS Department	Implementation of security regulations
6 Chartering Department	Chartering and charter compliance
7 Accounting Department	Budgetary control
8 Crew Department	Crew recruitment and manning of ships
9 Supply Department	Supply of deck stores, provisions and paints inquiries
10 Ship	Operation of ship with the highest level of safety in accordance with the company's stated principles, policies and objectives

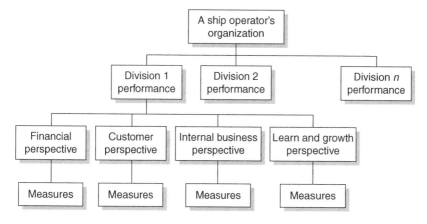

Figure 6.2 The organizational structure of a ship operator by divisions.

Additionally, he will have to choose the most appropriate operation for his ships in order to maximize the profit of the firm. Eventually, he should be able to respond to daily challenges and demands such as hiring, evaluating or firing employees.

The profitability of a ship operating company depends on the services that it provides (e.g. tonnage, speed, cargo suitability) and it is achieved by hiring the vessel or some space on board for a period of time. This hiring is legally bound by a contract which is named as charter party. The examination of the available charters and the suitability of the company's vessels are carried out by the Chartering Department. Additionally, one of the department's functions is to draft a reasonably executed charter party.

One of the most important assistants of the managing director is the operations manager. He is in charge of the operation and performance of each ship in accordance with its commercial and legal obligations. These activities include monitoring of sea voyage, cargo operations, bunkering and other minor operation issues.

Another important division is the Technical Department, which is generally tasked with the maintenance of machinery and structure of the company's fleet. In more detail, the department will have to daily supervise the safe operation, performance and maintenance of the engineering and technical systems of a ship. Furthermore, dry-docking and repairs are usually planned by the technical department.

A ship should constantly be supplied with various items in order to be able to perform its assigned duties. A list with supply items includes deck stores, provisions, machinery spares and paints inquiries. The task of supplying a ship is normally carried out by the supply department. Among other duties, there is also the cost-effectiveness, quality control of the supplies and delivery on time.

Recruitment and manning of ships is of vital importance for the ship management. Researchers have verified that more than 80 per cent of the accidents in the shipping industry are due to human error. The qualifications of seamen and their actual quality is a continuous process based on appraisal and evaluation reports. As a minimum, a company will have a crew manager appointed to monitor this process.

There are two positions in which every ship management company is bound by the law of the flag state with respect to the safety and security of each ship that it operates. Such activities were not unknown to the ship management companies. However, now they have to document their performance. The primer position is fulfilled with the monitoring of the company's safety management, implementation of safety and pollution regulations. The latter position ensures the implementation of security measures to vessels.

It is assumed that a ship management company, as a profit-making organization, needs budgetary control. This task is performed by the Accounting Department that, among its daily activities, has to provide the general manager with realistic economic data regarding the financial obligations of the company.

A vessel itself is considered by many people as an extension of a company's headquarters. The master of a ship is in command to operate the ship with the highest level of safety in accordance with the company's stated principles, policies and objectives. Of course, the responsibilities of a master are not limited to the execution of a charter party but also cover a range of daily activities, such as navigation, cargo operation and crew performance. A well-organized company is able to provide a ship with great assistance.

6.5.1 BSCs for divisions

The BSC has been applied to the divisions introduced above in the following sections. Therefore a measurement system could be established for the organization of a ship operator.

6.5.1.1 Managing director

For a managing director the financial performance of the company that he leads is a prime issue that will be reflected through his entire career. His direct obligation is to increase income by reducing the off-hire days of his ships. Lowering of capital costs by purchasing ships at the lowest possible price will also be a major priority. Forecasting of market cycles could assist in purchasing ships at low market values. Consequently, the reduction of administration costs could occur in many ways, but it should not affect the overall performance of the company (Lagoudis and Theotokas 2007). Lack of cash flow is something that can put at risk the future of the company (Engelen *et al.* 2006), especially when immediate cash may be necessary in order to meet unexpected issues, such as regulations' requirements.

From the customer perspective, an excessive number of delays and off-hire days could increase dissatisfaction of customers. Therefore, a ship operator should be able to identify the cause of such an impact that will also have a negative effect on the reputation and credibility of the company. However, to improve the quality of a ship's activities, it takes something more than quality carriage of goods (Celik 2009). Quality should also include excellent safety records and zero problems with PSC and flag authorities. A financial claim is a clear indication that there are managerial issues and defective ships.

The learning and growth perspective could easily be ignored, but it could also be the unseen cause for a series of managerial deficiencies. A first indicator would be complaints from existing personnel regarding the need for additional employees due to lack of knowledge, ageing of key personnel or excessive workload. Insufficient IT applications or excessive spending could also be another indicator of poor performance. When near misses occur, appropriate control options should be established to avoid the occurrence of a potential incident (ABS 2006). Numerous reported managerial errors or equipment malfunctions show a good flow of information, where nothing is hidden. Eventually, employees should be able to be innovative by introducing new ship standards and/or practices.

As a major part of the internal business, the managing director is to supervise the frequency and quality of risk assessment studies that are carried out in the company. The cooperation and information flow of managers among various departments and crew members should be considered of high importance for such studies (Wang *et al.* 2004). Planning and execution should be another indicator of good organization. When risks are identified, training could be a part of the available solutions in order to minimize risks. Management review is an ISM Code requirement and detailed reports should be prepared in order to evaluate the progress of the internal business process.

6.5.1.2 *Operation Department*

The contribution of the Operation Department to the financial performance of a company could occur by increasing a ship's profit by increasing operational efficiency. This is a list of the main cargo-related and navigational issues. However, the avoidance of delays and cargo damages should not generate unnecessary operational costs at the same time (Garcia and Rodriguez 1994). Administration costs can be measured through detailed budget control, while the monitoring of unexpected cash flow expenditures should also be quantified.

The customers, and especially the cargo owners, are expecting continual improvement of a ship's operational productivity. Such a task is becoming more expensive and harder to achieve with older ships (Turan *et al.* 2009) and incompetent crew members. The number of contracts (charter parties) is a further indicator that could be used with respect to the increase of a ship's competitiveness from the operational point of view. The operational quality of a ship could be measured by management deficiencies. Errors related to a ship's operation could also appear in financial claims.

The learning and growth perspective for the Operation Department will usually appear from the adequacy of the department's employees followed by a success plan. Their ability to adopt new information systems, networks and technology infrastructure could keep pace with technological innovations (Roumboutsos *et al.* 2005). The number of human errors regarding ship operations could also be used to evaluate the competency of the department's staff. Introduction of new ship standards and/or practices will demonstrate the knowledge growth of the department.

The internal business performance can be evaluated by the ability of employees to carry out risk assessment studies for operational issues in a reasonable period. Their efforts to develop plans should also meet deadlines while the plans should be easily executed by crew members. The training programme cannot be either excessive or expensive (Robert *et al.* 1996). Knowledge management techniques should exist together with cooperation issues. The above initial steps, once executed, should minimize efforts to review the internal business process.

6.5.1.3 Technical Department

The financial contribution could be measured by increasing a ship's profit via technical efficiency. The implementation of corrective maintenance usually leads to expensive repairs, significant loss of time/off-hire periods and a decrease in the ship's credibility (Turan *et al.* 2009). Therefore, any delays or off-hire days would have negative financial aspects. At the same time, the maintenance costs cannot be excessive. This could be a challenge for older ships so careful monitoring should be put in place. Administration costs and minimizing the need for immediate cash, so as to meet unforeseen technical issues, could be indicators of excessive costs of the department.

The company's customers expect that ships are maintained to high technical standards. Consequently, any low performance of the ship due to technical reasons would damage this expectation. In contrast, a reliable technical ship will contribute to the competitiveness of the company (Yang *et al.* 2011). A sound technical ship should also be manned by skilful seamen and meet the charter party requirements. Therefore, any agreement with a charterer should be monitored for its accomplishment. On the other hand, any ship errors from the technical point of view would damage the company's reputation.

The learning and growth perspective of the Technical Department is of high importance, as it very often keeps pace with technological innovation and regulatory changes. Therefore, competitive employees should cope with several issues including inspection, attendance and monitoring of technological issues. Occasionally there is a demand for advanced IT applications, such as a non-tank vessel response plan (NTVRP) for ships entering the US EEZ for stability calculations. A reduction of technical failures could be an indicator of a well-organized Technical Department. New ship standards and/or practices should regularly be adapted or introduced.

The internal business perspective should be rationally executed and documented as it could be used for legal issues in the case of a legal dispute. Even routine maintenance inspections should be based on previous risk assessment studies. The efforts to develop plans could be an indicator of the internal processes' efficiency (Oelcer and Majumder 2006). Training schedules should avoid being time consuming. The production of lengthy revision reports could indicate ineffective internal business process.

6.5.1.4 ISM Department

In terms of safety, regulatory compliance most of the time is not included in the financial performance of a company. On the other hand, profit is related to the safe operation of the ship. Every delay caused due to regulatory failure minimizes revenues, while ineffective implementation of maritime regulations increases costs related to the maintenance of safety standards. Therefore, profit could increase provided there is an additional rational administration cost. In the IMO (2005) report this administration cost was estimated at $4,000–4,500 per ship annually in order to maintain ISM compliance. The need for immediate cash to meet new regulations' requirements should be forecasted and kept to a minimum level.

In terms of customer perspective, apart from the cargo owners, this division will also have to satisfy the port authorities, flag states and classification societies. A poor regulatory performance of a ship will disturb these relationships or even put an end to them (Rodriguez and Hubbard 1998). On the other hand, a good regulatory performance increases a ship's competitiveness. The safety standards of a ship could improve, while its safety or the related managerial deficiencies recorded by customers could be a performance indicator.

In terms of the learning and growth perspective, a steady number of employees should be able to cope with the workload. Furthermore, they should be able to adopt new information systems, networks and technology infrastructure. The above skills should be reflected in the reduction of a ship's safety management deficiencies. Regulatory compliance requires the ISM Department to adopt or even introduce new ship standards and/or practices as a daily practice (Karahalios *et al.* 2011).

An important daily aspect is related to the internal business perspective. Employees of the ISM Department should be able to carry out risk assessments for a new regulation frequently, and then to develop executable plans in a reasonable timeframe. Furthermore, they should be able to simplify the training schedules and effectively monitor their progress (Triantafylli and Ballas 2010). The revision process should be formalized and link the efforts of other departments so as to improve internal cooperation with respect to the safety and protection of the environment.

6.5.1.5 Chartering Department

The contribution of a Chartering Department to a company's financial performance is to increase profit from ship hires. Although this depends on the market cycles, commercial opportunities always appear. An appropriate strategy combining voyage and time charter parties could secure revenues from ship hires (Kavussanos 1996). Costs could escalate if ships were chartered with terms that are inappropriate for execution. Cash flow should be monitored in order to avoid the need for immediate cash so as to meet contractual obligations.

Customer satisfaction is related to a ship's high performance as per the charter party agreements. The customers face significant commercial risks and, therefore, risk management in shipping has been critical for a long time (Tsai *et al.* 2009). An increasing number of chartering offers is an indication of a ship's competitiveness from the commercial aspect. Management deficiencies contribute to a poor image of a ship's quality standards. Customer satisfaction can be measured by monitoring ship errors with a negative effect on the charter party.

With regard to the learning and growth perspective, the need to hire additional employees in the chartering department should be low, while the opposite would be an indication of an unbalanced distribution of the workload. As with any other department, IT applications used should be at reasonable cost levels (Batrinca 2008). Any errors related to poor chartering options could be an indication of an ineffective department. Past experience in chartering aspects should contribute to the improvement of a company's ship standards and/or practices.

From the internal business perspective, the identification of potential threats in a new chartering agreement should be the equivalent of a risk assessment study. Careful planning should be used in order to minimize any commercial risk exposure due to inability to comply with commercial agreements. Education regarding the consequences of identified risks as well as commercial consequences should be carried out. Revision as a part of internal processes could point out problems in assessing risk during chartering and distribution of this knowledge to other departments.

6.5.1.6 Accounting Department

The financial performance of a company heavily depends on the Accounting Department. Monitoring and establishing rational budgetary control could increase overall cash flow control. Revenues are recorded on balance sheets as an appropriate evaluation of their fluctuations (Carruthers and Espeland 1991). As with any other department, it should have steady administration costs as well as the ability to foresee unexpected occurrences of immediate expenses.

A wealthy company creates a positive impression to its customers. Langfield-Smith (2006) noted that accounting information is a powerful influence in shaping managers' activities and relationships, while it also creates an external image of success. A ship that is operating with minimum expenses should do so without risking its ability to deliver services of high quality. Therefore, any cost reduction should be compared with any devaluation of its standards. In addition, the Accounting Department should be able to reduce a company's financial problems.

The performance of the learning and growth perspective can be evaluated by the need to hire additional employees in the Accounting Department. The necessity to hire more people or to purchase additional IT applications could hide risks of the department's decay. Nicolaou (2000) has demonstrated the significance of an accounting information system that could process financial information and support decision tasks in the context of coordination and control of organizational activities. Ship deficiencies due to poor accounting decisions are also an indicator of poor performance. The Accounting Department has a duty to innovate by introducing new standards and/or practices so as to minimize loss of money.

The internal business perspective could be used to monitor the efficiency of the department's procedures. The identification of potential financial risks and the development of appropriate planning are two measurable indicators for the employees. Risk assessment studies should be a part of the evaluation of the existing business model's vitality (O'Donnell and Schultz 2005). Regular training, including the hours required, is an indicator that can measure the competence of employees to share knowledge with each other. Complicated reviews of the internal business process can reveal a department's weakness in terms of managerial defects.

6.5.1.7 Crew Department

The contribution of the Crew Department in the financial performance of a company is to increase profit by hiring high-quality crew. A shipowner or crew manager can select and group seafarers according to manning costs, legal constraints and on board management experience (Wu and Winchester 2005). On the other hand, an effective crew performance can increase revenues by maintaining the ship in good standards and by providing essential information to headquarters. The crew costs, when uncontrolled, may reduce a company's profitability. Occasionally, for reasons related to crew misbehaviour, an immediate repatriation or delay may disturb cash flow, especially cash that is on board a ship.

The customer satisfaction should include cargo owners and government authorities. The customers expect crew efficiency to be up to their standards, which may differ significantly from a company's understanding. Therefore, any deficiency related to crew should be considered as a reduction of a ship's competitiveness. A high-quality crew will always improve the overall public image of a company. Crew-related errors must be investigated to find other related deficiencies, such as recruitment or appraisal procedures. The ISM Code involves management procedures for detecting and eliminating unsafe human behaviour from simple mistakes in arithmetic, judgement and deliberate risk-taking (Talley 1999).

In terms of the learning and growth perspective, the measure indicators could be the number of employees in the Crew Department. Any expenditure for hiring more people or purchasing additional IT applications should be monitored for its cost reduction. In addition to economic aspects, records of crew-related deficiencies should also be improved. The department's contribution to the growth of the company will depend on the employees' adoption and improvement of crew managing standards and/or practices.

Human error is related to the majority of accidents. In addition, human behaviour is unpredictable. As Talley (1999) noted, it is less expensive to change human behaviour than it is to redesign safety for ships. Therefore, the Crew Department should be comfortable in investigating such threats by evaluating the existing data. The modification of existing plans or the development of new ones demands an excessive effort. Providing training related to crew issues is a challenge that will reveal the competence of the department's staff. Excessive efforts to review the internal business process could be due to careless planning in the first place.

6.5.1.8 ISPS Department

Security is evolving into a major issue for ship operators and, consequently, it has an impact on the financial perspective. The secure operation of a ship will have the same result as a safe ship, avoiding costly delays or off-hire days. At the same time, costs related to security could increase, especially when a ship is operating in insecure geographical areas (Barnes and Oloruntoba 2005). The administration costs should be monitored through budget control. The need for immediate cash to meet regulatory security requirements could be an indication of poor financial performance.

In a similar way as other regulatory issues, several stakeholders should be concerned as customers expect a ship's high performance in terms of security. Most of the charter parties and the bills of lading incorporate the provisions of Hague/Hague-Visby Rules and, consequently, the ship operator is required to exercise due diligence in providing a seaworthy ship, which, in this context also complies with the ISPS Code. In the aftermath of the ISPS Code, major industry organizations, in an attempt to avoid delays and their related costs, have drafted new voyage and time charter clauses (Goulielmos and Anastasakos 2005). Third-party complaints, due to security aspects, could be evaluated as the signs that a ship's competitiveness is reduced. An increase in a ship's security standards would appear from the absence of its security deficiencies.

The qualifications of employees in the ISPS Department are clearly stated in the ISPS Code layout. Similarly, equipment is required to be installed on board ships, although the monitoring of ships requires additional IT applications. Such equipment should be regularly tested from ashore as well (Metaparti 2010). The number of security deficiencies, either managerial or technical, could show the learning and growth performance. Security at sea is a developing area which demands from an ISPS Department to cope with new standards and/or practices.

In terms of the internal business perspective, it is a regulatory obligation for the designated personnel to carry out risk assessment studies for security issues (Bichou 2008). The effectiveness of the ship security plan (SSP) should be tested and it should be updated with new information, while training should be compact and not time consuming. A review of the internal business process with the participation of crew members could reveal practical difficulties.

6.5.1.9 Supply Department

The financial contribution of the Supply Department could be essential. The right ordering of requisitions could avoid unnecessary purchase of new spare parts due to frequent malfunctions. Abdullah (2012) concluded that poor quality, high cost and late delivery are related to each other. A well-supplied ship would conform to charter party agreements, increasing, therefore, the revenue from the good operation of the ship. Fluctuations of administration costs should be closely monitored for their effect on the quality of materials and provisions supplied. Following introduction of MLC 2006, PSC officers can detain a ship if it is found with insufficient provisions. Any need for immediate cash, in order to supply a ship, should be considered as cost disbursement.

The customer frustration will occur when a ship's spares are insufficient or defective. The quality of equipment is a regulatory requirement and so it is frequently inspected by various authorities. On the other hand, a ship free of supply problems will increase its competitiveness (Mokashi *et al.* 2002). Any delay or malfunction of a ship due to a supply aspect could be measured as poor customer performance.

The learning and growth perspective could be measured by good personnel results. An increased number of employees or some unnecessary expenses for the purchase of additional IT applications could hide the risk of the department's decay (Turan *et al.* 2009). Furthermore, an indicator for this perspective should measure any complaints or defects of poor supply. The adoption of new ship standards and/or practices contributes to the growth of the department and, consequently, of the company.

With regard to the internal business perspective, the supply of any material should be a part of the risk assessment studies (ABS 2006). The proper choice and shipping of the most suitable material should be well planned, especially when the destination is a place unfamiliar to the ship operator. The training schedule should be closely monitored for its duration, cost and length; constant revision should be a formal procedure as the internal business process of a ship's supply is required to be proven in a legal dispute.

6.5.1.10 Ship

The financial performance of a ship is a main aspect, as this is the department that will have to prove daily that it can meet its commercial obligations. Therefore, the company's income depends on the ship's performance in terms of voyage execution, technical reliability (Glen and Reid 2010) and regulatory compliance (Knapp and Franses 2010). Keeping a ship in a good condition generates many costs, while their fluctuations should always be compared with the performance changes. Budget control for each ship should include its administration costs as well as any unexpected need for immediate cash.

The various customers that monitor a ship's commercial performance will be satisfied when its productivity (speed and capacity) is reliable (Engelen *et al.* 2006). Of course, the ship's competitiveness depends on the regulatory performance as well. A significant number of managerial deficiencies will mean a ship is listed as substandard. Furthermore, human errors on board are also a factor that, even if small in scale, would dissatisfy customers.

With regard to the learning and growth perspective, a ship should have a reasonable number of crew members. The employment of additional crew could be considered as an indication of poor management. Efforts have been made to reduce the risk through better technology, rules and supervision, as well as through mechanisms of compensation (Albayrak and Ziarati 2010). Technology is rapidly evolving in the shipping industry. However, the purchase of additional IT applications may eventually cause more hazards. Any near miss recorded should be investigated for its contribution to the learning aspect. Ideally, communication channels should be established in every ship in order to ensure that effective solutions are in place or can be adopted.

The internal business perspective could be measured by the ability of crew members to carry out risk assessments. This is an ISM Code requirement (Objective 1.2.2) that, apart from the office, should take place on board ships as well. The effectiveness of planning by a senior officer should also be measured. Effective training solutions should be proposed and implemented on any ship without the assistance of headquarters. The crew should be capable of reviewing the internal business process with reasonable effort.

6.5.2 *The weighting of each division*

Each division contributes to the operation of its organization in a unique way. However, all these division do not have the same weight in decision making. A hierarchy should be developed in order to include the authority among the divisions. Eventually, the weight of each division and its perspectives could be used to evaluate its contribution to the implementation of regulatory process. Karahalios *et al.* (2014) investigated the weighting of these divisions with respect to the implementation of a maritime regulation. It is expected that for a different problem these weight could be very different. The data were provided by a group of industrial experts, each being with a reasonable mixture of academic qualifications, professional qualifications and industry experience (Karahalios *et al.* 2014). The survey was conducted through research questionnaires in which industrial experts provided valuable feedback with regard to the regulatory authority of the representative stakeholders. Then, by applying AHP, the weighting of each division was evaluated. The results of this survey are shown in Figure 6.3.

According to the experts, it appears that the most important division in the regulatory process is the Managing Director, which is followed by the Operations and the ISM Departments. The fourth division is the Technical Department, with a

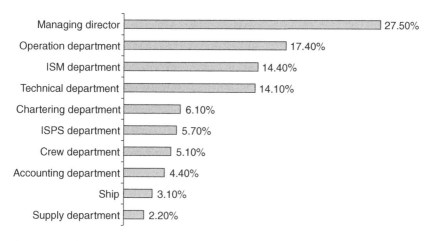

Figure 6.3 The weighting of divisions.

small difference from the ISM Department. These dominant divisions in total accumulate 73.4 per cent of the total weight. This is a reasonable finding, since failure to one of these departments will be very significant for customers and/or authorities. Technical reliability and proper management are the keystones for a ship operator. Proper documentation could also be a good supporting tool providing evidence of good management. The weight distribution shows that all divisions contribute to the regulatory standards of the ship operator.

It is noteworthy to discuss the key role of the managing director, although his weight is an indication that he is not the sole player in a shipping company. His duties may affect the performance of his company in terms of regulatory compliance. If the ships he chooses to purchase are old and very specialized, they will be inspected more often and rigorously, increasing the probability of being detained by authorities. In addition, he is responsible for choosing senior managers, having, therefore, the opportunity to find and retain the most valuable ones. It is his responsibility to monitor whether the high regulatory standards are followed by all divisions.

The list is completed with the remaining divisions who, although they have a significant role in the normal operation of a ship, have relatively low regulatory contribution weight. Among them, the Supply Department appears last in the list. The role of the Supply Department in purchasing quality material and provisions is of high importance for the smooth operation of a ship. However, it is closely monitored by other departments. Therefore, an incorrect order of a spare part, for example, should be detected by the Technical or Operations Departments.

In the middle ranks there is the Chartering Department with 6.1 per cent followed by the ISPS Department with 5.7 per cent. The weighting of the ISPS Department could be justified by the elevation of piracy incidents. The Crew Department has 5.1 per cent and is listed above the Accounting Department with

4.4 per cent. This is an indication that the weight of crew selection is higher than that of budget monitoring.

The ship is listed ninth in the ranking order with a relatively small weight. On the one hand, this could mean that the role of a ship is to follow orders from other divisions. On the other hand, the small difference with other divisions regarding its weight may be an indication that crew members are recognized by a ship operator as a part of the management team. Therefore, a sound organization should include the efforts of crew members as well.

6.6 The implementation generates benefits and costs for ship operators

A key point for discussion is that the success of a regulation's implementation can be evaluated by taking into account the benefits and costs of a ship operator. If the burden of a newly introduced regulation is not excessive for a ship operator, then he will be more motivated to implement it. Consequently, there is a greater probability that the regulation will be implemented adequately and in a reasonably short period. As was discussed in Chapters 4 and 5, the BSC approach could be used as a tool for such a cost–benefit analysis. A ship operator could apply this tool to conduct such analysis in all his divisions.

6.7 Perspectives and measures for evaluating the implementation of a regulation for a ship operator

The designed BSCs, which are displayed in Table 6.2, are based on the fact that every division must contribute to the same goal, which is the effective implementation of maritime regulations by the ship operator. The four perspectives are used in order to describe how every department should achieve this goal. However, the measures of every department vary considerably since the aims, targets and operation of divisions are usually very different. A proposed generic scorecard for a ship operator, which includes the selected perspectives and their definitions, is shown in Table 6.2.

Table 6.2 Perspectives for a ship operator

Perspective	Definition.
Financial perspective	Costs and profits that will result from the implementation of a regulation.
Customer perspective	The satisfaction of a ship operator's customers, as an outcome of the implementation
Internal business perspective	The procedure that should be followed to implement a regulation. Training, planning and review are considered as key elements of this perspective.
Learn and growth perspective	The required resources in order to implement a regulation. These resources include technology, human resources and knowledge.

6.8 Hierarchy development for evaluating maritime regulations' implementation performance from a ship operator's perspective

It is crucial for a ship operator to link his organization with the shipping industry. In Chapter 5, a hierarchy was designed for the shipping industry showing the commercial interaction among the stakeholders when implementing a maritime regulation. Although the ship operator is already part of this hierarchy, this graph should be extended as is shown in Figure 6.4, in order to include a detailed evaluation of the implementation performance of a stakeholder.

A detailed hierarchy for the ship operator is shown in Figure 6.5. For a successful implementation of a maritime regulation or any other goal, as it appears in Level 5, each division should contribute equally. Although each division has a different weight, they can all be positioned in Level 6. Then, a BSC approach is

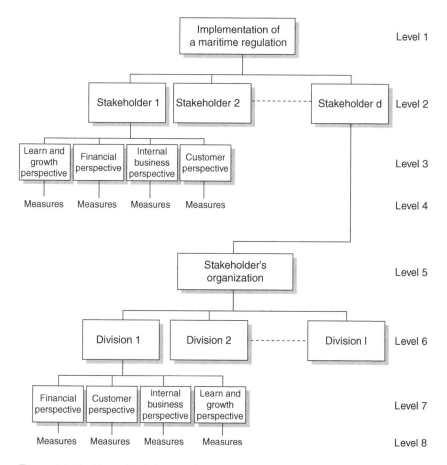

Figure 6.4 The hierarchical diagram for evaluating maritime regulations' implementation performance (source: Karahalios 2011).

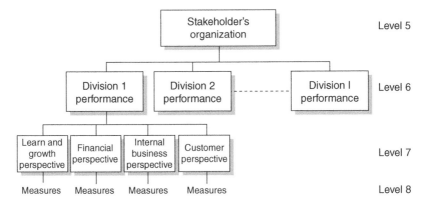

Figure 6.5 The hierarchy diagram for evaluating maritime regulations' performance from the stakeholder aspect (source: Karahalios 2009).

designed for each division positioned in Level 7, although the common perspectives for each of them may have different weights. Level 8 shows the measures of a division's perspective. The identification of such measures is useful in order to describe how a ship operator can achieve each perspective and, consequently, to successfully implement a new regulation.

Based on the weights of Karahalios *et al.* (2014), the organizational structure of a ship operator can be graphically shown by the diagram in Figure 6.5, which consists of four levels. However, each division contributes to the operation of a ship operator's structure in a unique way. Therefore, the divisions of an organization may not be of equal weight. Alternatively, by applying methods such as AHP, the weights of the divisions can be calculated depending on the structure and needs of each ship operator.

6.9 Selecting the perspectives and measures with the highest weight

Following the cascade approach of the scorecards, the measures of Level 4 can be used to monitor the performance of each division in the same organization. The measures used for the divisions of a ship operator are the same as those discussed in Chapter 5. A ship operator has limited sources of revenue, which mainly come from the hire days of the operating ship (Garcia and Rodriguez 1994). The maximization of its profit depends on the reduction of costs, such as maintenance, insufficient operation and damages. Therefore, in this research it is suggested that the profit of some divisions should be measured by the cost generated by failure of this division to meet a regulation, such as off-hire days and/or penalties from various authorities. In a similar way, it is difficult to define the productivity of some divisions. Thus, it is suggested that the productivity of every division from the regulatory aspect should be measured by the number of failures that generate costs to the stakeholder.

The scorecards are designed based on the fact that each division of a ship operator must contribute to the effective implementation of a maritime regulation. The four perspectives – financial, customer, learn and growth, internal business – are used in order to describe how each division can achieve the implementation. The measures of each division will vary considerably, since their functions and targets are very different. The scorecards' measures are based on the safety management system of the chosen ship operator as well as on the literature review. In this hierarchy, customers are identified as any other stakeholder of the shipping industry with higher regulatory authority or commercial advantage than a ship operator. The literature review was used to address the proposed measures of a ship operator's divisions according to their unique needs and obligations.

By following the cascade approach, several balanced scorecards should be distributed to each division. Assuming that, in this chapter, ten divisions have been selected and each one could have up to 16 measures then, in total, the organization will be evaluated by 160 measures. Such a detailed measurement will provide a detailed picture of the ship operator's performance with respect to the regulatory implementation. Karahalios *et al.* (2014) argued that in the real world rapid information assessment is an advantage. A self-assessment audit, where a company would have to rate its overall performance, would be time consuming. From the management perspective a company would not be willing to use resources for complicated measurement systems.

A ship operator is a decision maker that daily should make several decisions of a different nature. When there is a lack of data, he should follow strong indications. With respect to the problem of decision making, Gigerenzer (2007; Gigerenzer and Goldstein 1996) suggested that when there is a lack of both time and expertise, it may be useful to examine a single criterion each time until all criteria are met. In other words, a ship operator should take action in favour of the most important aspects of his business. When there is a major threat to one of the important aspects, an immediate solution should be provided. It goes without saying that the order of the important aspects that will be examined should follow a ranking order according to their significance. Otherwise, he is uncertain about the level of risk to which he is exposed until all the 160 measures are assessed.

Figure 6.6 graphically illustrates the above points. In a ship operator's organization, up to 40 measures could be in use. The weighting of each measure varies and the 15 measures with the highest weight constitute 80 per cent of the total weight. It is very clear that failure of one of these measures would be critical for the performance of the organization. Consequently, an indication for possible failures of these measures can help the ship operator make corrective actions where required. Therefore, the initial 160 measures should be reduced to a level at which a ship operator could have accurate and quick results regarding his company's performance with minimal effort. To demonstrate the significance of this interaction among the divisions of a ship operator, a research study was carried out by Karahalios *et al.* (2011), the results of which will be briefly presented below.

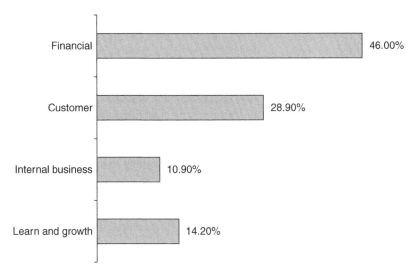

Figure 6.6 The weighting of a ship operator's perspectives.

Figure 6.6 shows that overall the perspective with the highest weight for the divisions' implementation of a regulation is the financial perspective, followed by the customer, the learning and growth and the internal business perspectives. These results indicate that the most interesting issue for the ship operator is the costs that can be incurred by each division as a result of the implementation of the new regulation. The difficulties generated by additional workload in order to fulfil the regulations' requirements and to improve the organization's functions are of lower priority. It is expected that for some divisions their priorities may be different. For instance, in the ISM department the customer perspective is ranked higher than the financial perspective.

For the managing director (Figure 6.7), the financial perspective appears to have the highest weight. When the customer satisfaction perspective weight is added, then its commercial implications affect him by 80 per cent. Internal business and learning and growth perspectives have similar but significant weights. This could be an indication that for the managing director both the organization of his company and the know-how are of almost equal importance.

The next interesting division for analysis is the ISM Department (Figure 6.8). From the analysis it is clear that the departments may have different priorities to each other, as in the case of the ISM Department where the customer perspective is ranked higher than the financial perspective. In this department the customer and learning and growth perspectives are ranked significantly higher, accumulating 66 per cent in weighting. This is an expected finding since the cost of implementing a regulation could not be higher than the expected implementation results. This is reasonable as the ISM department considers issues involving safety and pollution prevention more important than the cost reduction. The

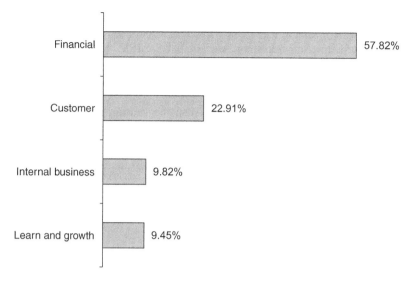

Figure 6.7 The weighting of the managing director's perspectives.

internal business has 10 per cent in the weighting, indicating that the process of complying with a regulation is not that significant, since the resources should be available.

The overall performance of the financial perspective (Figure 6.9) shows that cost is a paramount issue not only for the ship operator but also for its divisions. The costs that could be produced from the leading divisions have a significant effect on the decision making. The managing director's financial perspective is almost double that of the Operations Department, which is ranked second. The Chartering Department is in a mid-ranking position, since careless chartering could also generate significant costs.

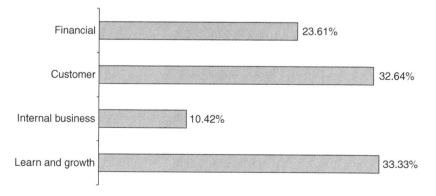

Figure 6.8 The weighting of the ISM Department's perspectives.

From the Customer satisfaction (Figure 6.10) perspective the leading division is the managing director followed by the Operations Department. Those two divisions are directly related to customers and are accountable for any poor performance of the ship. An interesting issue is that the ISM department, which represents the regulatory performance, is above the Technical Department. The remaining divisions have significantly lower weight in the regulatory process with respect to customer satisfaction.

The ISM Department is on top of the list in the learning and growth perspective (Figure 6.11), with a significantly higher weight. This is expected since

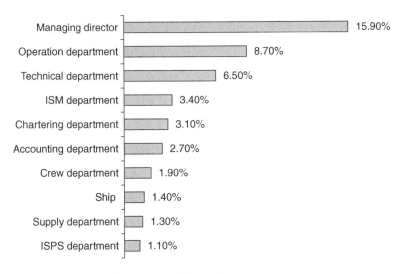

Figure 6.9 The overall weighting of financial perspectives.

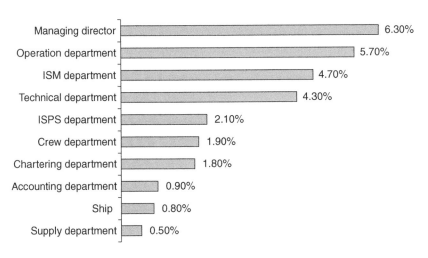

Figure 6.10 The overall weighting of customer perspectives.

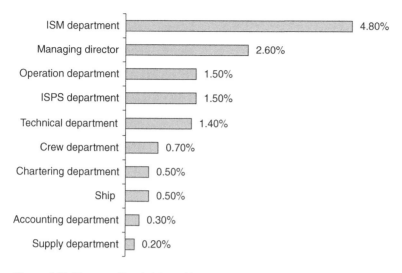

Figure 6.11 The overall weighting of learn and growth perspectives.

it is the department that should be updated and well informed of any regulatory issues so as to provide solutions. The managing director also has a significant weight in the process. Apart from the leading departments, the remaining division have significantly lower weights. This could be an indication that their knowledge in regulatory issues is not a main performance factor in the implementation of a regulation by a ship operator.

The internal business perspective (Figure 6.12) appears to have overall small weights. The dominant divisions are leading the ranking list again, since it is part of their daily operations to identify potential and existing hazards. The ISPS department could be higher, but the small value of its weight could be due to the fact that procedures are quite standardized in the ISPS Code. The remaining divisions are not daily involved in hazard identification, although their contribution is not negligible. Ships should have higher weight since, with ISM requirements, risk assessment should be carried out on board for any risky operation.

6.10   Evaluation of the ship operator's performance

The calculated weights of previous steps may be used to evaluate the implementation performance of a stakeholder regarding a maritime regulation. According to this approach, the initial BSCs should be modified in order to include the weights of their perspectives and measures. Hence, every time a measure of scorecards is filled, it will be possible to calculate its effect in the regulatory process.

A ship operator needs a tool that will allow him to monitor the regulatory implementation process at all levels within his organization. To meet the above steps/ objectives, the SHS was introduced by Karahalios *et al.* (2014) as a cost–benefit tool, measuring the commercial impact of a maritime regulation on the main

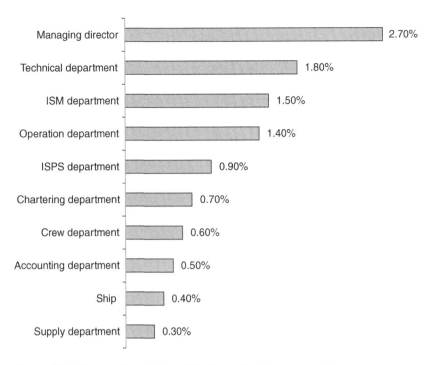

Figure 6.12 The overall weighting of the internal business perspectives.

stakeholders of the shipping industry. In this case study, the maritime regulation chosen for investigation of its implication to a ship operator is the SOLAS regulation II-1/19.1, as amended by Resolution MSC.216(82), and more precisely the Damage Control Information, introduced by the IMO. To avoid numerous calculations, the perspectives and measures that have been included were those with the highest weight. A case study survey was carried out by comparing the performances of four chosen companies towards the regulation II-1/19.1. The results of both surveys are included and explained in the subsections below.

The feedback will be entered in the system as values of the measures. However, the values of some measures may be different, as for example the number of accidents or amount of money. Thus, it is necessary to normalize these values on the same scale e.g. 0 to 10. The rating of each scorecard measure should be valued from 0 to 10, where the value 0 represents lack of any achievement and the value 10 represents absolute success.

By adopting this scale, the values that will be entered to the scorecards will represent the relative success of each measure in terms of achievement. Then, by using the weights of the parent perspectives, it will be possible to calculate the impact of each measure on the overall performance of the ship operator. The definitions of rates are shown in Table 6.3.

Table 6.3 An example of measures rates

Rate	Definition
9–10	Very high performance
7–8	High performance
4–6	Medium performance
2–3	Low performance
0–1	Very low performance

6.11 Setting the pass mark

A further question that is worth discussing is what the pass mark for each division, perspective and measure should be. Someone could easily say that 50 per cent is a good indication of acceptable performance. After consideration it would be fair to link this pass mark with the ship operator's expectations from his organization and divisions. As it was revealed by the experts of the survey, the overall performance of a ship operator's organization should have a minimal value of 7 out of 10. In terms of percentage it means an accomplishment of 70 per cent of the desired goal. Nevertheless, other ship operators may choose another, higher value. It should be stressed that a minimum performance for regulatory compliance could be settled much higher from a court. The sum of the weights from the four highly ranked divisions, as shown in Table 6.4, is 0.734. Therefore, it could be simply calculated that the higher ranked divisions should obtain a value equal to 5.91 in order to get an overall performance for the company equal to 7. Consequently, if one of these four dominant divisions achieves a value smaller than 5.91, then this is a strong indication that the ship operator did not perform well.

Table 6.4 Perspectives with highest weight

Division	Perspectives	Overall weights
Managing director	Financial	0.159
	Customer	0.063
	Internal business	0.027
	Learn and growth	0.026
Operation Department	Financial	0.087
	Customer	0.057
Technical Department	Financial	0.065
	Customer	0.043
ISM Department	Financial	0.034
	Customer	0.047
	Learn and growth	0.048
Chartering Department	Financial	0.031
Accounting Department	Financial	0.027

The above discussion could be extended to include perspectives. Perspectives with the highest weight could be used for a more comprehensive examination of a ship operator's performance. As can be seen from the figures above, the weights of 13 perspectives are 71.4 per cent of the total weight. By adopting this approach, we have a more representative sample for examination, since it includes lower-ranked divisions, such as chartering and accounting.

In order to determine a minimum average value of each of the 13 perspectives (P_{avg}), two assumptions are used. First, the remaining 27 lower-ranked perspectives from Table 6.4, that aggregate 0.286 of the total weight, are valued with 10. Second, the overall performance of the organization should not be less than 7. Then the minimum P_{avg} can be calculated by using the following equation:

$$P_{avg} = \frac{Overall\ performance - 10}{Weight\ of\ higher\ perspectives} + 10 = \frac{7-10}{0.714} + 10 = -4.21 + 10 = 5.79$$

Therefore, each of the 13 higher-ranked perspectives should achieve an average value of 5.79. Otherwise, even if all the other perspectives excel, the ship operator will not achieve a high performance. By adopting the above approach, Karahalios *et al.* (2014) limited the ten chosen divisions to four, which includes 13 perspectives, as is shown in Table 6.4. Therefore, this quick decision-making tool could be first used by the ship operator to concentrate on the area that he wants to research. Then, he must evaluate how this area is affected the most by the four aspects of the scorecard.

By selecting the higher ranked elements, a ship operator may easily have a pre-evaluation of his organization. With this method an accurate estimation could reveal red flags without excessive data analysis, something that is translated into numerous working hours and unnecessary costs. However, while identifying and measuring a major issue, such as cost performance of the Technical Department, we cannot reveal hidden threats. As it was shown in previous figures, the elements of the scorecards that should be measured are numerous. On the other hand, relying only on the 13 higher perspectives will be a 73 per cent evaluation of the ship operator's organization. The remaining 27 per cent leaves a high percentage of uncertainty for his organization's implementation performance, as is shown in Figure 6.13. Therefore, it is possible for a ship operator to end up with misleading conclusions for his regulatory implementation performance if he relies only on the analysis of the 13 perspectives. It is important to periodically collect data and assess in detail all perspectives for all divisions.

6.12 Evaluation of ship operators

A number of maritime experts, such as quality and safety managers from companies that vary in size and organization, participated in the study of Karahalios *et al.* (2014). The scorecards completed for the Damage Control Information

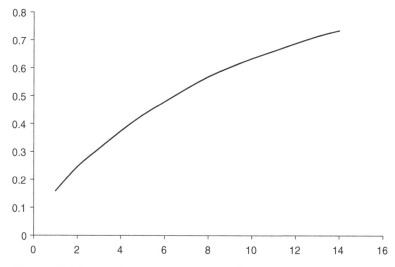

Figure 6.13 The contribution of perspectives to the total performance weighting.

requirement of SOLAS were used to compare the division performance rates of each ship operator in order to find which divisions face the most challenges. As it was shown, the divisions for all the ship operators have achieved values of less than 5.91, which was calculated in Section 4.3.1 as the minimum accepted value. Therefore, it could be argued that the regulation implementation is challenging for most of the divisions. For further analysis, the perspectives were compared with each other and the minimum P_{avg} value of 5.72 was not achieved in any of the perspectives.

Since the improvement of safety is costly and time consuming, even if the regulations had fewer requirements, for some divisions the rates still could not be much higher. However, a small increase in rates could make a difference. It is of high importance to underline that the results would be more accurate if the ship operators could provide numerical data, such as the amount of money spent or the number of failures related to the regulation.

A further finding was that the regulatory implementation performance appears to be easier when a ship operator has more employees ashore for each of his ships. Although the structure of the company varies, the ship operator who appears to have the highest performance has a large number of ships operating and staff working ashore.

This case study shows a detailed analysis of the factors that may affect the performance of the chosen divisions during the implementation of a regulation. It is very important to highlight that the total results from each ship operator are low. According to this study, there is an indication of how a simple regulation still makes ship operators achieve a low performance, especially when fewer people in an organization operate many ships.

6.13 The consequences of an accident

To date, the concept of documented management regarding either safety or quality has been introduced in the shipping industry. The ISO 9001 and the ISM are measured with this system as contributors to the financial perspective. This concept has been tested over the years and has shown some positive results in the shipping industry. One main negative aspect of these systems is that they require careful planning, monitoring and skilful employees to execute them. Their results will be shown in due time, and so, for the first year of implementation of such a system the results may be doubtful. Ship operators need to find gaps in their management systems regarding the introduction of a regulation based on accurate and reliable results and its compliance with the requirements of ISO and ISM Code systems. A ship operator needs to make decisions after the relatively easy extraction of the desired data.

In the modern, complex shipping industry, mistakes and omissions are often heavily punished by authorities. Therefore, the ranking of the priorities that a ship operator should consider when he implements maritime regulations is of great importance. In this section it was demonstrated how significant a detailed performance management system is for a ship operator when he evaluates his organization with regard to regulatory implementation.

Karahalios (2014) examined the performance indicators for their significance in the regulatory implementation, and especially those associated with accidents; the results are shown in Table 6.5. The effects of an accident on a financial performance of a ship operator are valued on average at 4 on a scale of 1–5. Loss of income and associated costs are of particular importance. The indicators of

Table 6.5 The average rate of indicators

Perspective	Indicators	Rate average
Financial perspective	Profit	4.75
	Revenue	4.37
	Cost	4
	Use of assets	3.12
Customer perspective	Productivity	4.5
	Competitiveness	4.75
	Quality	4.62
	Reputation	3.87
Learn and growth perspective	Human capital	3.37
	Information capital	3.5
	Organizational capital	4
	Innovation	3.25
Internal business perspective	Risk analysis	2.75
	Planning	2.5
	Training	2.5
	Review	2.75

customer perspectives are equally valued. The involvement of a ship in an accident will cause commercial damage to other stakeholders, with commercial implications, as explained in Chapter 4.

The learning and growth perspective is not as highly rated as the financial and customer perspectives, which represent the human element and know-how of a ship operator's organization, while the internal business perspective is lower rated. However, it could be argued that the risk analysis of a ship operator is a tool to minimize the probabilities of an accident's occurrence.

Karahalios (2014) examined the links between planning and consequences for a ship operator after a bulk carrier's collision. The involvement of a bulk carrier in a collision can have severe consequences for the environment, as well as for the safety of seamen. A collision of a bulk carrier may cause pollution due to the bunker quantity that it is carrying. The fuel could be spilled into the sea, producing significant environmental damage and high cleaning costs. The structural integrity of the ship may also be severely damaged due to the excessive forces applied (Lutzen and Pedersen 2001). In the case of severe structural damage there is a risk for the hull to fail and the stability of the ship to be reduced (Skjong and Vanem 2005). This is one of the main factors that could eventually cause the loss of a ship. If the collision occurs in shallow waters then the ship may cause a wreck, restricting navigation of other ships and becoming a hazard. Those risks eventually may put an obligation on a ship operator to begin emergency procedures. Such emergency evacuations in the case of passenger ships should be executed within a few minutes (Vanem and Skjong 2005). Therefore, the involvement of a very well-trained crew is required.

A ship operator, as per the ISM Code requirements, should be able to develop procedures based on data analysis for threats that a collision could generate. With respect to SOLAS, the ship should be maintained in a structurally sound condition and the crew members should be well trained in order to minimize the risk of loss of life. MARPOL include SOPEP requirements that necessitate that the ship operator equip his ships in such a fashion as to minimize the risk of oil pollution produced by a collision. However, even if there is not any oil leakage or injury, the ship will suffer damages that will affect its seaworthiness. This situation will cause a loss of money for repairs and a breach of commercial obligations.

The collision case is noteworthy for discussion since it may result in a combination of all the above hazards for each ship involved. The COLREGS state that a collision is a situation where the blame falls on both parties. Consequently, the legal exposure for a ship operator is that he must also compensate for the damages of the other ships involved. This means he must pay for his own damages and proportionally for the damages to the other party. In terms of risk assessment, the obligation of a ship operator is to examine threats with respect to the environment and safety. By examining the roots of the collision he will fulfil his obligations under the ISM Code requirement for hazard identification. The Code includes clauses that refer to crew selection, training, maintenance and planning.

However, the real problem for a ship operator will be the financial damages that he will suffer. This financial impact will be determined by how severe the damages to each ship and the environment were. This impact could be assessed by the financial perspective already explained in this chapter. It is, therefore, important for a ship operator to include financial damage in his risk assessment studies. The scale of Table 6.6, which includes safety, environmental and financial issues, could be used to categorize the severity of each incident (Lois *et al.* 2004).

A ship operator could use past cases to examine the probabilities of the damage severity for each hazard identified above. These past cases could provide data for case studies. Although there are some noteworthy databases, the one that is available is the GISIS provided by the IMO, which constitutes a report for 43 cases where a bulk carrier was involved.

The probabilities of each scenario are illustrated in Figure 6.14. By examining these data it appears that only in two cases were the damages negligible, allowing ships to make their voyages. Although no damage occurred, someone may expect that the involvement of authorities will cause delays, which, eventually, will produce costs. In terms of customer satisfaction, apart from the cargo owners and the charterers, the port state, the flag state and the classification society will be displeased with such an incident. It is highly likely that he will be liable to his contract obligations, which is a main violation of the ISO 9001:2008 standards. Furthermore, it is likely that such a regulatory failure will be penalized by the authorities. Corrective actions and further studies will also be required in order to investigate the cause of the incident.

Ten incidents also produced minor damages, which of course generate some repair costs. Therefore, apart from the corrective actions, the financial cost in these cases is more severe. In terms of weighting, the financial perspective and the customer perspective sum to a total weight of 0.75. Consequently, the most important managerial perspectives have failed.

In 16 collisions, the situation was escalated to critical, causing severe injury, major vessel damage and major environmental damage or missed voyages. Twelve

Table 6.6 Severity index

Scale	Definition	Examples
1	Negligible	Injury not requiring first aid, no cosmetic vessel damage, no environmental impact, no missed voyages
2	Minor	Injury requiring first aid, cosmetic vessel damage, no environmental impact, no missed voyages
3	Significant	Injury requiring more than first aid, vessel damage, some environmental damage, a few missed voyages or financial loss
4	Critical	Severe injury, major vessel damage, major environmental damage, missed voyages
5	Catastrophic	Loss of life, loss of vessel, extreme environmental impact

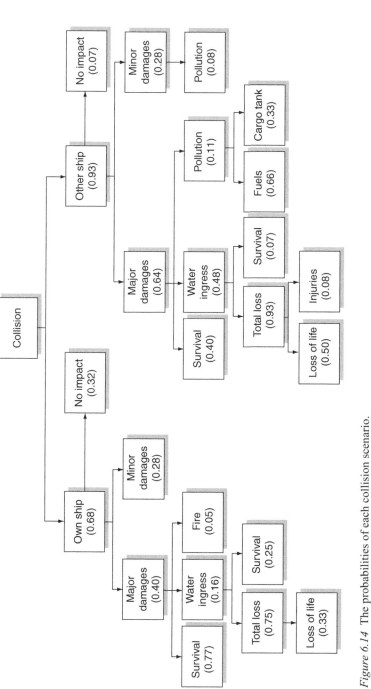

Figure 6.14 The probabilities of each collision scenario.

of those collisions caused severe structural damage to at least one of the ships involved. In these cases the delays produced will be higher as loss of freight could be involved. The repair of the damage will require a shipyard and, if the ship is unable to manoeuvre, this could involve towage. Therefore, the costs are significantly higher and the reactions from the customers will be worse. Only two ships flooded but were not lost. Flooding in cargo spaces could damage the cargo, producing claims against the ship operator. Another option is that the flooding could damage the machinery space, also generating significantly high costs. Similar consequences should be expected when there is a fire on board. Although only two cases of fire appeared, it is evident that there is a risk of this occurring.

In 17 cases the result to one of the ships involved in a collision with a bulk carrier was catastrophic, causing loss of life, loss of vessel or extreme environmental impact. Eight incidents had as a result the loss of the ship. From the financial perspective, loss of a ship will generate very high costs for the responsible party. Such loss may include cargo loss as well, which will significantly increase the compensation. Seven of the lost ships also resulted in loss of life, which requires an investigation by port authorities. A regulatory violation, such as ISM Code clauses or equipment malfunction, could lead personnel to face severe fines and/or criminal convictions. Two collisions caused pollution.

In terms of severity, Karahalios (2014) ranked the results of the incidents using the index of Table 6.6. This ranking is shown in Figure 6.14, where it is very clear how catastrophic the result for a ship operator could be if one of his bulk carriers was involved in a collision. Two main conclusions are taken from this ranking: the size of the vessel and the geographical area are deterministic factors for the severity of the consequences. When one of the vessels involved in an accident is very small, as for example a fishing boat, loss of life is a highly likely result. The passage of a ship in areas with significant fishing activity is an additional risk factor. These factors should be used by a prudent ship operator to revise navigation procedures.

Most of the collisions will generate critical or catastrophic results for the business of the ship operator due to ship damages, loss of life or marine pollution. By using scorecards, a prudent ship operator could assess what will be the economic impact from the different possible scenarios, since the financial perspective has the highest weight. The effect on customer satisfaction should be examined, taking into account the number of those that will be involved both at private and state levels. The collision cases showed the high-risk nature of the shipping industry. A ship operator should evaluate the commercial benefit that he gains avoiding any type of accident as a business strategy.

The extensive use of risk assessment studies is a solution towards this goal. The internal business perspective could be used to measure the effectiveness of a company in doing such studies. The growth of a company in a high-risk industry depends on the knowledge it could accumulate by proper organization and recruitment, as explained in the learning and growth perspective. A precautionary plan from qualified personnel is always a better solution to minimize the possibility of a catastrophic result, such as a collision.

References

Abdullah A. (2012). Maintaining of ships: the in-service support approach. *MIMET Technical Bulletin*, Vol. 3(1), pp. 18–25.

ABS. (2006). Guide for marine health, safety, quality and environmental management. Copyright. American Bureau of Shipping.

Albayrak T., Ziarati R. (2010). Training: onboard and simulation based familiarisation and skill enhancement to improve the performance of seagoing crew. In International Conference on Human Performance at Sea, HPAS 2010, Glasgow, Scotland, 16–18 June.

Barnes P., Oloruntoba R. (2005). Assurance of security in maritime supply chains: conceptual issues of vulnerability and crisis management. *Journal of International Management*, 11(4), 519–540.

Batrinca G. (2008). E-chartering web based platforms between success and failure. In 7th International symposium on marine navigation and safety of sea transportation, TransNav. *International Journal on Marine Navigation and Safety of Sea Transportation*, Vol. 2(3), pp. 293–296.

Bhattacharya S. (2012). The effectiveness of the ISM Code: a qualitative enquiry. *Marine Policy*, Vol. 36, pp. 528–535.

Bichou K. (2008). Security and risk-based models in shipping and ports: review and critical analysis (No. 2008-20). OECD/ITF Joint Transport Research Centre Discussion Paper.

Carruthers B.G., Espeland W.N. (1991). Accounting for rationality: double-entry bookkeeping and the rhetoric of economic rationality. *American Journal of Sociology*, pp. 31–69.

Celik M. (2009). Establishing an integrated process management system (IPMS) in ship management companies. *Expert Systems with Applications*, Vol. 36 (4), pp. 8152–8171.

Celik M., Lavasani S.M., Wang J. (2010). A risk-based modeling approach to enhance shipping accident investigation. *Safety Science*, Vol. 48, pp. 18–27.

Chantelauve G. (2003). An overview of maritime safety assessment trends in a stakeholder perspective. 14th European Safety and Reliability Conference, 15–18 June, Maastricht, Vol. 2, pp. 387–395.

Chen L. (2000). Legal and practical consequences of not complying with ISM code. *Maritime Policy Management*, Vol. 27(3), pp. 219–230.

Chu T.Y., Liang G.S. (2001). Application of a fuzzy multi-criteria decision-making model for shipping company performance evaluation. *Maritime Policy Management*, Vol. 28(4), pp. 375–392.

Engelen S., Meersman H., Voorde E.V.D. (2006). Using system dynamics in maritime economics: an endogenous decision model for shipowners in the dry bulk sector. *Maritime Policy & Management*, Vol. 33(2), pp. 141–158.

Fafaliou I., Lekakou M., Theotokas I. (2006). Is the European shipping industry aware of corporate social responsibility? The case of the Greek-owned short sea shipping companies. *Marine Policy*, Vol. 30, pp. 412–419

Garcia R.F., Sobral Rodriguez R. (1994). Global approach to ship operation optimization. *IEEE International Conference on Systems Man And Cybernetics*, Vol. 1, pp. 481–486.

Gigerenzer G. (2007). *Gut Feelings: The Intelligence of the Unconscious*. Allen Lane, London.

Gigerenzer G., Goldstein D.G. (1996). Reasoning the fast and frugal way: models of bounded rationality. *Psychological Review*, Vol. 103(4), pp. 650–669.

Glen D., Reid S. (2010). Tanker cost elasticities revisited. *Maritime Policy &. Management*, Vol. 37(6), pp. 585–600.

Goulielmos A.M., Anastasakos A.A. (2005). Worldwide security measures for shipping, seafarers and ports: an impact assessment of ISPS code. *Disaster Prevention and Management*, Vol. 14(4), pp. 462–478.

Håvold J.I., Nesset E. (2009). From safety culture to safety orientation: validation and simplification of a safety orientation scale using a sample of seafarers working for Norwegian ship owners. *Safety Science*, Vol. 47, pp. 305–326.

IMO. (2005). Role of the human element: assessment of the impact and effectiveness of implementation of the ISM Code in OECD countries and the employment function in the maritime sector. *Maritime Policy & Management*, Vol. 36(5), pp. 457–468.

Jensen J.I. Randoy T. (2002). Factors that promote innovation in shipping companies. *Maritime Policy Management*, Vol. 29(2), pp. 119–133.

Jensen J.I., Randoy T. (2006). The performance effect of innovation in shipping companies. *Maritime Policy Management*, Vol. 33(4), pp. 327–343.

Karahalios H. (2014) The contribution of risk management in ship management: the case of ship collision. *Safety Science*, Vol. 63, pp. 104–114.

Karahalios H., Yang Z.L., Wang J. (2011) A study of the implementation of maritime safety regulations by a ship operator. In *Advances in Safety, Reliability and Risk Management*, ed. Berenguer, Grall and Guedes Soares, Proceedings of 2011, Annual European Safety and Reliability Conference (ESREL), Troyes, France, 18–22 September, pp. 2863–2869.

Karahalios H., Yang Z.L., Wang J. (2014) A risk appraisal system regarding the implementation of maritime regulations by a ship operator. *Maritime Policy & Management*, pp. 1–25.

Kavussanos M.G. (1996). Comparisons of volatility in the dry-cargo ship sector: spot versus time charters, and smaller versus larger vessels. *Journal of Transport Economics and Policy*, pp. 67–82.

Klikauer T., Morris R. (2003). Human resources in the German maritime industries: 'back-sourcing' and ship management. *International Journal of Human Resource Management*, Vol. 14(4), pp. 544–558.

Knapp S., Franses P.H. (2010). Comprehensive review of the maritime safety regimes: Present status and recommendations for improvements. *Transport Reviews*, Vol. 30(2), pp. 241–270.

Knudsen O., Hassler B. (2011). IMO legislation and its implementation: accident risk, vessel deficiencies and national administrative practices. *Marine Policy*, Vol. 35, pp. 201–207.

Lagoudis I.N., Theotokas I. (2007). The competitive advantage in the Greek shipping industry. *Research in Transportation Economics*, Vol. 21(1), pp. 95–120.

Langfield-Smith K. (2006). Understanding management control systems and strategy. In *Contemporary Issues in Management Accounting*. Oxford University Press, Oxford.

Li K.X., Cullinane K. (2003). An economic approach to maritime risk management and safety regulation. *Maritime Economics and Logistics*, Vol. 5, pp. 268–284.

Lois, P., Wang, J., Wall, A., Ruxton, T. (2004). Formal safety assessment of cruise ships. *Tourism Management*, Vol. 25(1), pp. 93–109.

Lützen M., Pedersen P.T. (2001). Ship collision damage. Doctoral dissertation, Technical University of Denmark, Department of Mechanical Engineering.

Lyridis D.V., Fyrvik T., Kapetanis G.N., Ventikos N., Anaxagorou P., Uthaug E., Psaraftis H.N. (2005). Optimizing shipping company operations using business process modelling. *Maritime Policy Management*, Vol. 32(4), pp. 403–420.

Metaparti P. (2010). Rhetoric, rationality and reality in post-9/11 maritime security. *Maritime Policy & Management*, Vol. 37(7), pp. 723–736.

Mitroussi K. (2004). The role of organisational characteristics of ship owing firms in the use of third party ship management. *Marine Policy*, Vol. 28, pp. 325–333.

Mokashi A.J., Wang J., Vermar A.K. (2002). A study of reliability-centred maintenance in maritime operations. *Marine Policy*, Vol. 26(5), pp. 325–335.

Nicolaou A.I. (2000). A contingency model of perceived effectiveness in accounting information systems: organizational coordination and control effects. *International Journal of Accounting Information Systems*, Vol. 1(2), pp. 91–105.

O'Donnell E., Schultz Jr J.J. (2005). The halo effect in business risk audits: can strategic risk assessment bias auditor judgment about accounting details? *The Accounting Review*, Vol. 80(3), pp. 921–939.

Oelcer A.I., Majumder J. (2006). A case-based decision support system for flooding crises onboard ships. *Quality and Reliability Engineering International*, Vol. 22(1), pp. 59–78.

Panayides P.M. (2003). Competitive strategies and organizational performance in ship management. *Maritime Policy Management*, Vol. 30(2), pp. 123–140.

Panayides P.M., Cullinane K.P.B. (2002). The vertical disintegration of ship management: choice criteria for third party selection and evaluation. *Maritime Policy Management*, Vol. 29(1), pp. 45–64.

Plomaritou V., Plomaritou E., Giziakis K. (2011). Shipping marketing & customer orientation: the psychology & buying behavior of charterer & shipper in the tramp & liner market." *Management-Journal of Contemporary Management*, Vol. 1, pp. 57–89.

Progoulaki M., Theotokas I. (2010). Human resource management and competitive advantage: an application of resource-based view in the shipping industry. *Marine Policy*, Vol. 34, pp. 575–582.

Robert B., Gamelin C., Hausler R., Jarry V. (1996). Training concept for environmental emergency measures: structuring knowledge. *Journal of Contingencies and Crisis Management*, Vol. 4(3), pp. 175–183.

Rodriguez A.J., Hubbard M.C. (1998). International Safety Management (ISM) Code: A new level of uniformity. *Tulane Law Review*, Vol. 73, p. 1585.

Roumboutsos A., Nikitakos N., Gritzalis S. (2005). Information technology network security risk assessment and management framework for shipping companies. *Maritime Policy & Management*, Vol. 32(4), pp. 421–432.

Sampson H. (2004). Romantic rhetoric, revisionist reality: the effectiveness of regulation in maritime education and training. *Journal of Vocational Education and Training*, Vol. 56(2), pp. 245–268.

Scarsi R. (2007). The bulk shipping business: market cycles and shipowners' biases. *Maritime Policy & Management*, Vol. 34(6), pp. 577–590.

Talley W.K. (1999). The safety of sea transport: determinants of crew injuries. *Applied Economics*, Vol. 31(11), pp. 1365–1372.

Triantafylli A.A., Ballas A.A. (2010). Management control systems and performance: evidence from the Greek shipping industry. *Maritime Policy & Management*, Vol. 37(6), pp. 625–660.

Tsai M.T., Regan A., Saphores J.D. (2009). Freight transportation derivatives contracts: state of the art and future developments. *Transportation Journal*, Vol. 48, pp. 7–19.

Tsamourgelis I. (2009). Selective replacement of national by non-national seafarers in OECD countries and the employment function in the maritime sector. *Maritime Policy & Management*, Vol. 36(5), pp. 457–468.

Turan O., Ölçer A.İ., Lazakis I., Rigo P., Caprace J. D. (2009). Maintenance/repair and production-oriented life cycle cost/earning model for ship structural optimisation during conceptual design stage. *Ships and Offshore Structures*, Vol. 4(2), pp. 107–125.

Wang J., Sii H.S., Yang J.B., Pillay A., Yu D., Liu J.E.M., Saajedi A. (2004). Use of advances in technology for maritime risk assessment. *Risk Analysis*, Vol. 24(4), pp. 1041–1063.

Wu B., Winchester N. (2005). Crew study of seafarers: a methodological approach to the global labour market for seafarers. *Marine Policy*, Vol. 29(4), pp. 323–330.

Yang Z.L., Bonsall S., Wang J. (2011). Approximate TOPSIS for vessel selection under uncertain environment. *Expert Systems with Applications*, Vol. 38(12), pp. 14523–14534.

7 Evaluation of employees for their expertise in maritime regulations

7.1 Introduction

Regulations are introduced into the shipping industry as a result of accidents or pollution incidents. However, when there is a lack of data, the involvement of experts in providing qualitative and quantitative information is a common practice in regulatory processes. In a similar way, a ship operator needs personnel with adequate knowledge on regulatory implementation. Therefore in both cases it is necessary for a public or private organization to identify those individuals that have a degree of expertise. To date, there is no universally acceptable solution with respect to the problem of determination of an individual's expertise in an area. In the following sections some key points are discussed regarding the evaluation of a person's expertise.

7.2 The role of experts in regulatory compliance

When evaluating maritime regulations, the regulators have experienced some problems. In the IMO, by using the FSA studies, it was revealed that the results are very likely to depend on the different data that will be selected and evaluated (Rosqvist and Tuominen 2004). An example to illustrate this issue is the difference between the FSA conclusions made by Greece and the UK regarding the double-skin bulk carriers' efficiency (IMO 2004). Although the studies were carried out based on expert judgements, the results from the Greek research group were questioned by the UK group as follows:

> Regarding costs, the IC FSA study used a spectrum of owners, operators and shipyards to provide them and we believe them to be accurate. These costs are also used to compare with those used independently by the IACS and Japanese studies. However, the figures provided by the 'Hellenic Shipping Industry' experts differ widely, without explanation.

However, using statistics to process a large volume of data could be a critical issue that may affect the validity of studies. Especially for the ship's safety, the statistical distribution of the causes of shipping accidents is affected by the different viewpoints of accident analysis and investigation approaches (Celik *et al.* 2010). To address such limitations, alternative methods, such as the event-tree analysis, have been developed. This method starts with a hazard and works forwards to describe all the possible subsequent events, so as to identify the sequence of events that could lead to a variety of possible consequences (Aslan and Deha 2008). In the absence of databases or due to lack of time, a ship operator may have to rely on his managers to provide qualitative and quantitative information. For these reasons, many academics are using this approach, referred to as expert judgement.

The selection of experts in FSA studies is crucial with respect to the quality of their results (Rosqvist and Tuominen 2004). It is therefore important for ship operators to identify those people who would participate in risk analysis studies, especially when expertise in the maritime regulatory field is required.

The points that need attention in these cases are:

1   people who would participate should be sufficient in number;
2   participants need to have expertise in the appropriate field;
3   expertise should be proven.

A ship operator is also obliged to carry out risk analysis studies through a risk assessment requirement. Those studies should include data from previous accidents in order to determine their frequency and consequences. As Karahalios (2014) suggested, it is important for a ship operator to include commercial consequences of a hazard occurrence. Those databases should be used for assessing the regulatory performance of an organization. Comparison should also regularly be carried out with studies that have been published by international organizations. Hazards are usually associated with maritime regulations. However, these hazards may be linked with commercial management, such as the recruitment of crew members.

In order for a ship operator to fulfil these requirements, he depends on the size and structure of his organization. A large ship operator will have many employees with a variety of backgrounds to choose from. Examples of such employees may be some of the crew members who have already gained knowledge as per STCW requirements, and will be promoted to land jobs, while they are likely to be used by a ship operator as a source of qualified managers. Engineers, naval architects and graduates with shipping business degrees very often fulfil many other positions in shipping companies, as they have to carry out risk analysis studies as part of their daily duties, and occasionally train their subordinates. The mixture of these people will possibly form the structure of a ship operator's organization. However, in some cases it may be wiser to include external individuals to increase the internal validity of these studies. For a smaller ship operator this would be more difficult as well as time consuming, and so he may need to rely on the assistance of marine consultants.

7.3 Who is an expert?

An individual's expertise in a field is hard to determine. To qualify someone as an expert, people usually use certain criteria, such as relevant education level and experience in a certain field. Those main criteria are used by industrials and academics. However, when one of them is challenged, it appears that they may not be deterministic for the expertise qualification of an individual.

One of the most common criteria in determining the expertise of an individual is the amount of working experience in a field. The term 'experience' is usually used to describe the number of years an individual has worked in a field. The main supporting argument regarding experience is that people who do a task will keep improving until they eventually accumulate knowledge of almost everything related to this task. This term also implies a degree of success; if someone is not good in doing a job, then he will not build his career in this job.

Malhotra *et al.* (2007) carried out an interesting piece of research trying to associate expertise with experience in the oil and gas industry for the selection of quality practising managers. They found that more experienced people could perform better than those with limited experience in the same working environment. Their research was a good attempt to quantify and measure the expertise of an individual. However, those results were only indicative, because there were only 20 participants.

Another method for determining expertise is to look at the way in which individuals make decisions in their area of expertise (Rassafiani *et al.* 2008). Eighteen occupational therapists, having more than five years of experience working with children with cerebral palsy, participated in the research of Rassafiani *et al.* (2008). These therapists were required to make treatment judgements for 110 cases (20 of which were repeated) of children with cerebral palsy. Two groups of participants were identified: one with high consistency in decision making and the ability to discriminate between cases, and one with low consistency and poor discrimination. It could be argued that therapists in the first group had higher levels of expertise compared to therapists in the second group. Henceforth, the first group were considered as 'high performers' and the second group as 'low performers'. These two groups did not differ significantly on the basis of length of experience or work setting, but did differ in their type of decision making.

While experience seems to be important, some may argue that experience alone does not necessarily qualify someone as an expert. One must also comply with technological and regulatory changes. A variety of studies has shown that increasing experience is not always associated with better judgements (Witteman *et al.* 2012). For instance, the results of Witteman *et al.* (2012) showed that novice counsellors performed almost on the same level as very experienced counsellors.

Another criterion to qualify a person as an expert is their education level. Evidence of education level would usually be a university degree. It is expected that the higher the degree title obtained by a person, the more knowledge in a field is obtained by this person. Therefore, following this viewpoint, the expertise of a person is evidence-based (Germain and Tejeda 2012). Furthermore, in complicated industries such as shipping, there are a number of certificates that are used as training records. For instance, in order for a person to be a Company Security Officer, apart from any other education level, he also has to obtain a CSO Certificate.

In a similar way, a main certification standard for seamen is the STCW, which was introduced in 1978 (Triantafylli and Ballas 2010). Every seaman on board must hold certain certificates depending on his rank and duties. In order for a seaman to obtain a certificate, he must have some period of sea-going experience and attend some seminars. After passing an exam, he will obtain the appropriate certificate, which may sometimes be deterministic for the type of ship for which he can be recruited.

Therefore, setting a degree or a certificate of an individual as a criterion of expertise may exclude valuable people. In the aviation industry, Pauley *et al.* (2009) found that aeronautical experience was not significantly correlated with age and level of certification.

Another criterion that could be used to evaluate the expertise of a person is his consensus with other experts. The rationale behind this criterion is that when a person expresses his judgement of an issue, this judgement should not be very different from what other persons believe. As Weiss (2003) remarked, the experts in a given field should agree with each other; if they do not agree it means that at least some of the experts are not really what they claim to be. Rassafiani *et al.* (2008) described consensus reliability as the expected agreement among experts. In many studies consensus is considered of paramount importance. In the shipping field, for example, the safety standards of a ship are usually determined by the consensus among experts. Such studies also include assessment of risk factors (Wang *et al.* 2009), shipping registry evaluation (Celik *et al.* 2009) and assessment criteria for the sustainable competitive advantage of the national merchant fleet (Yang *et al.* 2011).

Although this is not conclusive, a person who states a different judgement is expected to bear the burden of proving such disagreement. Therefore, a practical issue when a group of experts is gathered in a brainstorming session, is that its outcome may not be the most appropriate solution, something that may threaten the validity of consensus reliability of such an outcome. Some academics have pointed out that a group of people may agree on poor answers (Weis *et al.* 2009). Therefore, although consensus could be a good indication, its validity is still under debate (Weiss and Shanteau 2003).

The problems with the validity of consensus may appear when a group of experts has to forecast events for which no previous knowledge exists. This will be the typical business environment for a ship operator, when he will try to foresee the market in order to make commercial decisions. Due to the complexity of events, it is possible for some of them to interrelate with each other, reinforcing or excluding one another. In that case, an invalid consensus could be reached by experts (Scapolo and Miles 2006).

In addition to experience and certification, an expert should also have discrimination, which is the ability of a person to identify differences on similar issues (Rassafiani *et al.* 2008). The value of discrimination is significant when it is repeated over time (Lee *et al.* 2012). For many researchers, the measurement of discrimination over consistency could identify an expert (Malhotra *et al.* 2007). In such research, candidates are required to distinguish similar but not identical cases. An individual with knowledge in an area should be able to identify issues that apply in general rules. In contrast, the expert should have such knowledge in order to identify differences in issues that are very similar and the average practitioner would not identify.

Of course, this discrimination requires a judgement to be repeated with consistency over time. Otherwise, a person's changing judgement after some time without any proper justification could be evidence of inadequate knowledge (Weiss 2003). An expert must make consistent decisions when repeatedly faced with the same or similar cases (Witteman *et al.* 2012). Many researchers suggest that the consistency of an expert's answers is an indication of his expertise (Weiss 2003; Shanteau *et al.* 2002). However, it is possible for a person who is using an incorrect rule to be inconsistent.

7.4 A survey approach to measure expertise

As is shown by the literature, it appears that typical qualifications cannot be used to determine the expertise of an individual. On the other hand, the ability of an expert to be consistent with his own judgements appears as a more reliable standard. Therefore, the following elements should be considered when choosing individuals to form a panel for group decisions and forecasting.

1   Select of candidates with appropriate formal qualifications.
2   Candidates should be able to demonstrate knowledge in a field by participating in a survey.
3   Estimate the consistency of all candidates.
4   Estimate the consistency of each individual candidate.
5   Evaluate the consensus of each individual with that of all candidates.

7.4.1 Data collection

To make sure that, when selecting participants to form a panel of experts, all available qualifications will be considered, a common approach is to conduct a survey, which could be in the form of a informal interview. Their answers could be used to measure the consistency of each individual. Then the answers provided by each individual could be compared to those given by other candidates in order to measure their consensus. If an individual's answers are very different from what the majority of other candidates have answered, this could be considered as a violation of the consensus criterion identified from the literature. A variety of books and guidelines should be consulted before the construction of the questionnaire. From these sources three fundamental issues were revealed:

1   The questions in a survey should be simple and appropriate for the level of the participants.
2   The personal details of participants, such as education and age, may reveal different schools of thought.

3   The structure of a questionnaire should be developed in different parts, each targeting a part of the research aims.

7.5 Mathematical approaches to evaluate expertise

Cochran, Weiss and Shanteau are three researchers that developed the CWS index, which is an attempt to quantify discrimination and consistency of an individual, in order to measure his expertise. This could be achieved by designing experiments in which practitioners in the same field are repeatedly questioned about several topics (Weiss *et al.* 2009). For instance, Witteman *et al.* (2012) applied the experiment which assesses the ability to consistently discriminate. The CWS index calculates expertise as the ratio between discrimination and inconsistence of an expert.

$$CWS = \frac{Discrimination}{Inconsistency}$$

In the use of CWS, the terms 'discrimination' and 'inconsistency' have been defined using terms related to the analysis of variance (Weiss *et al.* 2009). Discrimination is the variance among averaged responses to different stimuli, while inconsistency is the variance among responses to the same stimulus averaged across stimuli (Pauley *et al.* 2009). The larger the value of the index (i.e. larger discrimination and smaller inconsistency) the greater the exhibited degree of expertise is.

The index was designed to evaluate which of the participants in an experiment is performing better. This poses a limitation to its applicability, since it depends on the participants chosen for the experiment. Therefore, a careless choice of participants could indicate who is better among them but cannot determine that the participant who will achieve the highest score could be qualified as an expert.

As an alternative method, Germain and Tejeda (2012) proposed a psychometric scale. This scale consists of 18 items (Table 7.1) that measure the expertise of an employee. However, since it is a relatively new research approach, its value should be demonstrated in the future. Psychometric tests are broadly used in statistics in order to evaluate the consistency among respondents when they rate or evaluate a topic. A notable psychometric test is the Cronbach's alpha (α) value, which is a numerical coefficient of reliability that indicates the internal consistency of a model or survey. The values of this test range from 0 to 1. An alpha value greater than 0.7 is desirable for indices that are used as a scale (Kinnear and Gray, 2000). As the inter-correlations among test items increase, the Cronbach's alpha values will generally increase, and this is something that is known as an internal consistency estimate of reliability of test scores.

7.5.1 Selection of expert candidates in the shipping industry with E_{xp} index

A typical problem of qualifying a person as an expert for a specific field is that many people who are qualified for the same position may have very different academic and industrial experiences. As has been discussed in this chapter, many

Table 7.1 Psychometric scale that measures the expertise of an employee

---

1 This person has knowledge that is specific to his or her field of work.
2 This person shows that he or she has the necessary education to be an expert in his or her field.
3 This person has knowledge about his or her field.
4 This person conducts research related to his or her field.
5 This person has the qualifications required to be an expert in his or her field.
6 This person has been trained in his or her area of expertise.
7 This person is ambitious about his or her work in the company.
8 This person can assess whether a work-related situation is important or not.
9 This person is capable of improving himself or herself.
10 This person is charismatic.
11 This person can easily deduce things from work-related situations.
12 This person is intuitive in his or her job.
13 This person is able to judge what things are important in his or her job.
14 This person has the drive to become what he or she is capable of becoming in his or her field.
15 This person is self-assured.
16 This person has self-confidence.
17 This person is an expert who is outgoing.
18 This person can talk his or her way through any work-related situation.

---

managers in a shipping company may also have sea-going experience. For instance, a technical manager may be a former chief engineer or a naval architect or someone who has both qualifications. In a similar way, a safety manager of a shipping company may hold only a senior deck officer licence without any additional academic degree. When forming a panel, the exclusion of one group of professionals may deprive them from getting different viewpoints.

An interesting approach suggested by the author is to form a scale where all the formal qualifications could be evaluated overall (Karahalios 2009). In Table 7.2 a ranking scale is produced in a range of 1 to 5. The column with the heading 'Academic Certification' lists the available degrees. The adjacent column includes a list of the professional certifications, which include the STCW standards, the ship surveyors and especially the auditor's qualification, while the arbitrator's certification is added on top. The fourth column from the left side of the table includes the years of experience in a managerial position. An individual may have academic and/or professional certification, but not be promoted into such a position due to his age or lack of opportunities. This is the reason why the last column is added, as it includes the years of experience of an individual while not being in a managerial position. These criteria were selected due to their simplicity and their common acceptability. The values of the proposed criteria can be multiplied so as to obtain an Exp value. To illustrate, a person with seven years as a manager and 15 years of working experience holding an MSc degree will be:

$$E_{xp} = 4 \times 1 \times 3 \times 4 = 48$$

On the other hand, a person with a HND serving as a captain for 15 years will be:

$$E_{xp} = 1 \times 4 \times 1 \times 4 = 16$$

By using this scale, each qualification is increasing the significance of each participant. Therefore, there is a great difference produced among participants when experience or certification is different.

7.6 Estimate the consistency of candidates with AHP

Consistency of an individual can be estimated with the CWS index or AHP. In this book AHP is preferred because it is suitable when prior knowledge is poor and the data are inadequate or unavailable.

When experts of a panel reach an agreement, the result will be to rank priorities of the given problem. This ranking would then be considered of prime importance, as it will be used to make a decision. When such a decision is commercial, the future of the company or organization may be at stake. In a similar way, if this decision is a risk control option, it could bring legal implications to the company, unless it is made wisely. Therefore, the consistency of the group should be carefully examined. For instance, in the AHP method it is suggested that small changes in priorities, such as 20 per cent, should not cause rank reversal (Chang *et al.* 2007; Kahraman *et al.* 2007). An interesting case would be when the ranking of the priorities is changing among individuals. If such ranking changes are caused by some individuals, they should be examined, due to inadequate knowledge. It could also be the case that an individual with a very different opinion in group thinking is the real expert.

7.6.1 Conducting a survey

When a ship operator performs a survey, he can use his own personnel. However, there are some reasons why he could include external individuals. This approach would increase the expertise as well as cross-examine the

Table 7.2 Scale of experts criteria

Rate	Academic certification	Professional certification	Managerial experience	Experience (not managerial/sea service)
5	PhD	Ship surveyor/auditor	20+ years	20+ years
4	MSc	Captain/chief engineer	15–19 years	15–19 years
3	Postgraduate diploma	Chief officer/second Engineer	10–14 years	10–14 years
2	BSc	Deck officer/engineer	5–9 years	5–9 years
1	HND	Other	0–4 years	0–4 years

knowledge level of his personnel. Industrial experts who could contribute to this direction could include classification societies, shipping companies, academics and consultants. Their knowledge could be collected with a simplified questionnaire. In this case, anonymity is essential as it does not affect the opinion of the participants. However, personal details such as academic and industrial background could be proven to be essential for the evaluation of expertise.

The internal consistency could also be affected by the number of participants. A high number of participants may be unanimous even if their conclusions are not very suitable. Including a large number of people in that study may produce consensus results even if they are not experts. The second significant issue that is produced is that the individual consistency is more reliable than the overall. Therefore, the value of each person appears to be more important than that of the number of participants in a panel. By determining the inconsistent candidates, at least the most valuable individuals will be included in the panel. When examining the survey material it appears that the candidates could be inconsistent mainly for two reasons:

1 using extreme ranking when doing pairwise comparisons;
2 completing some pairwise comparisons carelessly.

When such inconsistencies among industrial experts exist, some may argue that they were not suitable for the selected topic. However, risk in the shipping industry is associated with the maritime regulations. An person within the industry should be aware of which stakeholder has higher authority in the regulatory regime. Another point could be that, due to the commercial interaction of the stakeholders, those in the industry may be confused about the regulatory authority of each stakeholder and/or his contribution to the current system. This is why the rank reversal appeals to the minor stakeholders.

In this chapter the following arguments are presented:

1 Considering a person as an expert should not rely only on his academic or industrial background.
2 Consistency with random judgements is very hard to achieve for an individual.
3 Consensus among a panel of experts is not a clear indication of good judgement.
4 It is very challenging to rely on a few industrial experts for decision making.

References

Arslan O., Deha E.I. (2008). SWOT analysis for safer carriage of bulk liquid chemicals in tankers. *Journal of Hazardous Materials*, Vol. 154, pp. 901–913.

Celik M., Deha E.I., Ozok A.F. (2009). Application of fuzzy extended AHP methodology on shipping registry selection: the case of Turkish maritime industry. *Expert Systems with Applications*, Vol. 36(1), pp. 190–198.

Celik M., Lavasani S.M., Wang J. (2010). A risk-based modeling approach to enhance shipping accident investigation. *Safety Science*, Vol. 48, pp. 18–27.

Chang C.W., Wu C.R., Lin C.T., Chen H.C. (2007). An application of the AHP and sensitivity analysis for selecting the best slicing machine. *Computers and Industrial Engineering*, Vol. 52, pp. 296–307.

Germain M.L., Tejeda M.J. (2012). A preliminary exploration on the measurement of expertise: an initial development of a psychometric scale. *Human Resource Development Quarterly*, Vol. 23(2), pp. 203–232.

IMO. (2004). *Bulk Carrier Safety. Cost Benefits of Double Side Skin Bulk Carriers Submitted by the United Kingdom*. IMO Publishing, London.

Kahraman C., Ates N.Y., Çevik S., Gülbay M. (2007). Fuzzy multi-attribute cost–benefit analysis of e-services. *International Journal of Intelligent Systems*, Vol. 22, pp. 547–565.

Karahalios H. (2009). An appraisal of maritime regulations in the shipping industry. PhD Thesis, Liverpool John Moores University.

Karahalios H. (2014) The contribution of risk management in ship management: the case of ship collision. *Safety Science*, Vol. 63, pp. 104–114.

Kinnear P.R., Gray C.D. (2000). *SPSS for Windows Made Simple: Release 10*. Psychology Press, UK.

Lee M.D., Steyvers M., Young M., Miller B. (2012). Inferring expertise in knowledge and prediction ranking tasks. *Topics in Cognitive Science*, Vol. 4, pp. 51–163.

Malhotra V., Lee M.D., Khurana A. (2007). Domain experts influence decision quality: towards a robust method for their identification. *Journal of Petroleum Science and Engineering*, Vol. 57(1–2), pp. 181–194.

Pauley K., O'Hare D., Wiggins M. (2009). Measuring expertise in weather-related aeronautical risk perception: the validity of the Cochran–Weiss–Shanteau (CWS) index. *The International Journal of Aviation Psychology*, Vol. 19(3), pp. 201–216.

Rassafiani M., Ziviani J., Rodger S., Dalgleish L. (2008). Identification of occupational therapy clinical expertise: decision-making characteristics. *Australian Occupational Therapy Journal*, Vol. 56(3), pp. 156–166.

Rosqvist T., Tuominen R. (2004). Qualification of formal safety assessment: an exploratory study. *Safety Science*, Vol. 42(2), pp. 99–120.

Scapolo F., Miles I. (2006). Eliciting experts' knowledge: a comparison of two methods. *Technological Forecasting & Social Change*, Vol. 73, pp. 679–704.

Shanteau J. (2002). Performance-based assessment of expertise: how to decide if someone is an expert or not. *European Journal of Operational Research*, Vol. 136(2), pp. 253–263.

Triantafylli A., Ballas A. (2010). Management control systems and performance: evidence from the Greek shipping industry. *Maritime Policy & Management*, Vol. 37(6), pp. 625–660.

Wang Y.M., Chin K.S., Kwai Poon G.K., Yang J.B. (2009). Risk evaluation in failure mode and effects analysis using fuzzy weighted geometric mean. *Expert Systems with Applications*, Vol. 36, pp. 1195–1207.

Weiss D.J. (2003). Empirical assessment of expertise. *Human Factors*, Vol. 45(1), pp. 104–114.

Weiss D.J., Shanteau J. (2003). Empirical assessment of expertise. *Human Factors*, Vol. 45(1), pp. 104–114.

Weiss D.J., Brennan K., Thomas R., Kirlik A., Miller S.M. (2009). Criteria for performance evaluation. *Judgment and Decision Making*, Vol. 4(2), pp. 164–174.

Witteman C.L.M., Weiss D.J., Metzmacher M. (2012). Assessing diagnostic expertise of counselors using the Cochran–Weiss–Shanteau (CWS) index. *Journal of Counseling & Development*, Vol. 90, pp. 30–34.

Yang Z.L., Bonsall S., Wang J. (2011). Approximate TOPSIS for vessel selection under uncertain environment. *Expert Systems with Applications*, Vol. 38, pp. 14523–14534.

Index

For Product Safety Concerns and Information please contact our EU representative GPSR@taylorandfrancis.com Taylor & Francis Verlag GmbH, Kaufingerstraße 24, 80331 München, Germany

Printed and bound by CPI Group (UK) Ltd, Croydon, CR0 4YY

01/05/2025

01858452-0008